THE SYMPHONY
OF MISSION

THE SYMPHONY OF MISSION

PLAYING YOUR PART
IN GOD'S WORK IN THE WORLD

MICHAEL W. GOHEEN
AND JIM MULLINS

Baker Academic

a division of Baker Publishing Group
Grand Rapids, Michigan

© 2019 by Michael W. Goheen and Jim Mullins

Published by Baker Academic
a division of Baker Publishing Group
PO Box 6287, Grand Rapids, MI 49516-6287
www.bakeracademic.com

Printed in the United States of America

Library of Congress Cataloging-in-Publication Data
Names: Goheen, Michael W., 1955– author.
Title: The symphony of mission : playing your part in God's work in the world / Michael W. Goheen and Jim Mullins.
Description: Grand Rapids : Baker Academic, a division of Baker Publishing Group, 2019. | Includes bibliographical references.
Identifiers: LCCN 2018059473 | ISBN 9781540960238 (pbk.)
Subjects: LCSH: Missions. | Evangelistic work. | Witness bearing (Christianity) | Vocation—Christianity.
Classification: LCC BV2061.3 .G64 2019 | DDC 266—dc23
LC record available at https://lccn.loc.gov/2018059473

ISBN 978-1-5409-6235-5 (casebound)

19 20 21 22 23 24 25   7 6 5 4 3 2 1

To Jenny and Elliana Mullins,
for displaying sacrificial and creative love

To Tom Shrader,
for his faithful and foresightful leadership
of Christ's church in Phoenix

CONTENTS

PREFACE

"Another book about mission?" you might be thinking. "Surely we don't need another. We just need to put into practice what we already know!"

We certainly sympathize with these thoughts. And in fact, this book is designed precisely to move God's people from theological reflection to faithful practice, from wrestling with the *idea* of mission to participating—faithfully and obediently—in what God is *doing* in mission. Harvie Conn, who has shaped both of us, says it well when he pleads at the beginning of his book on evangelism and justice, "And now to the streets and not, pray God, to the study."[1]

This book is a joint project between Mike Goheen and Jim Mullins. Mike is leading a creative experiment in missional theological education among the Phoenix area churches called the Missional Training Center (MTC).[2] He works with many pastors in this role, and Jim is one of them. Jim is the pastor of theological and vocational formation at Redemption Church, Tempe. He is on the board of MTC and plays a key role among the Phoenix area churches to catalyze and unify congregations in mission. He also helps lead the Surge School, a widely ecumenical endeavor that disciples hundreds of people annually in vocational mission. While both of us are deeply engaged in the mission of the church and in thinking about it in light of Scripture, it is especially Mike's theological reflection and Jim's imaginative implementation that come together in this book.

1. Harvie Conn, *Evangelism: Doing Justice and Preaching Grace* (Philipsburg, NJ: P&R, 1992), 10.
2. You can find out more about MTC here: http://www.missionaltraining.org/.

The book itself arises out of three things: our personal stories, how our stories intersect, and the need we discovered in our Surge School for a certain kind of book about mission. So we'll begin with our stories, each told in our own words.

Mike's Story

When (in the late 1970s) I committed myself to follow Christ, it was in a church that stood squarely within the revivalist tradition of the early twentieth century. My assumptions about the nature of mission and what it meant to participate in that mission sprouted from that soil. For me, mission was about evangelism, sharing a certain message that would enable people to go to heaven. In those days the animosity between the evangelical and ecumenical traditions was so bitter you almost had to experience it to believe it. Word and deed were seen to be in tension, and the church I was a part of was firmly and unapologetically committed to word over deed.

And so I became a zealous evangelist. I took a personal evangelism course in a local Bible college and memorized many formulas, including the Four Spiritual Laws and the Romans Road. I became involved in the Evangelism Explosion ministry in our church, diligently mastering all the techniques and becoming a trainer. I went into the homes of folks who had visited our church, urging them to believe in Jesus. I took every opportunity to share the gospel—or at least a narrow *version* of the gospel—with anyone who would listen, and often with those who wouldn't. In short, I embodied what one book of that time referred to as a "witless witness."[3] On the front of that book is a picture of an angry-looking man standing on the chest of another man who is pinned on the ground. The man who is standing has a large Bible raised high in one hand, while with the other hand he is aggressively pulling his helpless victim's tie. Now you might dismiss this picture as a mere caricature designed to get a laugh and catch the buyer's eye in a Christian bookstore, but it's more than that to me. You see, I remember a time on the streets of Miami when I came close to *being* that bully with the Bible as I badgered a young man with the "gospel" until he finally prayed the sinner's prayer. He said the words of the prayer, but he did so—I am sure—just to get rid of me. I'm not proud of that memory. But it is a reminder for me of a time when I was genuinely (though ignorantly) wrestling with the nature of mission, how I was to participate in it, and what it should look like in my daily life.

3. Fritz Ridenour, *Tell It Like It Is: How Not to Be a Witless Witness* (Glendale, CA: Regal Books, 1968).

But then another event occurred in my life a short while later that gradually worked loose some of my most deeply held assumptions about mission. A Haitian man appeared on the front steps of my church's conference center, his feet bleeding from a long walk. He was hungry. He had nowhere to live and no job. I brought him into the foyer of the conference center and seated him there while I set about figuring out what I could do to help. But before I came up with a real plan, I was summoned to the office of the senior pastor, where the whole pastoral staff had assembled to demand I remove this man from the premises. As a relatively new Christian, I was confused because these leaders whom I respected were apparently acting without mercy. "There are government agencies for this kind of thing," and "You can't help everyone, Mike," were some of the words I remember. I stubbornly refused to follow their direction, and a long drama ensued that eventually led me to find lodging and a job for the man on my own. But the whole incident shook me deeply. At that point, I didn't yet understand the twentieth-century theological history that had produced such a passionate division between word and deed. But I knew something was very wrong with a church that placed such a high priority on evangelism and yet had so little sense of justice and mercy. My views on mission were being challenged and broadened.

The tradition in which I grew up was also committed to cross-cultural missions. Accordingly, I decided that if my life was to count for anything, I needed to become a foreign missionary. With that in mind, I decided to head to Westminster Seminary, Philadelphia, to get the biblical training I would need for the task. I have no doubt that many of my ideas and convictions shifted during my three years there, but two such shifts in particular would play a huge role in my later life. First, I learned in the tradition of Herman Ridderbos and Geerhardus Vos to read the Bible as one story. Second, I was exposed to Harvie Conn's classes on mission. His views of holistic mission, his redemptive-historical approach to every issue, and his urging to read and absorb J. H. Bavinck's work combined to shape my views on mission profoundly.

When it came time to graduate, I was met by a group from eastern Ontario who challenged my commitment to go overseas. They argued that Canada was a far more needy mission field than any of the African countries I was considering. And, of course, they were right. I ended up church planting and then pastoring on the edge of Toronto. I'm afraid I did many—perhaps most—things wrong. Yet I learned a lot and continued to wrestle with the nature of mission, especially in relation to the church. My views of mission had been highly individualistic; now I had to find the right connections between my missional and pastoral activities. What, I began to ask, does the *church* have to do with mission?

A number of events in my life at that time were working together to reshape my understanding. First, I was invited to teach an introductory course on mission at the university level.[4] I didn't know where to begin, so I turned to Bavinck's *The Science of Missions* (since that is where Harvie Conn had told me to go). After reading that book again, I became convinced that one must begin by reading the Bible as one story in order to understand mission.[5] I also began to read David Bosch and especially Lesslie Newbigin. Newbigin offered a way of viewing mission that helped resolve a number of tensions I had experienced in my theology and ministry, especially the tensions between church and mission and between word and deed. Moreover, Newbigin challenged me to understand mission in terms of the church's role in the biblical story, and this resonated with what I had already learned from reading Bavinck.

This experience in the late 1980s led me to do a doctorate on the missionary ecclesiology of Lesslie Newbigin and eventually to move from the pastorate into the academic life. I developed and taught mission courses in a number of universities, wrestling with the nature and practice of mission with hundreds of students. But I also taught worldview; I had come to see the worldview emphasis that flowed from Kuyper, Bavinck, and others in the Dutch neo-Calvinist tradition as very helpful in my attempts to understand mission as holistic, including not only word and deed but also vocation and witness in the public square. This understanding was reinforced by my ongoing study of Newbigin. My classes in worldview were attempts to help my students take up their vocations, first as students and then as future professionals, as part of God's mission.

During this time I did not forget the church. Too much teaching about mission, including some versions of "vocation in the public square" in the Reformed tradition, neglects the local congregation. My continuing studies in Newbigin would not allow me to do that. I worked in two congregations as a preaching pastor with other pastors and leaders, and we did our best to enable the church to be missional. Questions about the fundamental nature of mission, about how the various members of the church should find their place in God's mission, and about what mission should look like as it is worked out in their lives continued to press on me.

One observation that troubled me at that point in my life and work was that most pastors had been theologically trained in institutions where mission

4. Twenty-five years later, this class would inspire *Introducing Christian Mission Today: Scripture, History, and Issues* (Downers Grove, IL: InterVarsity, 2014).

5. My book *A Light to the Nations: The Missional Church and the Biblical Story* (Grand Rapids: Baker Academic, 2011) was an effort almost four decades later to take the Bavinck storied approach to a biblical foundation for mission and to expand and contextualize it.

was not a central concern. When they graduated and took up their pastoral roles, they were not prepared to preach and teach, or to exercise pastoral care and discipleship, for the purpose of leading and forming *missional* congregations. And then the opportunity to do something to change this picture came my way unexpectedly. I was invited by some leaders in Phoenix to come and carry out some new experiments in theological education, and for the past eight years I have had the privilege of working in theological education with pastors and leaders from many confessional traditions by wrestling with the questions I have been asking all along: What is mission? How do we find our place—and how do we help people under our pastoral care find *their* place—in God's mission? What does "finding our place" look like in daily life?

One of the exceptionally gifted pastors I met in Phoenix was Jim Mullins. Jim had been grappling with these same questions for some time, and he had found the theological traditions that had nurtured me, and their expression in my writings, helpful. Jim was bursting with creativity, imagination, and energy and had been given a platform to do something with these gifts. He began to put into practice much of what we were discussing. He had stories to tell and concrete illustrations to stimulate the imagination. He was developing metaphors and exercises to help people take up their place in God's mission. So when the occasion arose to write a book with him that would enable us to express together what mission might look like when put into action, I was delighted to take the opportunity.

But before we speak more about the book, we need to hear Jim's story.

Jim's Story

What is God's mission?
What is my role within God's mission?
What does mission look like in daily life?

I have been wrestling with these questions for over fifteen years, but one day in particular stands out in my memory as a time when it seemed more important than ever to find the answers. I wish I could say that it was a day when my answers to those questions led me to glorify God and love my neighbor. It wasn't. In fact, it marked the beginning of what was to be my biggest failure in attempting to participate in God's work. The day was September 11, 2001.

I had been a follower of Christ for about two years and a college student for two weeks. With crusty eyes and disheveled hair, I stumbled half asleep into my Sociology 101 class at Mesa Community College. There was a commotion in the hallway—it sounded like someone was crying—and we trailed out after our professor to see what all the noise was about. A mix of students and faculty huddled around an old portable television on wheels that had been pushed into the hallway. They were watching the towers fall. Half of us stared at the television in shock; half of us scrambled to find an available telephone. We knew the shrapnel from this one day would affect the rest of our lives.

With each passing week after September 11, I became more of a disciple of television and talk radio. As I was exposed to images of angry Muslims with guns, my heart began to simmer with anger. That simmer became a boiling rage as I began to equate all Muslims with terrorists. Even though I had never met a Muslim in person, I said some of the most slanderous and ethnocentric things about Muslims that you could imagine.

Eventually I was called out by a few Christian friends who gave me a choice: I needed either to repent of my idolatrous and unloving heart or to disassociate from Jesus altogether, because I was running his name through the mud. I took several days to pray and reflect on Scripture, which led to a season of God exposing my sinful motives and leading me into repentance. The Spirit began to renew my mind and give me a different understanding of mission as I began to see God's heart for all nations. As I read the Gospels, I was gripped by Jesus's call to love our neighbors and enemies alike. He didn't just talk about peace and loving enemies but actually modeled it when he died for his enemies, including a vengeful sinner like me, on the cross.

My season of repentance led to the conviction that I should make a few Muslim friends. Eventually I moved into a predominantly international neighborhood near Arizona State University to extend hospitality and friendship to international students. This was an important time for me of reimagining the nature of God's mission. After living there for several months, I began to imagine what it would look like for a whole community of people to move into that neighborhood, live life together, and extend hospitality to the international students that God was bringing from all over the world—places like Saudi Arabia, Pakistan, and China.

Sitting at a coffee shop in that neighborhood, I wrote a vision paper. I started sharing it with my friends, inviting them to move in, extend hospitality, and proclaim the good news. We called ourselves the "Moravian Community," because a number of us had been reading about an eighteenth-century community of refugees in Germany called the Moravians, a group of ordinary people who believed in an extraordinary God. They were used by him to bring the gospel to the ends of the earth. We were captured by their story and prayed that God would use ordinary knuckleheads like us too.

About eighty people initially responded and joined the Moravian Community; about a third of them moved into the international student neighborhood.

We organized ourselves around a weekly prayer meeting, six different home groups, and daily interactions with international students. Our goal was to reflect God's hospitality by breaking bread, drinking tea, and helping these newcomers navigate the complexities of life in America. Hundreds of international students heard the gospel and saw it displayed by this peculiar community of ordinary people. We also had a vision of sending people to unreached countries. Eventually over twenty of the members of our community moved overseas to bear witness to Jesus. Even my wife and I led a team to Turkey and lived there for three years.

Our time with the Moravian Community and our three years in Turkey created a perfect opportunity to ask important questions about God's mission and how normal people like us should participate. Whether it was while eating bagels on Sunday mornings in Tempe, Arizona, or while snacking on Turkish simit on the streets of Ankara, my community of young, zealous followers of Christ kept returning to the same few questions:

What is God's mission?
What is my role within God's mission?
What does mission look like in daily life?

Over the past ten years as a pastor, I've found that most people who know and love God are asking the same things.

What is God's mission? Within the Moravian Community this question was framed in a number of different ways. Sometimes it came in the form of debating which needs were the most urgent in the world. Should we focus on poverty alleviation, church planting, or eradicating sex trafficking? Should we just focus on evangelism? Does God's mission include things like job creation, environmental stewardship, and peacemaking? Eventually we came to agree that all these things play a role in God's mission—but what should we prioritize? Some of us argued for unreached people groups in distant lands, others for the most vulnerable in our own area, and others for culturally influential cities.

We tried to figure out an answer by going to missions conferences and reaching out to nonprofits. Each one of them seemed to have a different sense of God's mission, or at least of what God cared about *most*. Each offered compelling biblical arguments, tearjerker videos, and some well-selected statistics. We walked away from each meeting and conference feeling that if we didn't sign up for their particular cause, we would be wasting our lives.

This constant exposure to missions marketing, combined with my lack of wisdom in my early twenties, gave me a serious case of Missional Attention Deficit Disorder. Not wanting to waste my life, I bounced from cause to cause and idea to idea, trying to drag the rest of the Moravian Community along with me.

For a while I thought, "Mission is about *unreached people groups*." I was deeply moved by the appeal of various missions agencies that told me about whole people groups without a single known Christian. They challenged me to leave my own country—where there was a church on every corner—and instead plant churches among the nations. They made a powerful appeal to young, zealous, single men like myself to live a "radical" life in the most dangerous places on earth. For a while I was captivated by this vision and challenged the Moravian Community to make it our highest aspiration to "get our heads chopped off in the name of Jesus." This sort of cause really seemed to attract zealous young men like me; unfortunately, it also seemed to deter wise young women from joining me on a date. But one courageous woman named Jenny gave me a chance. We were eventually married and decided that our young team should move to Turkey because it was 99 percent unreached.

Then for a while I thought, "Mission is about *church planting*." With the growth of the Acts 29 Network, many people were making the case that church planting is the most important approach to mission, because the church is sustainable and the church is the bride of Christ. Therefore, we decided not just to go to Turkey but to focus on church planting while we were there.

Then I thought, "Mission is about *campus ministry*." Months prior to moving to Turkey, I began meeting with leaders of large campus ministries who emphasized the importance of doing evangelism on college campuses because college is a crucial life stage. Having just graduated from college, many of the Moravians resonated with this idea, so we decided to try to connect with universities in Turkey.

Then I thought, "Mission is about *urban mission*." This next shift came when I started reading about the importance of mission to cities. These books argued that Paul's strategy was to focus on major urban centers because they were the centers of cultural influence. So the Moravians decided that we needed to do more than merely move to Turkey, do campus ministry, and try to plant a church. We needed to be in a large, influential urban center, like Ankara, the capital of Turkey.

Then I decided, "Mission is about *our daily work and vocations*." During my first few months in Turkey, I read several books about business as mission, the importance of providing jobs, and the opportunities to make disciples within the rhythms of everyday life, so the Moravians decided that we needed to dream up ways to start some businesses.

Then I thought, "Mission is about *living among the poor*." After being in Turkey for about a year, I began listening to sermons and lectures about God's heart for the poor and became convinced that we needed to move to an economically distressed neighborhood and live in solidarity with the poor, or even move to an altogether more economically distressed country.

Inevitably, about this time, my wife and teammates had had enough of me. I was wearing them out with a dizzying barrage of conflicting visions. Trying to figure out the most important aspect of God's mission, we hedged our bets by moving to an influential city in a country that was 99 percent Muslim to start businesses and do campus ministry and plant churches while I started looking for apartments in the poorest neighborhoods.

My disoriented team began to suggest that something must be wrong with the way I was viewing mission. In part, I was guilty of chasing the idol of significance rather than pursuing the heart of God. But mostly, I was bouncing around because I had confused the various missional *strategies* with the *scope* of God's mission. I thought then that God's mission must be about primarily one of these activities. I would eventually learn that God's mission is as broad as creation itself. And one of the ways I learned this was through Mike's writings.

During those three years in Turkey, I would often walk to my favorite café, open up my Bible, and try to find a verse with the answer to my questions about mission. One day I received an email from Chris Gonzalez, a pastor of Missio Dei Communities in Tempe, Arizona, and my good friend. Knowing the questions I was wrestling with, he recommended I read *The Drama of Scripture* by Michael Goheen and Craig Bartholomew. This book has had a profound influence on my view of mission (even though that isn't the primary aim of the book), because it so radically reshaped my understanding of the Bible itself.

I realized that I had treated the Bible as a collection of disconnected verses rather than as a unified story that gives meaning to all of life. This new way of reading the Scriptures created a massive shift in my understanding. I stopped looking for a few verses about mission and came to see the whole Bible as a story of a *missional* God whose goal is to restore a broken world. I came to see that God called a people—the church—to participate in his broad mission of restoration.

When I moved back to Arizona, I was delighted and surprised to learn that Mike had built a strong relationship with several churches there. He was instrumental in helping shape the Surge School structure, a discipleship program that I now help to lead. Eventually, he and his wife, Marnie, moved to Phoenix for part of the year to launch MTC to equip pastors and leaders for missional leadership in the local church. As I've participated in the work of MTC and been involved on the board of directors, I have come to know Mike as a friend and mentor. He's greatly influenced my understanding of theology and mission. Many of the stories I tell in this book are the results of what I've learned about mission from him. It's truly a privilege to write this book with someone who has had such a profound influence on my life.

Surge School

To understand the origins of this book it is important to understand the Surge School, which arose among a network of churches in the Phoenix area. Surge School is the brainchild of Tyler Johnson and Chris Gonzalez, who were looking for a way to lead their churches into a broader understanding and practice of mission. In 2008 it began with a handful of people from several churches. Today over three hundred people from more than forty churches participate each year. It is designed as an ecumenical discipleship program rooted in the local congregation.[6]

The curriculum is divided into four quarters. In the first quarter, participants learn to read the Bible as one story. In the second quarter, they consider how to root themselves in the gospel and live in that story. In the third quarter, they deal with the nature and breadth of the church's mission. And finally, in the fourth quarter, participants are challenged to discover how their particular callings fit into the mission of God. Many concrete questions arise from participants during the last two quarters as to what it looks like to participate in God's mission, especially in their vocations. Jim is one of the leaders of Surge School and has also led Surge tables for many years.[7] This book comes, in part, from his attempts to answer the many questions that arise and to offer stories to spark the imagination of what their participation might look like. Many of the stories told in this book are the fruit of Surge School and our mutual friends in the Phoenix area. Other stories come from Jim's or Mike's personal experiences.

6. You can learn more about the Surge School here: http://surgenetwork.com/surge-school/. You can view an older video regarding its impact on some of its earlier participants here: https://vimeo.com/72829264.

7. A Surge table is an intensive small group of participants in a nine-month discipleship program called Surge School. It's focused on viewing all of life through the lens of the biblical story, addressing idols of the heart, participating in mission, and discerning vocation.

This Book

In this book we deal with the three big questions we both have wrestled with.

What is the church's mission as it participates in God's mission? We hope to show just how big mission is. As the church participates in God's campaign to heal the world, mission includes all the approaches we mentioned above. They should harmonize, not compete with one another.

What is my role within God's mission? While most people don't suffer from the level of Missional Attention Deficit Disorder that Jim suffered from, many of us struggle to figure out where we fit within God's work. Even when we know that its scope embraces all of life, we are still left with the questions of our calling and where we should focus our energies. We wonder how our particular gifts, burdens, and experiences have equipped us to participate in God's mission. In this book, we provide opportunities to reflect on these issues.

What does mission look like in daily life? The question of *how* is not the most important question, but it might be the most overlooked. It's important to understand what God's mission is and how the particular good works we were created to do fit in, but we still need to address one more question: What does it look like to participate in God's mission through the daily rhythms of life? Rather than prescribing a script, examples of tangible practices are provided to help our readers creatively and prayerfully dream up ways to participate in God's mission that will be meaningful in their own life contexts.

The primary metaphor for this book is the symphony. Ironically, neither of us is musically gifted. Mike may have a slight advantage because his wife and all four of his children and their spouses are very musical. Because he loves them, he has developed some appreciation for classical music. However, Mike is the outlier, the one nonmusical person in a very musical family. And until recently, Jim had only limited exposure to classical music. Nevertheless, the metaphor came to him one day as he listened to Mike teach about mission while classical music quietly played in the background, making a sort of soundtrack for his teaching. Because Jim is a highly distractible but also imaginative man, his mind began to wander. Symphony, he thought, is actually a stellar metaphor for mission.

God's mission is like a symphony. He is restoring the harmony of creation to a world broken by sin. Just as a symphony brings together the string, brass, woodwind, and percussion instruments to make a beautiful sound, God's mission is to bring the various aspects of creation together in perfect harmony through the work of Christ, which is "to bring unity to all things in heaven and on earth under Christ" (Eph. 1:10).

God is the great composer of the plan to redeem, reconcile, and restore all of creation. This plan is the beautiful music of blessing that God plays for the nations, welcoming them to take their part in producing its harmony. God is also the great conductor: the Spirit guides the church in a wide array of activities that contribute to his mission, distributing various gifts and callings to his people. Just as flutes, drums, and trombones have distinct sounds to contribute to a symphony, things like poverty alleviation, personal evangelism, discovery Bible studies, and entrepreneurship all play complementary melodies and harmonies in the symphony of mission. To devalue any one of them is to diminish the overall work and distort the music of the gospel.

God invites us to join him, to participate in his symphony. In the first chapter, we provide a brief overview of the biblical story that describes the goal of God's mission, which is simply (and profoundly) to restore his good creation. Just as we can discern the heart of a composer by continually listening to his or her music, we can discern God's purpose and plan for the world by immersing ourselves in the biblical story.

When someone picks up a new instrument, they learn how to play basic notes arranged in a simple melody before moving on to complex pieces. For people called to participate in God's mission, the basic notes of simple faithfulness form the foundation on which all intentional and creative mission is built. Therefore, in chapter 2, we reflect on the simple attitudes and actions suited to the mission to which we are called. These attitudes and actions include being motivated by love, being empowered by the Spirit, understanding the comprehensive scope of mission, living in community, and being committed to incarnational presence. These are the basic, foundational notes in the symphony of mission.

We then turn to the issue of cultivating missional intentionality. We describe three major ways to participate in God's mission: stewardship, service, and spoken word. Chapter 3 provides an overview of all three of these "movements" in the symphony of mission. Each movement is important in itself and complements the others. When we lack stewardship or service or the spoken word, our participation in God's mission is incomplete.

Each of the next three chapters is devoted to one of those movements of mission. In chapter 4 we reflect on the stewardship movement and how we are called to display the glory of the Father through the work of our hands. In chapter 5 we focus on the service movement and how we display the love of Christ by washing the feet of the world. In chapter 6 we attend to the verbal proclamation of the gospel—what we call the spoken word movement—and how we're called to participate in the work of the Spirit by opening our mouths.

The next section of the book focuses on important practices for participating in God's mission. We start in chapter 7 with a reflection on calling—finding our place within God's mission—providing several practices, exercises, and insights to help discern what kind of instrument God has made each of us to be within his mission. Chapter 8 focuses on our specific contexts, defines specific areas of mission focus, and reflects on specific ways to perform the symphony of mission. Finally, the last chapter concludes with three practices—subversive Sabbath, praying like a human, and lament—to help the reader persevere through the challenges of participating in God's mission.

Ultimately, our aim in writing this book is to help God's people participate in the symphony of mission through all aspects of life. John Calvin once said, "The whole world is a theatre for the display of the divine goodness, wisdom, justice, and power, but the Church is the orchestra."[8] Along with Calvin we issue an invitation to see every aspect of life—from life at home to daily work, from private conversations to public discourse—as practice rooms, recital chambers, and concert halls in which to perform the symphony of mission. In sharing the following chapters, we hope we will all be able to discern our places in God's mission and together perform the music of God's glory, love, and power for a listening and watching world.

8. John Calvin, *Commentary on the Psalms*, trans. James Anderson (Edinburgh: Calvin Translation Society, 1839), 5:178. Calvin is commenting on Ps. 135:13.

ACKNOWLEDGMENTS

It remains for us to thank the many people in our lives who have made this book possible. As always I (Mike) am grateful for my family and the MTC board, who are so supportive of my work. But the writing of this book has also made me acutely conscious of and thankful for the many pastors I work with in various places, especially in Phoenix, Brazil, and Hungary. While I have attempted to keep myself deeply rooted in pastoral leadership in the local congregation so that my scholarship serves the church, I am aware that many of the pastors I serve know how to implement what I teach in ways that move far beyond me. That I have learned much from Jim's pastoral wisdom about what mission is and what it should look like is evident in the book that follows. The many gifted pastors I have partnered with have greatly expanded my understanding of God's mission and our place in it.

I (Jim) must express my deep gratitude for my wife, Jenny. This book could have been filled with hundreds of stories of her sacrificial love and hidden generosity. Her life is a beautiful commentary on the self-giving love of Christ. And my daughter, Elliana, has been my tour guide in the kingdom of God. Each Saturday morning as we spend time giving thanks to God, she expresses gratitude for the simple, overlooked, yet profoundly glorious aspects of creation—like pinecones, Tuesday afternoons, and geckos. Her unique lens for God's world has helped me see the goodness of creation and the possibilities of creative love, two themes that will be prevalent in this book. And it is to Jenny and Elliana that I want to dedicate this book.

I would also like to express my gratitude to the church in Arizona, especially those congregations that are part of the Surge Network. It has been a gift to be able to partner with them in displaying the glory of God in the desert. The idea for writing this book emerged from my conversations with the Surge team, especially Dennae Pierre, the executive director of Surge, whose leadership has been stellar and friendship, emboldening. God has also used Chris Gonzalez and Tyler Johnson in profound ways to launch Surge and MTC.

Words cannot do justice to my gratitude for Redemption Church and especially Redemption Tempe, where I have encountered countless examples of creative love. It has been a great privilege to serve alongside my fellow elders and pastors there. I'm sincerely grateful for the many friends who have read and provided feedback for portions of this book and especially for Sari Klontz, who truly knows how to cultivate goodness out of the soil of the English language. I must mention my gratitude for three mentors who encouraged me to write and whose lives profoundly influenced this book: Steven Garber, Rick Love, and Mark Rentz. I'm thankful for the generosity of Reese and Teena Dare, Ron and Gennie Fuemmler, and Chuck and Kathi Bishop for providing the space for me to have a few writing retreats. While much of my writing happened on Friday mornings at Crepe Bar, it was fueled by my conversations with my dear brothers on Tuesday mornings and my MTC cohort on Thursday mornings.

We are also thankful to Jim Kinney, who supported this project so fully and helped in the process of moving it to completion. Doug and Karey Loney have helped to make this manuscript much more fluent and clear. It comes from their ability to write and use the English language. It also comes from their knowledge of the subject matter in their own lives. We are indebted to them.

Together we dedicate this book to Tom Shrader. Tom went to be with the Lord in January 2019, and so he will not be here to see the release of this book. Thankfully we were able to read this dedication to him and share our gratitude for his work the month before he died. His work has and will continue to influence Phoenix in a rich variety of ways. There are few ecumenical networks of churches that have accomplished as much together or had so many congregations working together on so many projects. Much of this has been led by pastors, now in their late thirties and forties, who were discipled by Tom. He planted and pastored Redemption Gilbert (formerly East Valley Bible Church), which subsequently became a flagship church in the Surge Network. Tom planted many theological seeds that have borne much fruit in many churches in the Surge Network: an outward-looking, service-oriented church; a church that confesses Christ's lordship over all human life, including the public square; a church that disciples leaders; and a generous and self-giving church. He handed off the fruit of his own labors to younger men and supported their work as they recognized that changing times need fresh approaches and new directions. The work in Phoenix is the work of God's Spirit, but God used Tom as an instrument. We are thankful for Tom's work and life, and we dedicate this book to him as a token of our gratitude.

I

STORY

Listening to the Symphony

"First, we must learn to listen!" This was the mantra that Mr. Terry, my seventh-grade band teacher, would repeat each day to an impatient class of teenagers. Before we picked up the shiny new instruments our parents had purchased for us, Mr. Terry wanted us to learn how to listen to music. And so, for the first several weeks of class, he played famous pieces by Beethoven, Bach, and Mozart. He encouraged us to listen closely to the nuances of each movement. He helped us discern the sounds of each instrument and explained the historical context of each piece. By having us listen to these musical masterpieces, he was giving us the big picture and showing us what we were stepping into.

Inevitably, impatience would get the better of us. Whenever Mr. Terry stepped out of the classroom—even for a brief moment—dozens of us would flip open the cases under our chairs, pick up our instruments, and begin making truly horrible sounds. Wendell's trumpet sounded like an elephant with asthma, Dave made the drums sound like drunk thunder, and I slobbered and hooted on the reed of my clarinet.

Wendell, Dave, and I never really learned how to play those instruments. We wanted to perform without first learning how to *listen* to music. We eventually dropped the class, but several of our friends continued and actually learned how to play. By being willing to listen, they became able to participate. Later, when we were in high school, I would often listen to them play powerful songs

1

from their place in the stands of the football stadium. I was glad I could be on the football team, but I always wondered what it would have been like to actually learn how to play a musical instrument.

When it comes to the symphony of God's mission, we must start by listening. Though many of us pick up books like this one because we want to learn how to *perform* in God's mission, we first need to be *informed*, and that happens by listening. We need to listen to how God and his people have been performing the symphony of mission for thousands of years, to reflect on the biblical story and how it shapes us for mission. As we do this, we will understand the nature and scope of God's mission and how to join in. If we are unwilling first to listen to God's symphony, then our attempts to participate might just result in loud, obnoxious noise. But if we listen to the biblical story and allow it to shape the way we live in the world, we might just be able to join God in playing the music of the gospel for our neighbors.

In this chapter, we will take a look at the biblical story as a whole so that we can better understand the wide scope of God's mission. This chapter is not meant to replace the words of Scripture but to give an overview of its broad movements—creation, rebellion, and restoration—to shape our view of God's mission to restore and reconcile his good creation.

The Question of Mission

I asked several friends from different backgrounds what they thought of when they heard the word *mission*. Here were some of their responses:

Acts of rescue and bravery, like the coast guard rescuing a capsized sailor

Pithy corporate mission statements

California architecture

Indigenous people being stripped of their culture

Tortilla chips

Space travel

Mormon missionaries on bicycles

As you can see, the answers greatly varied. I'm also aware that even among my primary audience of Christians within North America, this word carries different shades of meaning. Some associate *mission* with planting churches overseas, while others associate being "missional" with hipster Christians drinking craft beer. Furthermore, I know that some of my Muslim friends might associate Christian mission with military crusades. The word *mission* comes with a lot of baggage.

But the word itself is a simple one and comes from a Latin word meaning "to send." And when we open the pages of the Gospels, we see that our God is a sending God. The Father sends Jesus into the world as the savior of the world, and Jesus sends his Spirit to continue his work in and through his people. Jesus also sends his people to bear witness to his saving work (John 20:21). In this chapter, we will observe how God's mission is to restore all that's broken in the world and how he creates a community to participate in that mission. Christopher J. H. Wright puts it this way: "Fundamentally, our mission (if it is biblically informed and validated) means our committed participation as God's people, at God's invitation and command, in God's own mission within the history of God's world for the redemption of God's creation."[1] In this book, *mission* always refers to God's continuing work to restore creation and to our own active participation in that work.

When I talk to some of my friends who don't yet know Jesus, they bristle at the idea of Christian mission. They think it's arrogant to try to change people's opinions about what they believe and to make claims about Jesus being the savior of the world. They will often say that faith should be private: "It's good if it helps you, but you should keep it to yourself." On one hand, I can sympathize with their concern. Many people have tried to promote Christianity in aggressive, harmful, or disrespectful ways, often doing more damage than good. However, in a sense we are all on a mission because all of us are attempting to figure out how this messed-up world could ever be made right. And if we think we have the answer, why would we want to keep it to ourselves?

Underneath the troubling thoughts that taunt us at night and the headlines that haunt our days, we are all asking the same question: How can things be made right? Every pill we pop, every tear we cry, every bullet fired from the barrel of a gun is another small monument to the mystery we are trying to solve.

Humanity has sought to solve the mystery of the world's brokenness in a myriad of ways. We've established religions and rituals to try to please God (or "the gods") in hopes of garnering favor. Some of the things that we treat as gods may not seem like gods, but when we trust technology or political ideologies to save us, they become the center of our lives and so function as our gods. Sometimes we promote them with the religious zeal of a missionary, even though they continually fail us.

---

1. Christopher Wright, *Mission of God's People: A Biblical Theology* (Grand Rapids: Zondervan, 2010), 22–23.

We've sought salvation in technologies that have certainly benefited the world but have never fulfilled their promises. Often they've simply made new and bigger problems. Nuclear fission brings heat to cold homes—but also the threat of a nuclear winter. The internet promises to bring us together, but it makes a world of lonely people who spend more time looking at glowing rectangles than into the faces of other people. In an attempt to solve the mystery of the world's brokenness, we've also established political and economic systems like communism, socialism, and capitalism, along with many other failed isms, that promise freedom but make us slaves.

Even modern-day health fads are attempts to solve the mystery of brokenness. But essential oils aren't potent enough to cover the stench of sin. Veganism will never find enough kale to cover our shame. A paleo diet cannot restore us to our original humanity. Crossfit cannot make us strong enough to carry the weight of the world's brokenness. Our world is marked by a brutal and comprehensive brokenness: we are spiritually cut off from God, socially separated from one another, and physically alienated from the flourishing we were intended to experience. All serious questions about how to restore goodness to this broken world reveal our longing for salvation, our desire for a mission worth pursuing.

God's Purpose and Plan

In Ephesians 1:11 we are told that God has a plan and that he is working it out in history. God's mission is the working out of his plan as it is narrated in the Bible, a plan that has a certain goal toward which he is moving, a destination at the end of a long historical journey.

What is this goal? The Bible describes it in many different ways. Paul tells us that when times reach their fulfillment, God will bring *unity to all things* in heaven and earth under Christ (Eph. 1:10). In another passage Paul says that God's goal is to *reconcile to himself all things* on earth or in heaven (Col. 1:20). Peter describes this same goal as the *restoration of everything* as promised by the prophets (Acts 3:21). Jesus tells us that the purpose of God's mission is the *renewal of all things* (Matt. 19:28). For many first-century Jews, the goal toward which God was moving was to establish the *kingdom of God*, and Jesus affirms this expectation when he announces the good news of the arrival of the kingdom (Mark 1:14–15)—though not quite in the way Israel expected. The prophets speak of the goal of history as the coming of *shalom*, the restoration of the original creational harmony among God, humanity, and the nonhuman creation (Isa. 9:7; 52:7; Zech. 9:10). Moses uses a similar term when he speaks of *blessing* as the goal of God's mission; the blessing that was enjoyed in the original creation by both nonhuman and human (Gen. 1:22, 28) will be restored first to God's people and then, through them, to the whole world (Gen. 12:2–3; Gal. 3:8–9).

Though these images differ slightly from one another and accent different things, together they point to the fact that God's mission is to restore the entire creation and the life of humankind to what God intended in the beginning. The goal of God is not to take a people out of this world to live as disembodied spirits in heaven but to restore a people to live bodily in the midst of a restored creation. God's mission is not merely to clean up some individuals so they can live with him in heaven but to clean up the creation so he can come back and live here with us. God's mission is to return the world to what it's supposed to be.

Creation: The Way It's Supposed to Be

In the beginning God created the world with astounding beauty and overwhelming goodness. Creation is God's masterpiece. Beethoven composed the Ninth Symphony, Coltrane wrote *A Love Supreme*, Hugo wrote *Les Misérables*, and Michelangelo painted the Sistine Chapel. But these masterpieces, as great as they are, pale in comparison with the first and ultimate work of art: God's creation of the world.

When you look at the first page of Scripture, you read that God is the creator of a "very good" creation. God creates his masterpiece by making light and darkness; the oceans and the atmosphere; land, water, and vegetation; the sun, moon, and stars; avian and aquatic life; and land animals. As he surveys every aspect of creation, he declares that it's good! His good creation contains both function and beauty, with things like trees, which give beauty to our eyes, food for our stomachs, clean air for our lungs, and shelter to protect us from harsh weather. Every morsel of goodness that you've ever enjoyed—from stargazing to playing a guitar—is the result of God's great work of creation. His work is perfect.

The most important character in the story of creation is God himself. The story is ultimately not about Adam and Eve, the serpent, or even the beauty of the garden, so much as about God. The earth is the arena where God will display his glory, majesty, goodness, and love. In this place there's perfect harmony among God, humanity, and the rest of his nonhuman creation. The whole earth is good and exists for God's glory.

The harmony and flourishing of the creation as it comes from the hand of God can be described by the Hebrew word *shalom*, a word that the prophets later used to describe creation regained. It describes the purpose of creation and the goal of God's mission. It carries the rich meaning of a world that experiences flourishing because of right and harmonious relationships among God, people, and all creation. Cornelius Plantinga puts it this way:

> The webbing together of God, humans, and all creation in justice, fulfillment, and delight is what the Hebrew prophets call *shalom*. In English we call it peace, but it means far more than just peace of mind or ceasefire between enemies. In the Bible shalom means *universal flourishing, wholeness, and delight*—a rich state of affairs in which natural needs are satisfied and natural gifts fruitfully employed, a state of affairs that inspires joyful wonder as the creator and savior opens doors and speaks welcome to the creatures in whom he delights. Shalom, in other words, is the way things ought to be.[2]

A world of shalom is marked by goodness and wholeness. The biblical story of creation invites us to imagine a world of shalom, where we delight in God, in one another, and in the nonhuman creation.

Flourishing in Relation to God

Genesis 1–2 describes life as humans experience and enjoy the intimacy of God's presence. Can you imagine what it would be like to experience communion with God without the distance, confusion, insecurity, and distortion of sin?

Instead of falling asleep in prayer, wondering if anyone is listening to your rambling, you would take naps in the perfect security of God's presence. Each moment would be filled with wonder as you explored God's great gift of creation, encountering oak trees in the forest and crawdads in the river. Each new discovery would cause your heart to beat strongly with worship, gratitude, and curiosity. Not only our prayers and encounters with nature, but all of our work and play, relationships and culture making, were designed to be pervaded by God's presence.

Each day you would stroll through a perfect park in perfect communion with God. Imagine a life without shame, where you truly knew God and were intimately known by him. Imagine the sum total of all the joyful relationships you've ever experienced. Those are mere hints of the infinitely deep joy that humanity is meant to experience in the unhindered presence of God. Think about every smile, warm embrace, rich conversation, and meal where you

---

2. Cornelius Plantinga Jr., *Not the Way It's Supposed to Be: A Breviary on Sin* (Grand Rapids: Eerdmans, 1995), 10 (italics original).

lingered long at the table because you didn't want to leave your company. The sum total of these experiences doesn't even begin to describe the type of flourishing that was known in the garden because of humankind's intimate knowledge of God.

Flourishing in Relation to One Another

God created the world so that men and women would flourish together in community in a vast array of relationships, not as isolated individuals. God says only one time before sin that creation is not good—when the first man is alone (Gen. 2:18)! He creates a companion for Adam, and he commands them to "be fruitful and multiply." But this is not a command just to add people to the world. The commands to fill the earth, subdue it, and rule it follow. In other words, the act of human intimacy leads to human communities and a variety of healthy relationships and institutions. Life in God's world was intended to be relational, and we were made to flourish together in a multitude and variety of relationships.

Can you imagine life without social strife? Can you imagine conversations in which you knew that you were fully loved and known by the listener? Can you imagine a world where all people selflessly served one another? Can you imagine a world where arguments, insults, divorce, abuse, war, school shootings, and racism had never been known? It's difficult for us to fathom life without these things—but in the garden it would have been impossible to imagine their existence.

Flourishing in Relation to the Nonhuman Creation

After each day of creation is described in Genesis 1, God declares the goodness of what has been made. Each aspect of his world was created to provide meaningful work and deep rest without the presence of pain and suffering. Can you imagine what that would be like? Imagine feeling the warmth of the sun without the threat of skin cancer. Imagine a hard day of work where every moment is full of meaning and purpose, void of pain and monotony. Imagine delighting in the fruits of your labor and then completing each day with a feast of celebration—in weather better than San Diego's and with cuisine better than the finest Michelin-rated restaurant. Each breeze would remind you of the life that God had breathed into your nonasthmatic lungs; with each bite of food, you'd taste the glory of God's creation.

Shalom is the harmony of all creation, where God orchestrates all of life to work together perfectly for his glory. Shalom means perfect fellowship between God and his creation and among all the parts of creation: lions and lambs, bermuda grass and tomato vines, men and women, children and parents, day and night, creativity and conservation, poetry and prose. Just as the goal of an orchestra is to bring all the instruments together in harmony to display the glory of what was composed, the goal of God's creation is to bring all aspects of life into harmony for the glory of the creator. Creation is a symphony of shalom.

Humanity: The Conductors of Creation

God is the composer of creation, but he doesn't choose to make music alone. He made humanity to be the unique part of his creation that joins him in his work. In Genesis 1 God declares each part of his creation to be "good," but the addition of humanity elevates the status of creation to "very good," because humans are uniquely commissioned to cultivate creation's potential. When God made Adam and Eve, he didn't create a mere audience for his own music but a class of apprentice musicians, commissioned to be the co-conductors of the symphony of creation.

Human beings have a unique vocation. We are given staggering authority (Ps. 8) and are called explicitly to "have dominion over" and to "subdue" creation (Gen. 1:26–28; 2:15). But these words have often been misunderstood. They aren't a mandate to scorch the earth through carelessness. Instead, they are an invitation to develop the hidden potential embedded in creation while caring for it (Gen. 2:15). These words call us to stewardship and summon us to join God in his work.

God didn't make a ready-made world. He created the raw material of all good culture and then commissioned humanity to be culture makers. From the soil of creation, humans were invited to make beautiful paintings, sturdy buildings, joyful playgrounds, efficient transportation, delicious recipes, and absorbing games. As they do this work with excellence, they display the majesty of the creator God whose image they bear. The first role we're called to play in the symphony of God's world is joining God in cultivating creational potential, opening up the order and beauty of the various aspects of creation through the work of our hands.

Our identity is as unique as our calling; we are the only part of God's creation made in his image (Gen. 1:26–28). There's something about us that uniquely displays what God is like. We are like monuments of God, placed in the world to pay homage to the true composer of creation. When humans fulfill their vocation, they display the brilliance of creation and the glory of God's character. This is the way it was intended to be.

After creating humans in his image and giving them the unique vocation of cultivating his world, "God blessed them and said to them, 'Be fruitful and increase in number; fill the earth and subdue it. Rule over the fish in the sea and the birds in the sky and over every living creature that moves on the ground'" (Gen. 1:28). The concept of blessing here is quite similar to that of shalom. In the Old Testament *shalom* carries the connotation of thriving and flourishing, of delight and joy, as we live according to God's intended design. We enjoy the divine favor and empowerment for satisfying fruitfulness that comes from a right relationship with God, with others, and with the nonhuman creation.

In the garden, Adam and Eve enjoyed the abundance of God's blessing, the perfection of God's masterpiece of creation. They walked with God, relating to him with perfect love, reverence, and worship. Their days were filled with fruitful work and harmonious relationship. They were safe, secure, loved, and flourishing in a world with the perfect balance of productive work and delightful rest. They dwelled in harmony with God, each other, and the physical creation. They experienced spiritual, social, and physical well-being as God intended. And with the ongoing blessing of discovering even more of the goodness of creation together with God and each other, they were heirs to a marvelous future.

Rebellion: Not the Way It's Supposed to Be

So all was well in the garden—until tragedy struck, when the harmony of shalom was shattered by rebellion.

God had given the whole world as a garden buffet to Adam and Eve to work within and to feast on. They had the freedom to explore and enjoy almost everything, to sink their teeth into every plant, except for one: the tree of the knowledge of good and evil (Gen. 2:15–17). Life in the garden was abundant and perfect. Employed as God's gardeners, their work was delightful and meaningful. The only possibility of pain, death, and decay was found in rebellion, in eating the fruit of that forbidden tree. The ripples of destruction from such an act would ultimately make their way through every aspect of creation, tearing the fabric of the perfect order and harmony of God's world, vandalizing shalom. Things would then *not* be the way they were supposed to be.

On that fateful day, Satan, in the form of a serpent, whispered lies to Adam and Eve. He said that the fruit forbidden to them wouldn't really bring death; instead, they could dethrone God with the special knowledge that came from the tree. Tragically, they listened to the snake instead of to the Source of all goodness in the garden.

Adam and Eve gave the middle finger of rebellion and plucked the fruit from the tree, expecting a greater degree of life. Instead, it tasted like death. While the juice of the fruit still dripped off their chins, the world began to unravel. Soon it was filled with all manner of evil: death, destruction, and decay. The world that had been filled with harmony and abundance was soon filled with alienation and scarcity. A world intended for joyful worship, intimate relationships, fruitful work, and sensual delight in the goodness of creation had been infected by idolatry, injustice, and the curse. All because of sin.

Idolatry

Adam and Eve, who had walked with God as friends in the cool of the day, were now hiding from him. There would be no more afternoon picnics with God in the garden. Their act of rebellion was just the first in a long, weary history of rebellion and idolatry.

God had given humanity skilled hands with opposable thumbs to fashion good and beautiful things, to throw footballs, build oak tables, hold babies, and mold the world into a full and flourishing place that glorifies God. But instead we used those adept hands to carve idols, little statues to be worshiped in God's place. We began to worship the objects of our creation rather than the creator of all things, and this misdirected worship continues today. True, we may not carve statues—but we still make idols. We are creatures who worship and serve. It's our nature, and we can't change it. But rather than worshiping and serving God as the author of creation, we worship and serve created things and center our whole lives on them (Rom. 1:22–23, 25). Our sinful hearts make gods out of money, power, nations, sex, and many other once-good things that we have turned into evil by giving them the place of *ultimate* things. And this idolatry drives our social and cultural life. No wonder the Bible speaks about sin most often in terms of communal idolatry!

Injustice

Another effect that came from the rebellion of humanity was social alienation and disharmony. When Adam and Eve began to blame each other, their argument was the first in a long line of relational pain. The self-sacrificing love that had characterized relationships between people turned to self-serving attempts at mastery. Because of that one act of rebellion in the garden, we now live in a sin-stained world, where our reality is one of conflict, injustice, fear, shame, and suspicion. Right now as you read these words, somebody is out there writing a racist comment on Facebook, someone is wounding a child with vicious words, someone is twisting together the wires of a bomb, someone is feasting and wasting their goods while another starves, and someone is lying in shame in a hotel room a few miles from their marriage bed. This is not the way the world is *supposed* to be. It's the way that it *is*—because of our sin and rebellion against God.

Adam and Eve didn't cease being image-bearers after they were evicted from paradise. They continued to fill the earth with people and develop culture. However, sin had infiltrated the heart of humanity, and idolatry had twisted every aspect of social and cultural life.

Genesis 4–11 provides a tragic overview of the spread of sin and its effects. The good gift of competition devolved into toxic rivalry; the good gift of work led to murder. Upon hearing of God's approval of Abel's excellent animal husbandry, Cain responded in a jealous rage that caused him to use the very hands that were meant to cultivate life as weapons to bring death to his brother.

Sin corrupts not only commercial life but also art, civics, and the full scope of human society. Cain, the former farmer (now with blood on his hands), became the founder of a city that would soon be filled with corruption (Gen. 4:17). Later we hear about Lamech, the author of the first poem after the fall (Gen. 4:23–24), celebrating his own brutality in a boastful song to his wives. Sin infiltrated every aspect of human life and culture—family, work, art, commerce, food, city planning—everything.

Sin is not just an individual act; it is also embodied in human communities and the cultural institutions that build systems and patterns of life to desecrate God's creation and devastate other image-bearers. Whole cultures form their lives around idolatry, and this leads to injury and injustice. Because of sin, we live in a world where entire systems are built around injustice, such as the global sex trade, companies that profit from abortion, and justice systems that give harsher sentences to the poor than the rich.

All of humanity deserves the judgment of God, and this is what we see in the story of Noah. God cleansed the earth with a flood, which hit the reset button on the world, intending to build a new humanity from the family that built the boat. However, Noah's family proved to be just as tainted by sin as their drowned neighbors; they too participated in idolatry, injury, and injustice (Gen. 6:5; 8:21). Yet rather than hitting the reset button again, God affirmed that he would continue his mission of filling the world with his glory as he blessed Noah and restated the cultural mandate to be fruitful and multiply (Gen. 9:1–17).

It's evident that the whole world is polluted by sin and needs to be rescued from the idolatry, injustice, and evil of the world. The very human beings who were created to reflect God's image became those who distort his image. Those who were made to care for God's good world have desecrated it. By the time we reach Genesis 11, we see the whole of human culture and society corrupting God's world. We see a world that desperately needs God to launch a rescue mission.

Curse

It is not just humanity that has been impacted by their own rebellion. Because humans were made rulers and stewards of the creation, the whole of that creation was drawn into the wake of human rebellion. A curse was placed on the nonhuman creation, and now it too (in the words of Alfred, Lord Tennyson) is "red in tooth and claw." Animals suffer, and the world convulses in earthquakes, tsunamis, and tornadoes. No wonder the whole suffering creation longs for the liberation of God's children, because it too will then be liberated from the bondage of the curse (Rom. 8:19–22).

The nonhuman creation is corrupted not only within itself but also in relation to humanity. The work of our hands is burdened by sin's effects. No longer is work delightful, joyful, and satisfying; too often it is filled with pain and boredom. Our selfish domination of the world and the culture making that ignores the biblical mandate of care and stewardship have created staggering problems—from hunger to AIDS, nuclear weapons to global warming, a dwindling energy supply to an impending water shortage, toxic chemical waste to the loss of protective ozone. We have become victims of our own exploitive and destructive desires.

Our bodies are wracked by pain and disease, and ultimately, we all face death. Right now, as you read this sentence, the physical effects of sin are wreaking havoc on the world. Somebody is sitting in a hospital hearing that their child has stage IV cancer; autism is muting the words of a beautiful person who just wants to be known; and bacteria in the very room in which you sit are seeking to assassinate you. Cancer, arthritis, flash floods, concussions, dehydration, diarrhea—they exist only because sin exists. Even if you have lived a relatively easy life or don't feel pain in this moment, you know that your day is coming. The eyes that you use to read this sentence will one day close.

These statements are not meant to bring gloom and despair—quite the opposite! When we know the bad news, we can finally hear the good news. When we feel the darkness, we can welcome the light. As we feel the bone-chilling cold of our reality, we long for the warmth. And there is good news, light, and warmth.

Restoration: Returning the World to the Way It's Supposed to Be

The creation groans—and we do too—longing for liberation from the pain and curse that have come on our world because of our foolish rebellion. We long for the world to be restored to the way it's supposed to be. And there is good news! The story of God's mission narrated in Scripture is precisely this good news: he intends to return the whole world and the entirety of human life to its original shalom and blessing, the way it's supposed to be. And we are called to participate in this mission. So let's listen carefully to the symphony, as it has been going on for some time, so that when our time comes, we can pick up our instruments and play our parts.

Israel

Rather than engaging in a solo performance, God chose to execute his mission in a peculiar way. He formed a human community set in the midst of the old world to be the nucleus of the new world he is calling into being. Sinful humans, who had rebelled against him and flooded the world with death, became his chosen instruments. Just like he composed the beautiful symphony of creation, he began to compose the masterpiece of re-creation, a symphony of mission aimed at restoring the corrupted creation. Like a composer picking out a pen to craft a masterpiece, God began by choosing a feeble couple, Abraham and Sarah, whose children would one day become a nation and begin the healing of a diseased creation. Indeed, quite strangely, God's mission began with the election of a childless couple who was trapped in the same idolatrous rebellion as everyone else (Josh. 24:2). In the story that unfolds from them we can listen to how God performs his mission through his people.

ABRAHAM AND HIS FAMILY

The human impulse is to use powerful tools for important tasks, but God's ways are often different. God launches his rescue mission by forming a community that would become his partner in countering the curse of sin. He doesn't adopt an existing superpower like Egypt but chooses one man, Abraham, from whom to build an entire nation.

God sends Abraham to another land, where he blesses him so that he might be a channel of that blessing to all the nations of the earth (Gen. 12:1–3; 18:18–19). Blessing is the human flourishing and delight that come when we live according to God's creational design. Blessing is the joy and satisfaction we find by living in right relationship with God, others, and the nonhuman creation. Thus, if creational blessing and shalom are to be restored, they can come only in a restored relationship with God, one another, and the nonhuman creation. And this is precisely what we see in God's promise to Abraham.

The promise to Abraham extends to a people who will come from his and Sarah's children, a people who will be restored in their social, economic, and cultural relationships, living according to God's original intention in a fruitful land that is itself both the gift and blessing of God.

But all of this can be enjoyed only in relation to the God who gives it. The promise first given to Abraham in Genesis 12 soon takes the form of a binding agreement: "I will establish my covenant as an everlasting covenant between me and you and your descendants after you for the generations to come, to be your God and the God of your descendants after you. . . . I will be their God" (Gen. 17:7–8). God is restoring a people to again love, serve, and worship him.

Blessing, then, is the restoration of relationship with God, one another, and the nonhuman creation. But this blessing isn't just for Abraham and his descendants, though it begins there. They are to be a channel of God's blessing to the surrounding nations, to all peoples on the earth. God chooses Abraham to "direct his children and his household after him" to keep the way of the Lord and do what is right and just. In this way they will display God's blessing, and God will, through them, bring blessing to all the nations on earth, for his love and care extend to them all (Gen. 18:18–19).

God's covenant people are to be the means by which God deals with the sin and evil of the world. The curse of Genesis 3–11 will be replaced by the blessing promised in Genesis 12. Abraham's family bore in their own lives the *promised* goal and purpose God has for the world. The blessing and shalom that will one day fill the whole earth when God *completes* his mission are to characterize God's people in the present as he launches that mission.

Such an exalted vocation! It almost sounds ludicrous to make this claim for God's people, especially when we read about the seemingly mundane and broken lives of Abraham, Sarah, and their descendants. Most of the book of Genesis narrates their story. What's clear from these chapters is that though God's people continually fail, God remains faithful to continue his mission and use his people. Genesis is not about the heroics of Abraham but about the loving heart of God, whose mission is to extend his blessing to all nations. He is El Shaddai, the one who has the power to overcome all barriers that stand in the way of restoring blessing to his creation (Gen. 17:1; cf. Exod. 6:2–3).

EXODUS

The Genesis story ends with a small tribe of Abraham's people making their way to Egypt to escape famine. Exodus opens four hundred years later and describes a vast number of people living in bondage to the Egyptian Pharaoh and the gods he represents. If Abraham's descendants are to be a people of blessing to the nations, they must first be liberated from the Egyptian gods. And so there is a dramatic showdown between Moses, who represents the Lord, and Pharaoh, the human representative of the Egyptian gods. God brings judgment on the Egyptian gods through a number of plagues aimed directly at their supposed powers (Exod. 12:12), and Israel is liberated from idols to serve the living God. Then, through Moses, God leads a reluctant and complaining people through the wilderness to Mount Sinai.

Why has God done all this for a small and little-known nation of slaves? Perhaps they wondered that too. The Lord tells Moses to answer this question with these words: "You yourselves have seen what I did to Egypt, and how I carried you on eagles' wings and brought you to myself. Now if you obey me fully and keep my covenant, then out of all nations you will be my treasured possession. Although the whole earth is mine, you will be for me a kingdom of priests and a holy nation" (Exod. 19:4–6). The language of being a treasured possession is the language of election. It is precisely because the whole earth belongs to God that he chooses Israel to be a priestly kingdom and a holy nation. The role of a priest is to be a representative of God to the people and a mediator of God's presence and blessing. Israel is to assume a priestly role among the nations, to be a unique and holy people who display the wisdom of God's ways and act as mediators of his presence and blessing among the nations.

Israel's participation in God's mission isn't based on merit, strength, or competence but is a response to God's redemptive grace. Before sending them to the land to take up their mission, God takes up residence in their midst in the tabernacle. The God who rescued them is present and powerful among them to enable them to carry out their priestly mission.

LAW

Since God's people are to bear the promise of blessing, they are called to live distinctive and holy lives, manifesting God's shalom in the midst of the nations. And so God lays out a vision of what a holy, priestly kingdom might look like, ruled by a law based on loving God and neighbor (Exod. 20–23).

The law was good news for Israel; they celebrated the law in song as a way of life more precious than gold, more sweet than honey (Pss. 19:7–11; 119).

It governed the worship and service of God and made provision for patching up the broken covenant when Israel disobeyed (Leviticus). It shaped all of Israel's cultural, political, social, agricultural, and economic life to manifest the shalom and blessing of God (Deuteronomy). It directed them in faithful stewardship of the nonhuman creation. God's laws were uniquely beautiful in comparison to the laws of other nations because they were built on God's creational intentions for all that he had made. For example, God's law cared for the weak and powerless rather than protecting the rights of the powerful, unlike the other law codes of the day (and today!). God's law gave a glimpse of what shalom was supposed to look like in the ancient Near Eastern cultural context and displayed the unique wisdom of God's ways to the surrounding nations (Deut. 4:5–8). As Israel embodied and obeyed these decrees in their communal life, they were showing the world a pattern of life filled with blessing that would lead to the flourishing of all creation.

The laws of the surrounding nations were centered on the whims of harsh dictators, but God's law was centered on God's will for creation. Some of these laws may seem obscure to us, but they were intended to counteract the evil and unjust practices that were so prevalent in that day. We can see this in a small sampling of those laws: God's people are called to love God (Deut. 6:4) and neighbor (Lev. 19:18), honor the role of family (Lev. 19:3, 32), care for the poor (Deut. 15:7–11), pursue economic justice (Lev. 19:13), extend compassion to the disabled (Lev. 19:14), display fairness in their legal system (Lev. 19:12, 14), practice commercial honesty (Lev. 19:35–36), maintain sexual integrity (Lev. 19:20–22), practice environmental stewardship (Lev. 25:4), and extend care and hospitality to immigrants (Deut. 10:18–19).

Many of these examples come from Leviticus 19. In this chapter, God gives his people a vision for holiness but first explains why holiness is so important: "Be holy because I, the LORD your God, am holy" (v. 1). God's people are to be the living analogy and visible example of God's holiness. If they obey these laws, they will display to the nations around them the God who is good, loving, just, wise, and merciful and who cares for the fullness of creation.

LAND

God promised Abraham that he would make his family into a people with a land of their own. Blessing, flourishing, and shalom mean taking one's place in the good creation, being at home in this world, as Adam and Eve were in the garden. Israel did not know this joy until well after the exodus. Abraham and the patriarchs wandered around Palestine with only the *promise* of a physical homeland (Heb. 11:9). The Israelites were landless immigrants in Egypt, and after they left, they wandered through the wilderness with no home to call their own. But this all changed when the Lord (keeping his promise to Abraham) took Israel into the land under Joshua (Josh. 21:43–45).

The land was given as a gift—the beachhead of the new creation—so Israel could know and manifest God's shalom. But as always in God's economy, a gift brings task, and privilege brings responsibility. Israel was to faithfully embody God's law in the land as a sign of God's purpose to restore blessing and shalom to *all* nations and the *whole* creation. But the land also came with temptation and danger. The peoples already living in the land promised to Israel were in bondage to the idolatry, injustice, and curse of Adam's rebellion. The danger was that Israel would fall into the same idolatrous patterns. Instead of being a light, they might be overcome by the darkness; instead of being distinctive, they might become immersed in the pagan idolatry of their neighbors.

The drama of Israel's vocation among the nations was to be played out in a very public way. Israel was located at the crossroads of the ancient Near Eastern world and thus in the military crosshairs of the more powerful and established nations surrounding them. They were vulnerable and needed to rely on God's provision and protection for their survival.

Today it's common for people to choose their homes based on the view. They want to look out their windows and see something beautiful: ocean or forest, sunset or elegant architecture. When God chooses real estate, he also chooses it for the view—but it is a completely different kind of view. He chose that particular plot of land for Israel so that his people would always be in view of the surrounding nations. Ezekiel writes, "This is what the Sovereign Lord says: This is Jerusalem, which I have set in the center of the nations, with countries all around her" (Ezek. 5:5). God placed his people in the sight of the nations like a glass house in Times Square, so that through them, all might see the distinctiveness of God and his law (Deut. 4:8–9). God's real estate business is missional to the core. Instead of giving his people a good view, he makes *them* the good view, which is a glimpse of the blessing and shalom that comes from God.

If they would choose to obey and live out their calling with faithfulness and justice, the surrounding nations would catch a glimpse of the way the world was intended to be under God's rule. But if Israel would succumb to the pagan idolatry of the surrounding nations instead and fail to live out their priestly calling as a holy nation, God's covenant judgment against Israel would be on display to the nations.

Sadly, Israel chooses the path of sin and disobedience. By the end of the book of Judges, God's people are not flourishing in the land. They are on a downward spiral into idolatry and injustice. Though they possess a beautiful law, they do not fully obey it and so fail their role in God's mission. Rather than being distinct and holy, they mimic their neighbors; rather than being a light to the nations, they sink into the darkness.

KINGDOM

The book of Judges narrates Israel's descent into apostasy and idolatry. The book ends on a surprising note—with the need for a king (Judg. 21:25). Somehow the author believes that a king might be the means of ending Israel's slide into covenant rebellion. The book of Samuel (which follows Judges) tells how God grants them a king so that they might fulfill their vocation to be a shalomic presence among the nations. Unfortunately Israel wanted the wrong kind of king, one like the leaders of "all the other nations" (1 Sam. 8:5, 20). Though God wanted them to have a king to mediate his rule and to enable Israel to live faithfully under his reign, Israel wanted a king to displace God and fight on their behalf. God grants their wish and gives them Saul. But, unsurprisingly, Saul's reign ends in failure and disgrace.

After Saul, God provides his people with David, a king who is after God's heart (1 Sam. 13:14) and is willing to lead his people into covenant faithfulness by defeating Israel's enemies, centering Israel's life on God's presence in the temple, and enforcing the law. Only under such a faithful king could Israel hope to fulfill their calling.

But even though David is faithful, he is also a man with clay feet, unable to live completely under God's rule himself, let alone able to empower Israel to do so. But God gives David a promise: he will provide Israel with a king who will be able to accomplish what David cannot. This king will rule over a worldwide and everlasting kingdom (2 Sam. 7:11–16). The promise God made to Abraham—that blessing would come first to Israel and then through Israel to the nations—would be fulfilled by a king in David's line. And in the Psalms and Prophets from that point on, Israel's hope is for a king descended from David who will usher in God's own kingdom: "Then all the nations will be blessed through him, and they will call him blessed" (Ps. 72:17).

King David commissions the building of the temple in Jerusalem, and it is eventually built by King Solomon. The temple was symbolic of God's unique covenant and presence with his people, a beautiful place of worship and the centerpiece of Israel's life. But the temple was never intended to be for Israel *alone*: it was to be, one day, a house of prayer for *all* nations (Isa. 56:6–8). God was establishing an island of worship in a sea of idolatry. He was calling his people to worship the true God in the sight of the nations and to invite those nations to join them (Ps. 67:4; 96:3–10).

Israel's worship wasn't just about performing rituals; it was intended to be a robust engagement with God through lives of public holiness, lives that would display the uniqueness of God's justice and mercy. The prophets boldly condemned the people of Israel when they practiced the rituals of worship while simultaneously practicing idolatry and injustice. God frequently expressed his anger and disgust with Israel when they observed the Sabbath, fasted, and sacrificed meticulously while oppressing the vulnerable. Worship is acceptable to God only when it is accompanied by a life of justice and righteousness (Isa. 1:10–17; 58:6–8; Amos 5:21–24).

The kingdom of Israel was supposed to be a light to the nations and an instrument of salvation to the ends of the earth (Isa. 49:6), showing the nations what shalom looks like under the reign of God. But instead of leading Israel to live under the rule of God, the royal descendants of David led the nation to covenant rebellion. The temple, instead of nourishing Israel with worship and sacrifice, became a place of perfunctory practice and false assurance. In order for Israel to fulfill their calling to manifest before the nations what God intended for human life, they needed something much greater: a greater evidence of the presence of God than even the temple; a greater King than even David.

EXILE

Eventually Israel's rebellion brings God's judgment. He raises up pagan nations to conquer them and remove them from the land. They had refused to be a light to the nations, so they were to be scattered among the nations. This judgment happens in two waves. In 722 BC the northern ten tribes (simply called Israel) are scattered by the Assyrians, and in 586 BC the remaining two tribes (called Judah) are conquered and carried off to Babylon in exile. This is a low point in Israel's history.

Because they had refused to serve the true God, they would have to live in a place drowning in idolatry. Because they had refused to be a blessing to others, they would themselves experience the curse of exile. Because they had marginalized the most vulnerable, they would learn to live on the margins. Because they had desecrated the good land, they would now plant gardens in foreign soil. It's hard to overstate the pain, shame, and disillusionment God's people experienced as they stumbled down the road to Babylon.

Life in exile came with hard questions about how God's people should live. Did they still have their vocation? If so, how could they be faithful from a position of weakness? What did faithfulness look like apart from the over-arching guidance of the law? Which aspects of Babylonian culture should be rejected and which should be embraced? What does a missional identity look like under the oppressive rule of a pagan king? How should they relate to their Babylonian neighbors? Israel faced two major temptations in exile. On the one hand, some of God's people were tempted to withdraw from public witness until the exile was over. Like turtles in their shells, they attempted to retain their ways as a disengaged subculture, avoiding contact with Babylonian life. On the other hand, some were tempted to assimilate into Babylonian culture and its idolatrous practices. Like chameleons, they blended in with their surroundings and lost their distinctive missional identity, which was rooted in their covenant relationship with God.

But through the prophet Jeremiah, God shows his people a third way—neither as turtles nor as chameleons—to remain distinct and be a blessing to the nations:

> Build houses and settle down; plant gardens and eat what they produce. Marry and have sons and daughters; find wives for your sons and give your daughters in marriage, so that they too may have sons and daughters. Increase in number there; do not decrease. Also, seek the peace and prosperity of the city to which I have carried you into exile. Pray to the LORD for it, because if it prospers, you too will prosper. (Jer. 29:5–7)

Although they are living in an idolatrous and unjust city, God gives them instructions to plant good gardens and build strong families. Doesn't that sound familiar? These are basically the same instructions that he gave to Adam and Eve in the garden. Even though Israel is living in a sin-stained world, they are called to continue to engage in the good culture-making work that was given by God in the garden. Even in exile, God calls them to be hints of hope and conduits of human flourishing.

When Jeremiah mentions the word *welfare* or *peace* in Jeremiah 29:7, he's using the Hebrew word *shalom*. Again, shalom refers to a flourishing world of right relationships among God, people, and the nonhuman creation. God's people were called to bear witness to the steadfast love of God by seeking the flourishing of the same people who killed their families and carried them into a foreign land. They were called to seek the good of Babylon even as Jerusalem lay in ruins. They were called to love and bless their most hostile enemies as they cultivated a small plot of God's garden in the heart of the city. They were called to live such distinctly good lives that they provided a taste of God's kingdom amid a buffet of idolatry, oppression, and injustice.

Eventually, the exile comes to an end, the temple is rebuilt, and Jerusalem is reinhabited. However, Jerusalem lacks its original grandeur and suffers under the oppressive authority of occupying powers for generations to come. Israel is still virtually in exile as they live under foreign kings as slaves on the land that God had given them (Neh. 9:36–37).

PROPHETS

Israel had been invited into God's mission, but they had failed their part. They were intended to be the solution to sin but were part of the problem instead. The word of Israel's prophets, the visionaries who looked forward to a day of restoration, was their only source of hope. The prophets spoke of a day when God would flood Israel with his presence, replacing war with peace, establishing perfect justice, and renewing all of creation. Wounds would be bound, families would be reconciled, suffering would become a discarded memory, and all nations would gather to participate in the joyful worship of God.

The prophets poetically described a day when lions would dwell with lambs and instruments of war would be refashioned into farming equipment; because there would be no need to engage in war, all people would live together in perfect safety (Isa. 2:4; 11:1–10; Zech. 9:10). The prophets described a shalom of holistic human flourishing that would come when God would restore the blessing for which the world was intended. The prophets expected this peace to come from a unique king, a "Wonderful Counselor, Mighty God, Everlasting Father, Prince of Peace," who would establish a kingdom defined by justice and shalom (Isa. 9:6–7). They expected this peace to be a work of God's Spirit poured out in power to renew the whole creation.

Of course, God could have bypassed Israel in his continuing mission to establish shalom. After all, he had given them their chance, given them everything they needed to accomplish their mission. But he does not abandon them. God says to Israel, "I am going to act and prove myself holy *through you* so that the nations will know that I am the Lord." He promises to gather Israel and restore them by cleansing them from their idolatry, giving them new hearts, and putting his Spirit on them. Then Israel's covenant identity would be restored: God would be their God and they would be his people (Ezek. 36:23–28). Through them, God would fulfill his mission: the nations would be blessed and restored to creational life. God would restore and renew the whole creation and the entirety of human life to what he had always intended. This was the good news that Israel longed for during the time of the prophets (Isa. 52:7–10).

Interlude

Israel waited and waited and waited—for four hundred years. One oppressive empire followed another, finally culminating in Rome, the most cruel of all. But many in Israel kept reading their Scriptures. Their historians promised that blessing would one day fill the earth. Their psalms enabled them to sing with hope that God's kingdom would one day come. Their prophets filled them with the vision that God would return, rule the earth through his Messiah, and renew the earth by his Spirit. But when? How? And how were they to live until that day?

These questions were answered differently by various factions in Israel, and this often led to conflict, sometimes violent conflict, among them. But in spite of these differences, Israel shared the common belief that their God would return to Israel and act to restore his kingdom there. However, they also shared something much less noble. Under the oppression they had experienced first from Persia, then Greece, and finally from Rome, their prophetic hope had warped into an ethnocentric hatred for their oppressors, and their concept of God's kingdom transformed into a lust for nationalistic privilege. God would certainly return but *just for Israel*—or worse, just for a specific *faction* within Israel. Israel had lost her sense of missional vocation.

Meanwhile, all Israel waited for God's story to reach its climax.

Christ

And that climax *does* arrive, but in a way very different from what anyone in Israel could have imagined. Israel had been chosen by God to be the means by which he would deal with the sin of the world and restore creational blessing to his whole creation. Then Jesus comes, *representing* Israel, taking their vocation on himself and fulfilling it. But he does so in a very unexpected way.

Jesus seizes the primary image of Israel's hope: the kingdom of God. When Israel had imagined the kingdom, they thought God would destroy the pagan kingdoms that stood in opposition to him and restore his own righteous rule (Dan. 7:1–14). This powerful work of God by the Spirit in the Son of David was, they believed, to take place at the very end of history. But when Jesus comes, he announces that the kingdom of God has arrived *already* (Matt. 4:17, 23; Mark 1:14–15; Luke 4:43). "The restoration of creational blessing and shalom is present in me," Jesus says. The end-time salvation had arrived.

The salvation Jesus announces is comprehensive. Luke, for example, speaks of a salvation in which humanity is restored to God and to just relationships among themselves. Salvation is demonstrated in the mighty acts of Jesus. Here we have a window into the new creation (Luke 7:20–22). Salvation is forgiveness of sins (religious), liberation from demonic power (spiritual), restoration of the marginalized and ostracized (social), justice for the poor and food for the hungry (economic), liberation from political oppression (political), the end of natural disasters (natural), and healing of the body (physical). Salvation turns back and erases all the evil consequences of human rebellion against God.

Yet as Jesus was proclaiming the arrival of God's kingdom, the evidence of sin and evil remained. What sense did it make to say that the kingdom of God was present already (Matt. 12:28)?

Many within Israel wrestled with that same question. Israel understood history (based on the teaching of their rabbinic scholars) as two ages: the old age and the age to come. The old age (introduced by the sin of Adam) is dominated by evil, death, and suffering. The age to come, ushered in by the Messiah in the power of the Spirit, would erase all evil, death, and suffering and restore creational blessing (see fig. 1.1).

Even Jesus's own followers had trouble understanding how Jesus could be the expected one while the evil of the old age remained (Luke 7:18–23). To explain, Jesus offered insight into the nature of the kingdom through parables (Matt. 13), and his teaching would come more fully into focus after the Spirit was given at Pentecost (Acts 2). The post-resurrection picture offered by the New Testament writers is that, indeed, the kingdom *has* come, ushered in by the life, death, and resurrection of Jesus. God's power to heal and renew has been unleashed. But the evil powers of the old age remain. The two ages overlap: the power of the Spirit to restore blessing and shalom is already present in the world, but sin, demonic powers, and cultural idolatry remain as well (see fig. 1.2).

Why is the final coming of the kingdom delayed? The Gospels provide an answer: so that Jesus might gather Israel with the hope of gathering the nations in the future. And so, in his early ministry, Jesus begins to gather a community to inherit the kingdom (Matt. 21:43; Luke 12:32). He is the shepherd of the

Figure 1.1

Rabbinic Expectation

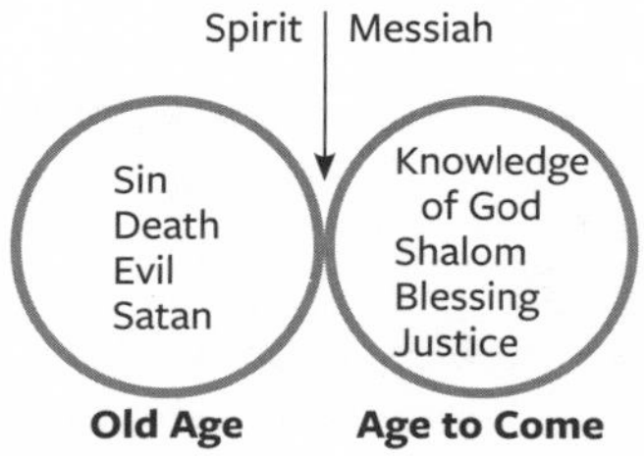

Spirit | Messiah

Sin
Death
Evil
Satan

Knowledge
of God
Shalom
Blessing
Justice

Old Age   **Age to Come**

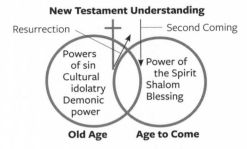

Figure 1.2

The climactic events in the arrival of the kingdom of God are the death

end-time, promised in Ezekiel, Jeremiah, and other prophets to gather the lost sheep of Israel and restore them so that they might fulfill their vocation (Jer. 23:3; 31:10; Ezek. 34:11–31; Mic. 5:4; Zech. 9:16; Matt. 15:24). The kingdom comes to this gathered disciple community as both gift and task. They take on the mission of Israel to be a light to the nations (Matt. 5:13–16). Jesus challenges the ethnocentric hatred within Israel and restores his little flock, now the true Israel, to a mission of suffering love for the nations, including those who hate them (Matt. 5–7). They are to make known the blessed and shalomic life of the kingdom made present in Jesus in the power of the Spirit.

The climactic events in the arrival of the kingdom of God are the death and resurrection of Jesus. In the death of Jesus, the sin, suffering, and evil of the old age were defeated. In the resurrection, the age to come was inaugurated. The death and resurrection are cosmic events: turning points in world history. They settled the goal of history; the resurrection life began in Jesus and will one day fill the earth. But until that day, the gathered and restored community is sent to every part of the world to make known the good news: God reigns victorious, and his gracious rule will one day cover the earth.

The Gospels end with Jesus sending his newly gathered and restored "Israel" to the nations. Against all expectations, it will not be a glorious kingdom established in Jerusalem that draws the nations of the earth but a sent people in whom Christ dwells by his Spirit. This sent community is the gathered and restored community of Israel. But as they go to the nations, the kingdom will take on more of a gentile shape. Jesus's mission of gathering will continue in this new era in history until he returns to complete the work he began.

The Church

We have been listening to God's symphony of mission, waiting our turn to play our part. That symphony moved through Israel to Jesus. Israel's mission to bear the promise of God's ultimate purpose for the whole world was ful-filled in Jesus's mission. But there is still more music to hear before we can take up our own instruments. Jesus handed off his mission to his newly gathered and restored community, inviting them to continue what he had been doing in Israel, to extend it to the ends of the earth. We cannot immediately jump from Jesus to our own part. The New Testament offers about a century of mission history in which the early church faithfully carried out its mission. Together with the mission of Jesus and the mission of Israel, the mission of the early church demonstrates the trajectory that leads us to God's ultimate purpose for creation.

Jesus confined himself to the lost sheep of Israel, but his completed work meant that blessing could extend to *all* nations. The New Testament makes clear that this new covenant community continues the mission not only of Jesus (John 20:21) but also of Israel (1 Pet. 2:9–10). Whereas Israel bore the *promise* of God's purpose for the world, the people of God today bear a *foretaste* of God's purpose for the world. The *promise* was fulfilled in the death and resurrection of Jesus. Because the Spirit has been given, the church has become a *foretaste* of new life and now bears it in every part of the world for the sake of all nations.

Shortly after his resurrection, Jesus spent over a month with his new dis-ciple community, but they were still confused. He appeared to them as the Resurrected One and talked with them about the coming of the Spirit and the kingdom of God (Acts 1:1–5). In Israel's vocabulary the words *resur-rection*, *Spirit*, and *kingdom of God* meant the end was about to dawn. So the disciples asked the most obvious question in the world: "Now you will restore the kingdom to Israel, right?" The answer to that question set the stage for the continuing mission of God's people until the end of the age (Acts 1:6–8).

In a nutshell, Jesus's answer was, "Yes, the kingdom *is* come—but in a way you never expected!" Jesus then articulated his agenda. First, the ultimate end would continue to be held off (Acts 1:7). Second, the Spirit would be given as a foretaste, down payment, and firstfruits of end-time shalom. The power of God's ultimate salvation would be given *already* in a provisional way in the midst of history. Third, this gift of salvation would constitute his followers' very identity as a witnessing community. "You *will be* my witnesses" was not a command but a declaration of fact. Having received a foretaste of the coming salvation, they would thereafter witness to it with their lives, and that witness would overflow into words and deeds that also pointed to what Jesus accomplished. And finally, this witness would begin in Jerusalem and move to the ends of the earth (Acts 1:8).

While all of this sounds quite familiar to us, it would have been astonishing to those early followers of Jesus. The words of Jesus changed the shape of the mission of God's people; the music of his symphony modulated into a different key.

The mission remained in Jerusalem for a short time as Jews were invited and gathered into the new covenant community. But gradually it moved outward, and gentiles were added. Soon the church was predominantly gentile, and the change in the composition of God's people was becoming clear. This change raised concern among Jesus's earliest followers. For thousands of years, God's people had been an ethnically Jewish people, unified by their place on one piece of land; now they were becoming a multiethnic and nongeographical entity. For fifteen hundred years the law had shaped the religious, cultural, political, economic, and communal lives of God's people; now they were to live under the laws of others, laws shaped by pagan idolatry. Many Jewish Christians simply were not ready for such a radical change. The ensuing controversy led to a council in Jerusalem where it was affirmed that God's people would take many cultural forms in the various cultural settings of the world (Acts 15). Somehow God's people needed to live faithfully in every dimension of their lives—including the social, economic, and political dimensions—within cultures organized to serve gods other than the Lord God. This was incomprehensible to Jewish believers at the time, and only when we feel this fully justifiable incomprehensibility can we understand the painful tension that we ourselves must live with in the idolatrous cultures in which *we* are set.

We might ask how the church was so faithful in its mission in that first century. The first answer Luke gives is that it had an *attractive life* of generosity, justice, mercy, joy, and power—and that this was the most powerful witness to the kingdom (Acts 2:43–47; 4:32–35; 11:19–29). But added to this distinctive life were the church's *words* of witness (Acts 4:32–35). It is not possible to separate the two, for it was the church's *life* that made its verbal testimony so compelling. Other places in Acts also show that the witness of life led to the witness in word. But if the church was to be faithful to Jesus's mandate, its mission of witness needed to extend "to the ends of the earth." So where Christian communities were not already established to make the good news known, the church sent out some of their own to be off-site witnesses. Paul and Barnabas, and then Paul and Silas, were sent off to plant new witnessing communities. When their initial work was done in each of these new places, the people of the newly planted church were left to be the witnesses for that area.

One more important point needs to be made about the communal life of the church as witness. Today, "church" can refer to a private body in which certain religious practices take place. But the word *church* (*ekklēsia* in Greek) was chosen for the early believers precisely because it identified them as a *public* body. The church was the beginning of that new humankind that would one day fill the earth. The church is God's people living as God intends across the whole spectrum of their lives. Thus, we see the church gathered on Sundays to renew their lives by the Spirit, to live the life of the kingdom more and more. Then, Monday to Saturday, the same church is scattered throughout its members' various vocations, bearing witness to the lordship of Jesus in all the places its members find themselves. Lesslie Newbigin puts it this way:

> Is it not an illusion that constantly fogs our thinking about the Church that we think of it as something which exists manifestly on Sunday, is in a kind of state of suspended animation from Monday to Saturday? The truth of course is that the Church exists in its prime reality from Monday to Saturday, in all its members, dispersed throughout the fields and homes and offices and factories, bearing the royal priesthood of Christ into every corner of His world. On the Lord's day it is withdrawn into itself to renew its being in the Lord Himself.[3]

The apostle Peter urges the individuals who make up the church to take up their callings in public life as a witness to the gospel (1 Pet. 2:8–17). He speaks of being holy "in all you do" (1:15) and of a "way of life"[4] and "good works"[5] in the public square. Christians were to participate in all aspects of their cultural lives distinctively because they were aliens to the idolatry of the Roman Empire, living out a different story.

The book of Acts ends on a somewhat strange note. A fast-paced, gripping narrative seems simply to grind to a halt with an anticlimactic ending. Yet this ending is purposeful: Luke is using a literary technique to say that the story he has been telling is not over. He invites his readers to participate in what God is doing and tacitly challenges us to find *our* places in the continuing story.

Consummation

The day is coming when God's mission of restoration will be complete. The apostle Peter describes this day as the future *restoration of all things*: "Heaven must receive him [Jesus] until the time comes for God to restore everything, as he promised long ago through his holy prophets" (Acts 3:21).

---

3. Lesslie Newbigin, "Bible Studies: Four Talks on 1 Peter," in *We Were Brought Together*, ed. David M. Taylor (Sydney: Australian Council for the World Council of Churches, 1960), 96–97.

4. Six times Peter speaks of a way of life (1:15, 18; 2:12; 3:1, 2, 16).

5. Six times Peter speaks of good works (as a verb: 2:15, 20; 3:6, 17; as an adjective: 2:14; as a noun: 4:19).

The prophets he refers to had described a coming restoration and the mending of all that was broken. The prophets pointed to a day when God himself would reign over all nations, bringing a final peace through his power, lifting up the oppressed, humbling all oppressors, and remaking the world in perfect shalom. War, terrorism, racism, hunger, and genocide would all vanish under God's peace. In Isaiah 65, we see a vision of the new heaven and new earth as a place of joy instead of tears (vv. 18–19), life instead of death (v. 20), homes instead of homelessness (vv. 21–22), productive work instead of wearisome toil (v. 22), blessing instead of the curse (v. 23), the attentive presence of God instead of his absence (v. 24), and safety instead of danger (v. 25).

We don't know exactly what this new heaven and new earth will look like. But the final chapters of the book of Revelation invoke this vision again in a glimpse of what's coming when Christ returns. Heaven and earth reunite, and the presence of God repairs all that is broken and restores all that was lost in the fall.

> And I heard a loud voice from the throne saying, "Look! God's dwelling place is now among the people, and he will dwell with them. They will be his people, and God himself will be with them and be their God. 'He will wipe every tear from their eyes. There will be no more death' or mourning or crying or pain, for the old order of things has passed away." He who was seated on the throne said, "I am making everything new!" Then he said, "Write this down, for these words are trustworthy and true." (Rev. 21:3–5)

This is a description of complete and final restoration. Notice that this passage doesn't say God is making all *new things*; it says that he's making all *things new*. This wording is important; it's the difference between replacement and restoration. God isn't throwing his creation in the dumpster; he's pulling it out of the recycling bin. Describing this future restoration, Al Wolters says, "God does not make junk, and we dishonor the creator if we take a negative view of the work of his hands when he himself takes such a positive view. In fact, so positive a view did God take of what he had created that he refused to scrap it when mankind spoiled it, but determined instead, at the cost of his Son's life, to make it new and good again. God does not make junk, and he does not junk what he has made."[6]

The rebellion of humanity brought pain and misery to the world. In Revelation we see that a day is coming when idolatry will be replaced by a palpable sense of God's presence. The hands that once carved false gods out of wood

6. Albert M. Wolters, *Creation Regained: Biblical Basics for a Reformational Worldview*, 2nd ed. (Grand Rapids: Eerdmans, 2005), 42.

will be lifted in praise to the One who is on the throne. Wounds will be healed and tears wiped away. Graveyards will become monuments to life, hospitals will be repurposed as playgrounds, and Band-Aids will become stickers that remind children of the God who heals the nations. Former enemies who once lobbed insults like bombs will become reconciled friends who craft encouraging words with poetic eloquence. Warring nations will find peace under the reign of their true King, replacing weapons of war with instruments of worship and clenched fists with hands of friendship.

Participating in the Symphony of Mission

What does this story mean for us? Where is our place in God's mission? When we listen carefully to each development in Scripture, we hear a story about God's mission of reconciliation, a beautiful symphony where God recovers every aspect of life and restores it to the original harmony for which it was made. This mission has been accomplished through the work of Christ. However, we are called to be more than spectators. We are to be the orchestra through which he brings the music of the gospel to the listening world, each of us an instrument created for specific contributions to the overall harmony.

Just as God formed the nation of Israel to be his instrument of mission, Jesus assembles the church as his instrument of reconciliation in the world. When the apostle Paul uses the language of "reconciliation," he describes what God is doing not only *for* us but *through* us. We are reconciled to God in Christ; we become a new creation and then are commissioned to *join* his work of reconciliation (2 Cor. 5:17–19). Paul describes us as being "ambassadors" on behalf of our reconciling God (5:20). We don't fully establish the kingdom, but we do build embassies (outposts of flourishing) in a world of spiritual idolatry, social injustice, and physical curses. We are called to scatter into our neighborhoods and workplaces to provide a foretaste of the future shalom that Jesus will fully establish when he returns. This means that our participation in God's mission should promote the spiritual, social, and physical reconciliations implicit in the gospel.

We have a mission to pursue humanity's reconciliation to God. God is speaking to the world, offering peace and forgiveness, appealing to people to turn from the idols that enslave them and turn instead to the God who offers true freedom. God is the one who speaks these words of invitation and reconciliation, but he chooses to speak through *our* mouths (2 Cor. 5:20). Therefore, we participate in God's mission by proclaiming the gospel in words and pointing people to Christ, the one who reconciles us to the Father through his life, death, and resurrection. Because of our commitment to being God's ambassadors of spiritual reconciliation, we should value preaching, evangelism, counseling, Bible translation, and the many types of ministry that use language to urge people to be reconciled to God.

As ambassadors of peace, we are to provide the world with a glimpse of the kingdom by promoting peace in our communities (Rom. 12:17–21). However, this is not to be a shallow peace that glosses over injustice. We are called instead to exercise a holistic kind of love for our neighbors, a love that considers the fullness of their lives as well as the systems that harm them. We are called to bear witness to the future social flourishing of the kingdom by working for our neighbors' flourishing now, both in our interpersonal relationships and in our engagement with society. Because of our commitment to being God's ambassadors of social reconciliation, we should value the many aspects of mission that promote the flourishing of society and our relationships with one another—from peacemaking to policy making, from welcoming refugees to protecting the unborn, from the hospitality of the dinner table to the diplomacy of the negotiating table.

We have a mission also to pursue reconciliation between humanity and the nonhuman creation. Our world is suffering greatly beneath the weight of a worldview that exalts humanity to the place where it dominates the earth for its own benefit. Our mission is to struggle toward a reconciliation that brings care and stewardship to the nonhuman creation as well as compassionate care for the suffering of human beings. In the Gospels we clearly see that Jesus in his earthly ministry pushed back against the physical effects of the fall. He restored sight to the blind and hearing to the deaf. He healed disease, fed the hungry, and conquered death by raising Lazarus from the grave. The day is coming when physical death and pain will be no more. In the meantime, as God's people, we are called to bear witness to the future fullness of the kingdom by meeting the physical needs of our neighbors. Because of our commitment to being God's ambassadors of reconciliation, we should value the many aspects of mission that address physical needs, such as providing housing for those who are homeless, employment for those who need work, food for the hungry, and art for a world in need of wonder.

If God's mission is indeed to reconcile all that was broken through the fall and to restore shalom to creation, then our participation in that mission should be as broad as the world's brokenness. As witnesses to the full gospel of Christ, we are called to engage all of life for the glory of God and the good of our neighbors.

2

SIMPLICITY

Learning the Notes

Surrounded by mangled wrapping paper, I glanced one last time at my father's beaming, slightly manic smile. I tossed the bow to the side, then flipped the flimsy silver latch on what was clearly a guitar case. As I flung it open, I saw a candy red electric guitar autographed by a rock star from the 1980s named Ted Nugent.

Of all the gifts I had received in my ten years of life, this one was supreme. Truthfully, I wasn't much interested in rock music or playing the guitar. (As much as I tried to hide it, my baggy pants and frequent outbursts of MC Hammer lyrics betrayed my preference for other types of music.) I just wasn't a fan—but my father was. Watching him watch me open this birthday present brought me the sense of a deep connection with my dad. In possession of the most expensive gift I'd ever received, I willed myself to become an instant fan of rock music and decided—that day—that I was going to learn how to play the guitar.

Over the next several days my head filled with visions of rock-and-roll grandeur. I imagined myself twisting my fingers along the neck of the guitar, growing out long hair to flip from side to side, and making the kind of music that would merit opening for my dad's favorite bands—Led Zeppelin, Ted Nugent, and ZZ Top. I imagined seeing my dad in the crowd with his squinty eyes, intense smile, and Elvis-impersonator hairstyle, delighting in

his firstborn son's music and watching me play that bright red guitar with
such mastery that people would start to call me the white Jimi Hendrix.

I had pretty much everything I needed—a guitar, an amp, and a book with
the chords for some of the greatest songs in history. I was ready to go! Except
for one little thing: I didn't know the slightest thing about playing guitar.

Within a week of returning from summer vacation at Dad's house in Colorado, I tracked down a guitar instructor and asked him to teach me to play.
He insisted that I needed to learn the rudiments of music first, the notes and
rhythms that are the foundation of every song.

But I was impatient and gave up. This was the beginning of a yearly cycle.
Usually I would rediscover that guitar in the closet sometime during the summer, begin plucking around, and then zealously declare myself a future rock
star. I'd find another guitar teacher, pay them for a few sessions, and give up
after several weeks without learning to play even one song. I passionately
wanted to make music for my father, but I wasn't patient enough to learn
the basics.

When it comes to mission, many of us want to do something great for
God, to enjoy his smile as we make the music of mission. However, many
of us vacillate between passion and apathy because we overlook the basics.
We're unwilling to put in the time to learn the rudiments of mission—those
specific notes and rhythms on which the music rests. Beginning in the next
chapter, we will journey toward finding our places within God's mission and
discovering tangible ways to love our neighbors. We will reflect on creative
ways to proclaim the gospel: how to display God's glory through the work
of our hands and how to show Jesus's love through acts of sacrificial service.
These things are like melodies in the symphony of mission. But before we can
ever play a melody, we need to learn how to play the basic notes and learn
the rhythms that bind them.

In this chapter, we will reflect on six things that are the foundation of all
missional engagement. Think of them as the basic sounds that together make
up the harmonies within the symphony of mission. Each will be represented
by a simple but easily overlooked word:

With—Mission must include incarnational presence.

From—Mission must be empowered by the Spirit.

And—Mission must be comprehensive in scope.

Us—Mission must be communal.

Be—Mission must include a distinct way of life.

Why—Mission must be motivated by love.

Just as we must learn the basic notes in order to play beautiful music, we must learn to understand the meaning of these basic words if we are to bear witness to the glory, love, and power of God.

With—Incarnational Presence

One of the most mysterious and profoundly beautiful aspects of God's mission is his choice to accomplish his mission through the incarnation, by becoming fully human and dwelling among his creation. God didn't accomplish his mission from a distance but came to the world in the flesh, drawing near to humanity with a beating heart and breath in his lungs. Taking up the language of Isaiah, Matthew calls Jesus "Immanuel," which means "God with us" (1:23–24). In the incarnation, Jesus dwelled *with* us to show us the glory of God and to enter into the brutality of humanity.

The humanity of Jesus wasn't merely a mask to hide his divine identity. The incarnation wasn't a cosmic episode of *Undercover Boss* in which the creator of all things pretended to be human to get a closer look at his creation. Jesus was truly and fully human—with chapped lips, childhood friends, and the occasional need of an afternoon nap.

Jesus's humanity was full and gritty. Splinters pierced his skin during his carpentry work long before nails pierced his flesh during his work on the cross. Before the glory of the resurrection, Jesus rose from bed nearly twelve thousand times, rubbed the sleep out of his eyes, and stepped into the mundane rhythms of humanity—working and playing, learning and teaching, laughing and crying. He's the God who multiplied fish for the masses—he was also the human with tilapia in his teeth.

For many of us, a lifetime of singing Christmas hymns and seeing nativity scenes has reduced the strangeness of the incarnation. However, people in Jesus's day were not expecting God to come in the flesh. The incarnation was an unfathomable idea. What they *did* understand was that "presence" is central to the mission of God. In Israel's history, God dwelled with his people in the tabernacle and the temple. He was "with" his people—protecting, guiding, empowering, and displaying his glory. The presence of God was central to their identity and mission. But they were in awe of the reality that God would come so near to humanity as to reside among his people.

For first-century Jewish people, it would be hard to imagine God coming closer than the tabernacle or temple. But in the incarnation, God didn't just come *close* to humanity; he actually *entered into* human life: "And the Word became flesh and made his dwelling among us. We have seen his glory, the glory of the one and only Son, who came from the Father, full of grace and truth" (John 1:14). The Greek verb for "dwell" in this passage connotes God setting up a tent and living in it among us. Eugene Peterson's *Message* paraphrases the same passage this way: "The Word became flesh and blood, and moved into the neighborhood." In Christ, God moves into humanity's neighborhood. No longer do we come to a large and ornate building to encounter the glory of God; the glory of God comes to us through the dusty hands and feet of Jesus.

Jesus's life wasn't sanitized. He entered into a world choked by the thorns and thistles of idolatry, sickness, pain, and injustice. He didn't run from the mess; he ran toward it. He touched those with contagious diseases, he wasn't afraid to be seen with the sexually shamed, he hung out with the homeless, and he carried the kingdom through the weak and undeveloped arms of children. He didn't merely come near the suffering of others; he *experienced* suffering so that he could relate to the hardest parts of human life. Solidarity *with* us came before salvation *for* us.

Consider the many ways he can relate to human suffering through his incarnation.

Traumatic childhood. Like many children who are abused by the very adults who are supposed to care for them or like the people abused by the governments that are supposed to keep them safe, Jesus was the intended target of Herod's genocidal edict to kill the firstborn of each household (Matt. 2:14–18). His early memories were likely filled with the death of his childhood friends and the panic of fleeing his home. Before Jesus could die for them, the babies in Bethlehem died around him.

Refugee. Herod's edict also made Jesus a refugee. Can you imagine suddenly waking up in the middle of the night to leave your home and relocate in a foreign land? This is the experience of millions of refugees around the world and was the experience of Jesus, who had to flee from Israel to Egypt as a child.

Homelessness. Even though Jesus is the creator and owner of the world, he had no place to lay his head. He was dependent on the hospitality and generosity of others. In this way, he can relate to those who wander and don't know the comfort of a home.

Abuse. Jesus can relate to those who have experienced abuse. He was repeatedly hit by Roman soldiers, forcibly nailed to the cross, and stripped and shamefully exposed in front of the whole city.

Terminal illness. Even though he didn't have a disease, Jesus trembled in the garden of Gethsemane the night before the cross, deserted by his friends and facing torture and death. He can relate to those who suffer alone and know that death is near.

Injury and disease. Jesus reaches out to those with arthritis with hands that were pierced; he walks to the paralyzed with feet that were immobilized by nails; and he preaches peace to those with stage 4 lung cancer with lungs that were filled with blood.

Through his incarnation, God suffers with us.

Not only is the incarnation good news for us, but it also provides a template for how we engage in God's mission (John 20:21). Just as the ministry of Jesus was marked by real, physical presence, we are invited to participate in God's mission by being present among those to whom we are sent. This means that we really enter into people's lives by spending time with them, understanding them, and intertwining our lives with theirs. Much of mission is just showing up! It's about sharing meals, celebrating holidays, and sitting in hospital waiting rooms—being present. And the authenticity of our being present is tested when suffering comes. Will we still show up when life gets messy, when our neighbors are diagnosed with cancer or are struggling financially? Will we settle for acquaintances based on trivialities, or will we truly get to know people? When we show up authentically in the lives of others, we provide a glimpse of the God who showed up to be *with* us in Christ.

From—Empowered by the Spirit

To engage in God's mission we must know the source of our strength. God's mission calls us to do things that seem humanly impossible, such as giving up our comforts, participating in the transformation of lives, being spokespersons for God, and challenging the very powerful idols and idolatrous systems that are behind almost everything in life. Church history is riddled with stories of seemingly simple and undistinguished people doing the difficult or impossible, like contracting diseases from caring for the sick and subverting empires without picking up a sword. How did they do it? Where did their strength come from?

We need to know where our motivation and strength come *from*. Scripture is very clear that we aren't just doing something *for* God; he supplies the ability to do it. In rich agrarian language Jesus describes our relationship with him as like that between a grapevine and its branches: "I am the vine; you are the branches. If you remain in me and I in you, you will bear much fruit; apart from me you can do nothing. If you do not remain in me, you are like a branch that is thrown away and withers; such branches are picked up, thrown into the fire and burned" (John 15:5–6). How fruitless the life of a Christian is apart from the life of Christ! When we seek strength from something else, we're like a branch that has been snapped off the grapevine. The disconnected vine has no life and cannot bear fruit. It just withers and dies. Apart from deep fellowship and dependence on Christ, we cannot offer the fruit of good works or the sweet wine of the gospel.

Mission is often filled with two kinds of stories. On the one hand, there are stories of impressive, talented people whose ministries start out strong. They want to change the world for God but eventually fizzle into cynicism or drift into temptation when the world doesn't change for them. These people often rely on their impressive résumés rather than on the power of Christ, and in the end they can do nothing. But there are other stories in which God seems to delight in using unimpressive people to display his glory, the powerless to display his power, and those of low position to be the heralds of his kingdom. These people don't begin with the illusion that they are strong enough on their own. They know that they need to be in constant communion with God to accomplish even the smallest thing.

For example, even though the apostle Paul had an impressive résumé, he refused to rely on his advanced training and high status in the Roman world. He knew that, when he had been apart from Jesus, he had been a terrorist who had persecuted the church. But God rescued him and then worked through him to build the church. Paul knew that he needed to be in constant communion with God and was fully dependent on God's grace to participate in God's mission: "For I am the least of the apostles and do not even deserve to be called an apostle, because I persecuted the church of God. But by the grace of God I am what I am, and his grace to me was not without effect. No, I worked harder than all of them—yet not I, but the grace of God that was with me" (1 Cor. 15:9–10). He preached, taught, and admonished so that others might become fully mature in Christ—but he did none of this in his own strength. He insists, "I strenuously contend with all the energy Christ so powerfully works in me" (Col. 1:29).

Matthew shows us that the calling to make disciples is dependent on the power of the risen Christ continuing his mission to make disciples through us (Matt. 28:18–20). Luke and John make clear that it is the power of the Spirit that enables us to do our part (Luke 24:48; Acts 1:8; John 20:21–22). All missional engagement must be empowered by the risen Christ through the Spirit. And this means that one of the first notes we must learn to play in God's symphony is prayer. In both the life of Jesus and the life of the early church the kingdom came as the Spirit worked in response to prayer:

> If the church is indeed to be Jesus' agent in bringing his whole agenda to his
> whole world, it needs his own Spirit. Indeed, if the church attempts to do what

has to be done without constantly seeking to be filled and equipped by Jesus' own Spirit, it is committing blasphemy each time it opens its mouth. This is not a plea that all Christians should enlist in the charismatic movement. Rather, it is a plea that all Christians, particularly those involved at the leading edge of the church's mission to bring healing and renewal to the world, should be people of prayer, invoking the Spirit of Jesus daily and hourly as they go about their tasks, lest they be betrayed into the arrogance of their own agendas or into the cowardice of relativism.[1]

Crying out to God in prayer shouldn't be a last resort. It's not plan B— it's the whole alphabet. As we come to God understanding our dependence on him, he will often guide us into creative and strategic ways to love our neighbors. But creativity and strategy can never replace the work of the Spirit initiated through prayer.

We saw a great example of this several years ago when a group of believers in East Phoenix realized that a massage parlor in their neighborhood was most likely a front for prostitution, sexual exploitation, and possibly even sex trafficking. They tried to reach out to the authorities but didn't have concrete evidence of anything unlawful. So they started researching and strategizing. They began to write a vision paper about how to expose the hidden exploitation in their neighborhood. However, before they could even finish the first draft, the massage parlor closed down suddenly. They later discovered that while they had been strategizing, there was one woman from their group (her name was Erin) fervently praying each day that God would close down the parlor, expose sin, and protect the women being exploited. God answered her prayers with a potency that could never be reproduced by even the greatest human strategy. Apart from the power of Christ, we can do nothing; when we are connected to the vine, we can bear much fruit in God's mission.

And—Comprehensive in Scope

Let's start with a little thought experiment and play a game of "Would You Rather?" If you had to choose between the following, which would you choose?

Bed or breakfast? Imagine showing up for vacation and thinking you are staying at a bed and breakfast—only to find out that it's a bed *or* breakfast. The hosts inform you that you have to choose between fasting for the weekend

1. N. T. Wright, *New Tasks for a Renewed Church* (London: Hodder & Stoughton, 1992), 86.

while sleeping in one of their soft beds or having gourmet meals each morning after trying to sleep on the hardwood floors. Which would you choose?

Gas pedal or brake pedal? Imagine you are buying a car and the dealer tells you that in your price range you can only afford a car with *either* a gas pedal or a brake pedal. You would have to choose between reckless speed (and danger) and the drudgery of pushing your car everywhere you go—though you would be confident that you could stop the car whenever you want. Which would you choose?

If you had to choose one of the following options for the rest of your life, which would you choose? To live in a building made with just nuts or just bolts? To speak with only verbs or only nouns? To sleep or be awake? To eat or drink? To inhale or exhale?

These choices are absurd—even comical—to imagine because they are examples of things that were made to go together. One should never have to choose between them. One without the other diminishes both. We were meant for *and* not *or*.

The same is true with finding our place in God's mission. We don't have to choose between the various and vital aspects of God's work. Our witness is greatly diminished when we exclude important parts of mission from our lives, whether serving the poor, verbally proclaiming the gospel, or working as good environmental stewards. We are still carrying the baggage of twentieth-century church history, when the evangelical and ecumenical movements reacted against each other, each stressing *one* aspect of mission to the exclusion of another. It's time to drop the baggage.

Many followers of Christ today are still tempted to choose between various aspects of God's mission, to elevate one aspect and downplay others. Some of us are all about justice and mercy but downplay the importance of proclaiming the gospel. Others emphasize the verbal proclamation of the gospel but devalue tangible acts of service and stewardship. But God's mission is comprehensive. It's a mission of *and*, which knits together all the dimensions of God's work to renew his whole creation. Our witness should be defined by *and* as well. Here are some ways in which that plays out.

Word *and* deed. In the ministry of Jesus, word and deed went together. His words explained his deeds and his deeds authenticated his words. The apostle Paul is clear that the gospel needs to be proclaimed and displayed by good works (Rom. 15:18). To separate one from the other is to willfully diminish God's mission and distort the gospel. Lesslie Newbigin writes, "In the communication of the gospel, word and act belong together. The word is essential, because the name of Jesus cannot be replaced by anything else. But the deed is equally essential because the gospel is the good news of the active presence of the reign of God, and because this presence is to be made manifest in a world that has fallen under the usurped dominion of the evil one."[2] Words and deeds are not opposites; they belong together. Good news dances with good works to celebrate and make known the reality that God is restoring all that has been shattered by sin, demonic powers, and structural idolatry.

Staying *and* going. What's the priority? Should we as the church focus on sinking our roots deep into the places where we live, or should we leave our homes to take the gospel to unreached places? Many mission-focused organizations try to make the case that one of these should be prioritized over the other. However, we should see that the whole earth belongs to God, and he can raise up people as his witnesses for all places. For example, the apostle Paul was sent to preach the gospel to the ends of the earth (Rom. 15:20) and so kept pressing on to unreached people groups, but the apostle James stayed in Jerusalem his whole life. Which of these two giants of faith had it right? *Both* did! God cares about the depth and breadth of mission and so raises up one person to stay and another to go.

Respect *and* boldness. When it comes to bearing witness to Jesus, most people lean toward either respect or boldness. But, of course, we need both. On the one hand, our demeanor should reflect the kindness and gentleness of our God, who cares deeply about all people, lest we forget that the qualities of kindness and gentleness are fruits of the Spirit. Arrogance is out of place; it must give way to humility. Our gestures, tone of voice, and posture of listening should indicate that we truly value our neighbors and see them through the lens of dignity that comes from being made in God's image. They are not merely potential missional conquests or points on an evangelistic scorecard. Such treatment of God's image-bearers is sinful and needs to be expunged from our lives.

On the other hand, the message of the gospel is scandalous, and to present it faithfully in its costly demands requires a great degree of boldness. We are summoning people to turn away from false gods and center their whole lives on Christ. This bold, life-orienting message is inherently offensive because it seeks to displace whatever else has been central in their lives. Many of us are tempted away from the boldness of this message because we don't want to offend. We often think we're being respectful, when in reality we're acting out of fear or self-preservation. Such an approach is selfish rather than loving: it's always loving to tell the truth. You cannot have respect without boldness, and you cannot have boldness without respect.

2. Lesslie Newbigin, "Cross-Currents in Ecumenical and Evangelical Understandings of Mission," *International Bulletin of Missionary Research* 6, no. 4 (1982): 148.

Vertical *and* horizontal. Some will stress our call as Christians to reconcile humanity to God. Others will stress our need to be concerned for social reconciliation or for the reconciliation of humanity to the nonhuman creation. But environmental stewardship should not be seen as an opponent of evangelism. Caring about racial reconciliation shouldn't be considered a distraction from reconciliation to God. Every dimension of brokenness simultaneously calls out for liberation from sin and its curse.

When we address all of these needs as a church, we provide a harmonious witness that sings of the broad scope of God's mission, which brings restoration to all created relationships. It reconciles us to God, turns enemies into brothers and sisters, and heals the physical wounds of creation. We won't know the fullness of shalom until Christ returns. But in the meantime, we are called to bear witness to him by providing a foretaste of shalom in every aspect of life.

When we choose *or* over *and*, we are rejecting things that matter to God. Certainly, as individuals we will have different gifts, experience varying opportunities, play different roles, emphasize different dimensions, focus on particular interests. Let us beware of asking the whole orchestra to sound like a trumpet or a viola. Let us beware of remaking the shape of God's mission in the image of our personal theological or experiential preferences.

Us—Connected to Community

Mission cannot be carried out alone; it is not a solo act but a group performance. We need to be in community with other believers because our life together nourishes our connection to God and bears his witness to the world. We need one another in order to know God and to make him known. Under the influence of the individualism of the West, many of us have come to think of mission as an individual endeavor. We see community as an elective part of the Christian faith that may encourage us but isn't as essential as our personal walk with God and intentional witness. However, God does not carry out his mission by commissioning a roster of individual contractors; instead, he adopts a family and incorporates them into his family business of blessing the world.

Paul speaks through the metaphor of a body to describe the communal nature of the church's mission (1 Cor. 12). Each body part has its particular function, but it only works to the degree that it's connected to and in sympathy with the other parts of the body. Just as a room full of scattered body parts would indicate that something has gone very wrong, a world full of disconnected followers of Christ is an indication that the church is injured and the mission maimed. God has made some people to be evangelists, but he has given other people the gifts of compassion and mercy and still others the gift of administration. We need each gift, each part of the body, to be working together to enable the whole to be a conduit of blessing and shalom.

Over the years, I've known several Muslims who have come to believe in Christ. I've made a habit of asking them who was influential in their faith journey. Invariably, they describe an encounter with a whole community rather than any one individual. For example, my friend Abdul came to the United States as a refugee and encountered God's generosity and hospitality through a man named David, who invited Abdul to come live with his family. Next, Abdul encountered the wisdom and compassion of God through Joan, a woman in David's small group who helped Abdul find a job and learn a language in a foreign country. Abdul had a difficult time understanding what he was reading in the Gospels, but there was one person in their community, John, whom the Spirit used to explain the good news. This was a team effort.

Knowing that most Muslims have a hard time wrapping their minds around the cross and the Trinity, I asked Abdul how he came to understand those things. He said that it was ultimately God who opened his eyes. But the Spirit used the sacrificial love of that community to be a living analogy of the sacrificial love of Christ. Regarding the Trinity, he said that there wasn't a single apologetic argument that made sense to him. But he came to see the Triune God by living among this community of Christ followers, who were all individuals yet displayed a type of oneness that he had never seen before. There wasn't a single individual who could sufficiently proclaim and demonstrate the gospel to Abdul, but God used the varied gifts and shared life of this community to make himself known.

Be—a Distinct Way of Life

From the calling of Abraham to the gathering of God's people at Pentecost to the end of the age, we see that mission is a communal vocation. It is not just one of the many activities of the church but is its central *identity*, the very purpose for which God created the church. As Christopher Wright says, "Mission was not made for the church; the church was made for mission— God's mission."[3]

3. Christopher Wright, *Mission of God's People: A Biblical Theology* (Grand Rapids: Zondervan, 2010), 62.

Mission is what the church *is* as much as it is what the church *does*. Mission is not just about doing; it's about being. While we should live within our particular cultures and affirm all that's good in them, we are also supposed to be a contrast community, a distinctive people, different from the world around us in the way we display shalom in all of life. "You are a chosen people, a royal priesthood, a holy nation, God's special possession, that you may declare the praises of him who called you out of darkness into his wonderful light" (1 Pet. 2:9). With these words Peter describes the identity of the church by adopting the Old Testament imagery that described Israel's unique role among the nations. Peter is reminding the church that they were chosen to be a unique community of light in contrast to the surrounding darkness. Believers have been born anew into the resurrection life of the end times (1 Pet. 1:3), which makes them strangers in and aliens to the idolatrous life of the Roman Empire (2:11). Christians must be holy and distinct in their personal and communal conduct (2:11), their work lives (2:18–21), and their participation in the public square (2:13–17). In all areas of life, the church is called to honor the institutions of the culture it lives within, but it is also to be a community that recognizes God as the supreme authority. He's the one who gives Christians a distinct story and calls them to distinct lives with the aim of displaying his distinct character to the world (2:12).

Peter was addressing a church that needed to live within Roman culture in a way that was both respectful to local authority and unapologetic in its ultimate allegiance to God—this living in two worlds produced a unique way of life. The same is true for the church in the twenty-first century. However, instead of living among Roman idols, we have the idols of the West: consumerism, technicism, nationalism, and freedom. Our response to the question, "What is the chief end of human life?" should be, "To know God our Creator."[4] But the culture that surrounds us answers the same question in many different ways: "The chief end of human life is to enjoy the goods and experiences of creation," says consumerism. "To depend on technology to enrich my life and satisfy my deepest needs," says technicism. "To offer loyalty to my country and its worldview at all costs," says nationalism. "To be free to be and do whatever I please," says the modern ideal of personal freedom. Each of these answers takes what had been a good aspect of creation and gives it a significance it was never meant to bear. To treat created things as if they were the chief end of human life is idolatry. Nothing in God's good creation should become the ultimate focus of our lives. But all human cultures are shaped by idolatry. This is the "world" of Romans 12:2 that Paul warns us against

4. This is the first question and answer for children in Calvin's Geneva Catechism.

being conformed to. These idols will always fail to give the life, satisfaction, and joy they promise and will instead deliver pain, distortion, and injustice.

The patterns of our surrounding culture, which have been shaped by service to the wrong gods, are not to be the patterns of life for the people of God. As God's people, we bear witness to the world by being a community that has a unique pattern of life, shaped by a different story, with a different center. Our life is to show the world the uniqueness of God and the goodness of his ways. When we do this, we give the world a preview of what life will look like when Jesus returns to restore shalom to the world.

What should this distinctive life look like in the twenty-first century? How should we, as a community, display the uniqueness of God and the destructiveness of idols in our own day? We can't give a definitive answer to these questions—such a life of faith is bound to look different in each community and context in which it's lived—but perhaps the fruit of the Spirit can stimulate our imaginations (Gal. 5:22–23).

Love. Imagine if we were a unique community that focused on sacrificially and selflessly serving others rather than ourselves. Imagine a church known for its self-giving love in a world of selfies. Instead of being focused on self-preservation, what if we were risk takers for the flourishing of our neighbors? What if the world knew that in every place of pain the body of Christ would be present, praying and pouring out its resources, binding the wounds of a bleeding world? What if all our actions, from choosing where we live to choosing how we vote, were shaped primarily by our concern for others? Instead of obsessing over our self-image, what if we were known for seeing the image of God in all human beings and, therefore, were a community obsessed with knowing, loving, and serving others?

Joy. Imagine if the church were known by what it was *for* instead of what it was *against*. What if we had eyes of wonder that saw every good thing in this world as a gift from God, and what if we were constantly grateful for simple things, like the smell of orange blossoms, the backspin of a basketball, or a long conversation with a friend? What if we became the kind of community that could remain joyful in the midst of suffering because of our hope in the One who will one day wipe away all tears and make all things new?

Peace. Imagine if the church were known as a community of peacemakers in the midst of this conflicted world. Imagine if we were marked by listening, confessing sin, speaking truth, and extending forgiveness. What if those qualities were to spill over from the church community into the streets?

Patience. Imagine if the church were known as the people of patience in a world of hurry and immediate gratification. What if we were known as the people who put away their cell phones and paid attention in a world of distraction? What if we were willing to spend years walking with someone through depression or addiction? What if we were known as the people with hospitable ears, who were always willing to listen?

Kindness and Goodness. Imagine if the kindness and goodness of God were experienced through the kindness and goodness of the church. Imagine if the body of Christ became the unique community that had eyes to see the most vulnerable, hands to carry burdens, mouths to speak the truth in love, arms to embrace the hurting, and minds to constantly dream up creative ways to fill the earth with God's good gifts.

Faithfulness. Imagine if the church were known for being a distinctly trustworthy community. What if employers searched for new employees, and nonprofits tried to find volunteers, from within the church—because they knew that these people would show up and do their best work faithfully day after day? What if we were known for raising steady families, where divorce was rare, marriages were strong, and children felt secure?

Gentleness. Imagine if the church were a people of nuanced and gentle public discourse. What if we refused to engage in vitriolic rants online and instead had wise and measured words in all our conversations? What if we were known for refusing to adopt the bitterness of either the Right or the Left?

Self-control. Imagine if the church were known for saying "enough" in a world that says "more." What if our joy in the simple things subverted the emptiness of consumerism by showing that a deep contentment is possible in Christ? Imagine if we had such contentment that we didn't need to chase every dollar, watch every Netflix series, or win every argument.

Can you imagine a community overflowing with the fruit of the Spirit? It would be distinct from all other communities and would display the uniqueness of God's ways. It would challenge our culture's idols and show the emptiness of their promises. It would provide a feast for the world. To the degree that the church does display this kind of mutual love, it bears witness to the uniqueness of God's kingdom and offers an alternative way to live in the world. We provide a glimpse and foretaste of the coming shalom.

Why—Motivated by Love

The foundation for all missional engagement is knowing *why* we are participating in God's mission. The what, where, and how of mission must be built on the why, or our missional endeavors will crumble.

What is our motivation for mission? The answer is simple yet profound: it's upward and outward love. Our primary motivation for mission must be to love God and our neighbors. Some might suggest that we are motivated by the glory of God, the fear of the Lord, or the desire for obedience, and these are all good biblical reasons to engage in mission. But each of these reasons is only one aspect of love. When asked what was the greatest commandment, Jesus said, "'Love the Lord your God with all your heart and with all your soul and with all your mind.' This is the first and greatest commandment. And the second is like it: 'Love your neighbor as yourself.' All the Law and the Prophets hang on these two commandments" (Matt. 22:37–40). This is our ultimate motivation for mission. Jesus shows how the upward love for God and the horizontal love for our neighbors should be the driving force in all of human life, including in our intentional participation in his mission.

There is an order to love. Before we can love God and make known his love to the world, we must encounter the love of God for ourselves. His love comes first, and our love is a response to his: "In this the love of God was made manifest among us, that God sent his only Son into the world, so that we might live through him. In this is love, not that we have loved God but that he loved us and sent his Son to be the propitiation for our sins" (1 John 4:9–10 ESV). Before we can love God, we must deeply know his love and mercy, which is supremely displayed by the sending of the Son who brings us from death to life.

Before we can participate *in* God's mission, we must know that we are beneficiaries *of* God's mission. We are not the rescuers; we are the rescued who merely bear witness to others who also need to be rescued. We are the beggars who tell other beggars where bread can be found. We respond to the love of the Father by participating in the work of the Father, not as slaves or even employees but as adopted children, working in our Father's family business. Perhaps 1 John 4:19 summarizes the motive for mission best when it says, "We love because he first loved us."

The apostle John shows that loving God and being loved by God are the first things. But we cannot love God without loving others: "If anyone says, 'I love God,' and hates his brother, he is a liar; for he who does not love his brother whom he has seen cannot love God whom he has not seen. And this commandment we have from him: whoever loves God must also love his brother" (1 John 4:20–21 ESV). God's love cannot be contained. Containing his love would be like trying to capture Niagara Falls in a shot glass. His love must overflow from us into the lives of our neighbors. If we do not love our neighbors, we do not know the love of God.

Paul agrees with John when he says that the love of Christ is what launches us into the love of our neighbor. "For Christ's love compels us, because we are convinced that one died for all, and therefore all died. And he died for all, that those who live should no longer live for themselves but for him who died for them and was raised again" (2 Cor. 5:14–15). The love of Christ makes loving others possible. In Jesus's sacrificial love on the cross, Paul sees the breadth of God's love for the world. And now Paul turns to love the world with the same breadth. He also sees the cross as the model for how to love. God gave himself to us in sacrificial love, so we respond by giving ourselves back to him in worship and by giving ourselves to our neighbors.

When I was in Rio de Janeiro, I was impressed by the statue of Christ the Redeemer, high above a city of incredible beauty that is pockmarked by violent and impoverished favelas. I saw in that statue not merely a tourist destination but a vivid picture of God's love and mercy for the city. His hands stretched out, you could almost hear him inviting a burdened and yet beautiful city to run to his arms for forgiveness, cleansing, and healing. But as I looked up, my wife saw something else: reflected in my sunglasses was an image of Christ the Redeemer. This is how I must see this broken and yet beautiful world—through the lens of the love and mercy of Christ.

If love isn't our motivation, we can be sure that we are not participating in God's mission. We are loving and serving something other than God and are loving ourselves rather than our neighbors.

It may seem strange to think of feeding the hungry, preaching the gospel, or pursuing justice as serving a false god, but the scary reality is that these things can, though they look good outwardly, still be driven by idolatry. To build a house for someone without a house is a good thing, right? But if we're building a house while being driven by the idol of significance, we may just be building a temple of self-worship. We may even reveal our craving for the praise of others as we carefully humblebrag on Instagram. Furthermore, our missional engagement could be motivated by the idol of consumerism, especially the brand of consumerism that compels us to collect experiences. Many Christians have embarked on short-term missions trips, or have moved to culturally influential cities, with noble missional language, but their primary motivation is to see the world, live in an important city, or even be seen by others as a strategic player in God's mission.

Paul, in his well-known description of love in 1 Corinthians 13, insists that all good works, missional engagement, and acts of worship are nothing if they aren't rooted in love. Apart from love, our verbal witness can sound like an annoying, clanging gong. Even if we give all we have to the poor, we gain nothing if it is done without love. Much of this book is about how we can participate in God's mission, but all of the hows are worthless if they aren't motivated by the why: love for our God that overflows into a love for our neighbor.

In this world of sin and evil, there are great temptations to drift from loving God to loving an idol, from loving my neighbor to using my neighbor. That's why we need to be attentive to our motives. Our hearts easily deceive us: "The heart is deceitful above all things. . . . Who can understand it?" (Jer. 17:9). We must regularly ask God and other believers to help us see ourselves and expose our sinful motives. We must continually repent of our love of idols and marinate in the love of Christ in order to reorient our hearts toward God and neighbor.

Conclusion

Just as a budding musician must learn to play the basic notes before being able to play complex melodies, we must be sure that we continually pay attention to the core commitments of mission. I have represented these through simple words:

With—Mission must include incarnational presence.

From—Mission must be empowered by the Spirit.

And—Mission must be comprehensive in scope.

Us—Mission must be communal.

Be—Mission must include a distinct way of life.

Why—Mission must be motivated by love.

The missional engagement of each Christian community and each follower of Christ will look different depending on context and the unique gifts that God has given each of them. However, they should all include these six core commitments. All of our missional activity is worthless apart from incarnational presence, the power of the Spirit, a big vision of the gospel, mutually encouraging community, flow from a distinctive way of life, and love. All the missional strategy and creativity in the world will come to nothing apart from these six things.

3

INTENTIONALITY

The Movements of Mission

The Symphony and the Sanitation Truck

Each morning, Bruce steps into his truck, prays for God's blessing, fires up the engine, and begins his route. While most other drivers find little meaning in their work, Bruce knows that he's embarking on a mission. The hands that grip the steering wheel were created to display the glory of God. He knows that inside the size-thirteen boots that press against the gas and brake pedals are mangled feet with formerly broken toes, thick calluses, and bunions. Yet these feet have a rugged beauty, much like the beauty of the cross, because they will carry him to unforeseen opportunities to serve his neighbors in the name of the God who washes feet. Before putting the truck in gear, he lifts his coffee to his mouth, praying that he will have an opportunity to proclaim the gospel with the same lips that are being slightly seared by his piping-hot, gas station coffee. Bruce isn't a fan of classical music, but as he begins his day, he knows that he gets the privilege of participating in the symphony of God's mission. His 420-horsepower engine plays percussion in God's song of salvation to the nations.

Taped to his dashboard are several index cards with quotes and Scripture verses to remind him of the sacred work of driving a sanitation truck. One of the first cards he reads each morning displays this quote from Rev. Martin Luther King Jr.:

> If it falls to your lot to be a street sweeper, sweep streets like Michelangelo
> painted pictures, or Beethoven composed music, sweep streets like Leontyne

Price sings before the Metropolitan Opera. Sweep streets like Shakespeare wrote poetry. Sweep streets so well that all the hosts of heaven and earth will have to pause and say: "Here lived a great street sweeper who swept his job well."[1]

Bruce isn't exactly a street sweeper, but in a way, he is responsible for the cleanliness of the streets as he spends his days navigating narrow back alleys and using a robotic arm to scoop up the accumulated refuse of his neighbors. Another index card bears the words of Genesis 2:15: "The LORD God took the man and put him in the Garden of Eden to work it and take care of it." As he reads these words, Bruce is reminded that just as God placed Adam in the garden of Eden, so he has placed Bruce in that truck. Bruce's particular plot in God's garden happens to be the back alleys of his city. He cultivates that space for the glory of God. The broken glass, old furniture, weeds, and cinder-block walls are the materials of his sanctuary, a sacred space that belongs to God. He collects the trash with trembling reverence.

Every plastic bag or dirty diaper that Bruce keeps off the streets is an offering to honor his King. He sees himself as beautifying God's good earth and protecting the masterpiece of God's creation. Because of this, he's more motivated and joyful than all of his coworkers. He doesn't just "do his job." He is master of his craft as a driver, attentive to every tight turn and every detail. If this were just a menial task for him, he might be tempted to do the bare minimum. But he's working before the face of God, lifting up each trash bin with that robotic arm as if his own hands were raised in worship.

His coworkers may give him a hard time for his strange love of sanitation, but behind their banter there's a deep level of respect. Several of them treat Bruce as a mentor and a man of integrity who can speak into many aspects of life. His coworkers often show up at his house during the weekends to eat pancakes with the rest of his family. Bruce and his wife have three of their own children, but there are eight seats at their kitchen table. Each week they ask God to fill those seats with people who need a sense of family. Often the seats are filled by Bruce's coworkers, especially the younger ones who have become estranged from their own families. Bruce and his wife know they've

---

1. This quote, attributed to Martin Luther King Jr., is widely available on the internet, but the reference is never given. It is difficult, therefore, to confirm the exact words he used as well as where and when he actually said them. The best we can say is that the quote seems to be from a speech given at Barratt Junior High School in Philadelphia on October 26, 1967, six months before King was assassinated. See "What Is Your Life's Blueprint?," Martin Luther King Jr. and the Civil Rights Movement, *Seattle Times*, accessed June 28, 2018, http://old.seattletimes.com/special/mlk/king/words/blueprint.html.

been adopted by the Father through Christ, so they take a posture of adoption toward all who need a family.

Not only does Bruce give of his time for the sake of his coworkers; he also intentionally chooses the hardest routes. By bearing the burden of a difficult route, he imitates the self-giving pattern of the cross. Driving his garbage truck isn't just a means of serving his coworkers; it's Bruce's way of washing the feet of the city. As he drives through each alley, he prays over the homes there, prays for the flourishing of the city. He imagines what would happen if nobody were to pick up the trash. Life would become miserable as God's good world would be covered in garbage, and the stench would offend the nostrils of the whole neighborhood. Disease would drive people from their homes. By removing trash from the streets, Bruce tangibly loves his neighbor.

His coworkers often ask Bruce why his life is so different, why he loves his job so much, and why he goes the extra mile to serve others. It would be easy for Bruce to give them a stale, memorized gospel presentation. Instead, Bruce has reflected deeply on the redemptive analogies that are embedded in his context. So he often takes his coworkers to the back of the truck to look at the trash and says something like this:

"The reason I find so much joy in my work is that I believe every inch of this world belongs to God and that by keeping the city clean, I'm serving him. He made us to flourish, but everything got messed up a long time ago. All the proof you need is in the back of this garbage truck. When you look back here, you see a lot of formerly good things that are now broken, rotting, and decaying. What used to be a nourishing meal is now rotting meat; what was a good chair is now splintered wood. You and I both know that what's happening in the back of this truck isn't limited to the garbage bin. It's happening in countries at war, in the cancer growing in Dave's liver, in the corruption of politics, in the strain on our marriages, and in the pain we feel in our knees. Sin isn't just a list of bad things you shouldn't do but a disease that infects all of creation, starting with every human heart.

"It would make sense for God to crush this whole world and all that's broken. However, he doesn't intend to throw the world in the garbage heap but plans to recycle, renew, and restore all things.

"When Jesus came into this world, he entered the garbage bin of this earth to make all things new. He didn't just snap his fingers to make things better. He stepped into the trash compactor in our place: 'He was pierced for our transgressions, he was crushed for our iniquities; the punishment that brought us peace was on him, and by his wounds we are healed' [Isa. 53:5]. Essentially, whenever you see that hydraulic trash compactor crushing the brokenness, you should be reminded of what Jesus did on the cross. He was crushed so that we, along with the world, don't have to be. In his resurrection, he shows the power of God to deal with the brokenness of sin, Satan, and death—and to renew the world."

After one of these conversations with Bruce, some people roll their eyes or politely try to change the subject. But sometimes people want to learn more, and Bruce invites them to his small group at his church so that they can experience community and see the gospel lived out in the lives of many different people. And occasionally, Bruce has the privilege of baptizing one of his coworkers in the community pool at his apartment complex.

Obviously I've just given you a condensed description of Bruce's intentional participation in God's mission. It doesn't account for the daily grind and the ethical complexities faced each day. The real conversations I've summarized here probably sounded more organic in their immediate contexts. However, in this broad outline of Bruce's life we see a rich participation in the mission of God. Participation doesn't take a lot of money, influence, or credentials. It doesn't mean you have to move to another city or join another organization. Rather, we just need to approach our normal lives with missional intentionality.

The Movements of the Symphony of Mission

What can we notice about Bruce's participation in God's mission? You probably noticed that his life displays the gospel from many angles. He displays God's character through his good work, his sacrificial service to his coworkers, and his gospel analogies from within his context to verbally proclaim the gospel. Rather than pitting these aspects of mission against one another—debating which one is most important—he embraces all three of them, knowing that work, service, and evangelism were intended to work together to bear witness to God and offer a glimpse into the shalom that is the goal of the true story of the world.

Just as the earliest symphonies had three movements each—three distinct pieces of music that combined to tell one musical story—the church has three broad movements of witness that combine to tell a story of renewal. We'll call these the movements of stewardship, service, and the spoken word. They are the three major ways God has given us to participate in his mission. Think of these movements as the melodies we perform within the symphony of mission. Just as a symphony would be incomplete if it were missing one of its three movements, our witness will be deficient if it lacks stewardship, service, or the spoken word.

So then, here are the three movements of mission, with an accompanying diagram (fig. 3.1), that will occupy us for the rest of the book:

Stewardship: displaying the glory of the Father through the work of our hands (Gen. 1–2; 1 Cor. 10:31; Eph. 5:1–2)

Service: displaying the love of Christ by washing the feet of the world (Mark 10:35–45; Rom. 12:14–21; Col. 1:24–27)

Spoken Word: displaying the power of the Holy Spirit by opening our mouths (Rom. 10:10; Col. 4:2–6; 1 Pet. 3:15)

All three movements are vital to God's mission. They invite us to weave our words and our works together to point to the glory of God in Christ. Ideally, each individual believer and each Christian community will seek ways to participate in all three of these movements to intentionally display God's glory through the stewardship of their work, his love through their service, and his power through their sharing of the gospel in words.

This chapter provides a brief overview of each movement and some examples of what it looks like when all three work together in harmony. The next three chapters (4–6) will look at each movement, reflecting on how we can reorient our lives to be more intentional in all three areas. In the case study above, you may have noticed that Bruce knew he couldn't do everything. God's mission is broad, but Bruce's life is limited. He therefore needed to focus most of his efforts on one area of life—namely, his work. Chapters 7–9 reflect on our callings in order to discern what specific part of God's mission we should each focus on.

Figure 3.1

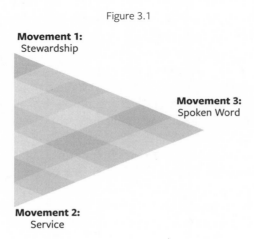

Movement 1:
Stewardship

Movement 3:
Spoken Word

Movement 2:
Service

Stewardship

How does the world come to see the glory of God? In large part, through the fruitful work of human hands. God's first invitation to join his symphony is an invitation to work, to develop the hidden potential that he's embedded in creation. In doing this work, we display and magnify God's character. The scientist who discovers and writes about the role of bats in the ecosystem is discovering and magnifying the brilliance of God's created order and reflecting the wisdom of God. The mother who teaches her child how to read displays the glory of our communicative God. When entrepreneurs provide meaningful jobs for families, they display the glory of the Great Provider.

The calling to work is the first command God gives to humanity, the first invitation to participate in his work in the world. Before sin entered the world, God had already invited us to sink our hands into the soil of the earth and to cultivate something good, something to serve our neighbor and to provide a picture of what God is like. He invites humanity to participate in his great symphony by calling us to engage in excellent work that puts his glory on display. "Work" does not refer only to employment; it refers to any human activity that's productive and that positively contributes to God's good world, whether it's parenting, yard work, art making, civic engagement, or any of the many other ways we can find to contribute to the flourishing of creation. God plays the music of creation and then invites us to join his symphony through the stewardship of creation—cultivating, caring for, and creating within his good world.

What does this stewardship look like? When we engage in good cultural work, we provide the world with a glimpse of what God is like. We function as little creational pictures of the great creator God. Just as a picture can't hope to display the fullness of what is being photographed, we must acknowledge that our lives at their best can provide only a snapshot of what God is like. However, a lot *can* be conveyed about a person or place through a picture. You can get a sense of the beauty of a mountain range, of the bond between friends, or of the joy of a family vacation through just a few pixels on a screen. And our lives *can* function as miniature portraits of God's glory. Through good and intentional work, we make the invisible God visible.

How does the world come to see the glory of our compassionate, faithful, sovereign, and restorative God? His compassion can be displayed through special education teachers like our friend Jessi, who spends her day truly seeing those from whom the world turns away. She may well spend her days getting scratched, cleaning up bathroom catastrophes, or hearing a child cry for several hours straight. But God wipes away those tears through her hands, expresses his favor through her smile, and displays his faithfulness by showing up, day after day, in Jessi.

How does the world behold the glory of God's order? Each day, he puts it on display through the well-ordered spreadsheets of accountants and the well-pruned hedges of landscapers. His creativity comes out through the crayon rainbows of a child's drawing and the flavors, textures, sights, and smells of good food from a master cook. God displays his creativity through the creativity of people made in his image.

Each day, God heals through the hands of doctors, protects through the hands of parents, feeds through the hands of farmers, and brings order to the world through the hands of anonymous administrators who work under the glow of fluorescent lights. When we do good work, we become living analogies of God's character, display the brilliance of his creation, provide a foretaste of God's kingdom, and serve our neighbors. When our participation in God's mission lacks intentionality in our daily work—whether paid or unpaid—we diminish our credibility and distort the character of God in front of a world that needs to behold his glory.

Service

How does the world encounter the love of Christ? God displays his love primarily through the cross of Christ, that ugly Roman instrument of torture that was so beautifully repurposed as God's instrument of defeating sin, Satan, and death. God displays his love for us by suffering for us. He didn't die for the deserving; when we were still God's enemies, he loved us and rescued us through his own brutal death.

Few things are more beautiful than sacrificial love, and the human heart's craving for this kind of love is displayed through the stories we tell. Whether it's heartwarming stories of first responders who run into collapsing buildings to rescue their neighbors, of injured athletes who persevere through accidents and broken bones, or of great literature like *Les Misérables* that endures for centuries because of sacrificial characters like Jean Valjean, the human heart is drawn to acts of self-giving, sacrificial, and costly love.

Though we find ourselves moved by these stories of sacrifice, we often find it hard to believe that *God* loves us so deeply and tangibly. There's something so good about the idea that God loves us that, for many, it seems too good to be true. The beauty of God's love is confounding. In this cynical world we tend to think of God's love as if it were something from a fairy tale: it would be nice, but that sort of thing doesn't happen in the world we know.

So how can the world come to know the love of Christ *by experience*? What's the best apologetic for proclaiming the cross to a cynical world? The best commentaries about the cross are not written in books; they are written on the scars of Christians throughout the world. The primary way the self-giving love of Christ is displayed to the world is through the sacrificial service of God's people. As we pour our lives out on behalf of our neighbors, we dramatize what Christ has done on the cross.

The service movement of God's symphony sounds when we display the love of Christ by washing the feet of the world, sacrificing for others so that they might see a living analogy of God's love. We can dramatize the suffering of Christ and join in the fellowship of his sufferings by intentionally bearing our neighbors' burdens. The "suffering and sacrifice" mentioned here refer to the kind of generosity that compels us to take all we have—time, money, influence, relationships, talents—and leverage it for the sake of someone else. As followers of Christ pour themselves out, the world catches a glimpse of the God who poured himself out on the cross.

What does this look like? The love of Christ was put on display when the early church welcomed people with diseases into their homes and nursed them back to health, often at the risk of contracting the illnesses themselves. The love of Christ is shown when a business owner, like our friend Michel, chooses to hire refugees, even when they have a steep learning curve and he might lose some of his customers because of the nationalistic sentiment in the US. When an entrepreneur like Bill loses out on thousands of dollars of profit because he honors his word and gives a contract to a company as promised—even though a lower bid comes in later—Christ's love is on display. When followers of Christ mow the lawns of senior citizens, use their spare bedrooms for foster care, or risk their reputations to become a voice for the voiceless, the notes of the service movement can be heard. When God's people are so compelled by the love of Christ that they sacrifice their time, money, comfort, reputation, and property for the sake of others, they join God in his mission and make the beautiful sounds of sacrificial service.

Spoken Word

How does the world come to hear about the one true God? Ultimately, it is through the power of the Spirit. However, the Spirit speaks to the unbelieving human heart most often through the instrument of human language.

We need words. It's not enough for people to see the glory of God on display through our good work or to encounter the beauty of sacrificial love through our service. They must also hear the good news about the God who is the fountain from which these things flow. People need the verbal explanation of the gospel that connects our good works to the good news about the life, death, and resurrection of Jesus. They need to know that our good deeds are not rooted in our own winsome personalities, nor are they the product of some generic deity. They point to something greater: the glory and love of God in Christ.

God chooses to reveal his uniqueness through words: verbs, nouns, adjectives, sentences, paragraphs, chapters. These are the weak instruments used by the powerful Spirit to reveal the character of God, to give new life, and to extend an invitation to covenant relationship. Words don't save people; God does. However, the Holy Spirit works powerfully through our words to bring home the gospel to people's hearts and so make them his children.

The third movement is about the witness of the Holy Spirit in words that announce the good news of the life, death, and resurrection of Jesus to a lost world. This is often referred to as evangelism. It's when we open our mouths to provide commentary about the wonder of God's creation, connect the pains of the world to the presence of sin, and announce Jesus as the only remedy for this wounded world.

Stories of Symphonic Mission

Each of these movements—stewardship, service, and the spoken word—plays an important role within God's mission. However, each is incomplete without the others. They are singular melodies and not complete symphonies in themselves. They must be present together to truly display the full beauty of God to a listening world. If you came to a great concert hall to hear Beethoven's Ninth, but the orchestra walked out after having played only the first movement, you'd feel a bit cheated, wouldn't you?

Sadly, this seems to be how the North American church often engages in mission. Only part of the composer's vision is delivered. Some groups emphasize evangelism and church planting and leave it at that. Other groups focus on community development and mercy ministries; still others focus on good work or art or governance. But what if these areas of emphasis were brought together in every industry, city, and neighborhood? All three ways of participating in the mission—stewardship, service, and spoken word—are necessary if we want the world to behold the glory of the Father, the love of Christ, and the power of the Spirit.

What does it look like to perform the melodies of stewardship, service, and spoken word together in the rhythms of daily life? Several examples of symphonic mission will be provided in this section. All of these examples are based on true stories, some of them slightly modified (when they are the stories of people who prefer anonymity) or edited for the sake of clarity. Some of these examples are small-scale initiatives that don't need a large budget. Others are full-scale businesses. The intention is to show that symphonic mission doesn't depend on the size or structure of your organization but on your attentiveness to what the Spirit is doing in your particular context and your intentionality in responding.

Grays Baseball Team

A Google search of "parents fighting at sporting events" produces tens of thousands of hits. You can see depressing videos of children watching as their fathers or mothers throw a can of beer at a referee, take a swing at another parent, or shout ugly threats at the opposing team. AAU basketball players are getting paid under the table by shoe companies, kids are pressured into specializing in one sport by the age of ten, coaches are shaming eight-year-old children through obscene verbal tirades, and freshman quarterbacks already know where to find performance-enhancing drugs. These are all signs that something is broken in youth sports. The obsession is so pervasive that in the United States many families spend more money on youth sports than on anything else but their mortgage.

Many kids and families are trying to find meaning, identity, and life in something other than God. They have taken the good gift of sports and turned it into an object of worship. It's easy to identify this as a problem and critique the idolatry of youth sports, but what would it look like to engage in sports in a countercultural way that gives people a taste of the kingdom?

The best example we have seen of this type of engagement is found in a competitive youth baseball team called the Grays. If you were to attend one of their games or practices, they would probably seem like a fairly normal baseball team, at least at first glance. But if you looked more closely, you'd catch a glimpse of God's character and hear an echo of the way the world is supposed to be. The coaches and players would be the first to tell you that the Grays are not perfect—and that's true. But many people in the community where they play will tell you that something truly unique is happening with the Grays.

The coaches started this team by imagining what baseball might look like in the fullness of God's kingdom. What if sports hadn't been distorted by the fall? The coaches imagined joy-filled games that allowed kids to experience some of the gifts of creation, that functioned as an echo of the character of

God, the giver of those gifts. Having control over an excellent curveball is an echo of the God who is sovereign over all things, the great author of the laws of physics. A game-winning, powerfully hit home run in the bottom of the ninth inning is an echo of the mighty hand of a God who rescues his people. The way in which the game of baseball affirms the individuality of the players while bringing them together as one unit provides a glimpse of the mysterious beauty of the Trinity. Good baseball is a means of cultivating creation, enjoying God's good gifts, and displaying God's character.

The Grays are devoted to coaching and playing to the best of their ability. However, they do this in a unique way. Many coaches seek to motivate kids through fear and shame, and they urge hatred toward their opponents. But the coaches of the Grays have built a culture of being a "team for others." This happens in a number of ways. For example, they have a team rule that prohibits boasting about oneself. Instead, players are encouraged to honor their teammates for both good character and good play. After most practices and games, they have a time when they encourage and honor one another. And being a "team for others" goes beyond the team itself. They also ask how they can seek the good of their parents, umpires, and even the opposing teams. The Grays are taught to thank the umpires, give fist bumps to opposing players who get a good hit, and yell out encouraging words to opposing players, saying "Next time, bud!" when they strike out. Even their competitiveness is rooted in a "for others" attitude. They play their best baseball in order to bring joy to the game and to draw out the potential of their opponents, helping them play *their* best baseball.

This attitude is also embedded in the way the coaches have structured their team. Three of the four coaches on the team played Division 1 baseball, and one is an Arizona Hall of Fame coach. They could easily leverage their backgrounds to recruit some of the best players in the state and win praise for themselves. But they have chosen to die to that desire for the sake of community and their commitment to the kids on their team. Most teams cut their three weakest players each year and hold open tryouts for replacements. But the Grays don't cut players. They are committed to keeping the community and friendship intact and to developing *all* of their players.

Many youth baseball teams play all year round, but the Grays coaches think it's better for kids to experience other sports and for baseball not to take too much time away from the kids' families. So they play for just one season each year. The result is that the Grays don't win as many games as they might otherwise. But they have created such a unique culture that the best players on the Grays typically don't leave the team, even when they have the chance to join some of the best teams in the league. This culture of seeking the good of others provides a living analogy of the self-giving love of Christ. It stands in contrast to the self-centeredness that's pervasive in most youth sports, and it provides a glimpse of God's kingdom.

Even though the Grays aren't an explicitly Christian team that quotes Scripture or uses explicitly theological language, the distinct culture of this team has exposed people to the beauty of God's kingdom in the creational goodness of baseball and the joy of serving others. The team is coached by several followers of Christ, but they make sure that kids from all backgrounds are welcome on the team. The impact has been profound, extending beyond the baseball diamond. It has shaped the culture of families, who have taken the "team for others" mentality into their homes, calling themselves "families for others." Parents from the opposing teams have also taken notice and say the attitude of the Grays is "beautiful." Umpires have noted the uniqueness of this team, and some were overwhelmed when they were thanked by players— because their job tends to be so thankless. (One umpire said he hadn't been thanked in fifteen years!) The beauty of sacrificial love provokes questions among those who don't follow Christ. Parents sometimes ask, "Where did you get this philosophy of being a 'team for others'?" In response, the team's coaches are able to quite naturally point to Jesus, the ultimate expression of sacrificial and self-giving love.

How do the Grays participate in God's mission?

Stewardship. The Grays display the good gifts of creation by joyfully playing baseball and working toward mastery over the various skills that are needed. Through excellent teamwork that honors the uniqueness of individual strengths, they display the beauty of our Triune God.

Service. They are a "team for others," called to put the interests of their teammates, parents, umpires, and opponents before their own interests. While they do play their best and seek to win, they do not seek to win at all costs. They are willing to sacrifice potential wins and fame in order to have time with their families and to keep friendships intact. When the Grays love their opponents, they reflect the one who suffered on behalf of humanity even when humanity made itself his enemy.

Spoken Word. When people inquire about the unique culture of the Grays' "others first" philosophy, they are able to point to Jesus, who washed the feet of humanity and suffered on the cross.

The With Collective

Summers in Phoenix can be brutally hot. While this is inconvenient to most of us, it can be deadly to those who are experiencing homelessness. In

2016 there were 130 heat-related deaths in our city. The cruel reality of this fallen world is that the same sun that provides energy for our air-conditioned homes and growth for the vegetables on our plate can kill those who don't have a roof over their heads or food on their plates.

Several churches, such as Missio Dei Communities, have recognized that when homeless people die in the blistering Arizona sun, life isn't "the way it's supposed to be," and they have formed missional communities to address this problem out of love for their neighbors. They started by partnering with the city government and local nonprofits to create an initiative where each church becomes a temporary homeless shelter for one day a week. The church provides an air-conditioned place to sleep, a refreshing shower, and a meal for the guests.

One church called their night "The *With* Collective" to remind themselves that they were not merely doing things *for* the homeless but were walking *with* them as friends. Just as God came to be *with* us through the incarnation, this ministry needed to be marked by true friendship and presence. So this church went the extra mile by intentionally sharing meals with their guests. Rather than serving food from behind the table in the food line, each volunteer made up a plate and joined the feast, seeing the table as a place for building friendships not just distributing food.

Everyone—guests *and* hosts—around the table was in need of food, friendship, and the deeper feast of knowing God. Around the table, they would share stories, tell jokes, pray, and occasionally shed tears over the harsh realities of this world. Deep friendships formed and extended beyond the weekly meal. Some of the guests built such a bond with the volunteers that they were invited to move in with them. Just as God provides us refuge, these local Christians opened their spare bedrooms to new friends. Others would meet up to play pool, have a picnic, or go job hunting. By intertwining their lives with the lives of others, these followers of Christ displayed genuine love. They poured out their time, money, homes, food, and hearts. They reimagined simple things—a quiche recipe, a spare bedroom—as instruments of love.

One day someone asked, "Why do homeless people typically get such poor-quality food at nights like this? Doesn't that implicitly communicate that they are less important than we are? Jesus calls us to love our neighbors as ourselves, so why don't we give them the same meals we prepare for our families? What if we started giving our best—making the recipes we would make if Jesus were coming over for dinner, meals to honor our guests as the image of God?" And several people took up that challenge, making their favorite recipes, sometimes cooking food that would take days of preparation. They even recruited a local chef to bring her most creative and extravagant recipes. To this day, the best cheesecake I've ever tasted came from The *With* Collective and not from a five-star restaurant.

If the guests asked why The *With* Collective made such high-quality food, the reply was something like this: "Our God is preparing an extravagant and eternal feast for us. It will include the finest food, the absence of pain, joyful friendships, and, most importantly, the joy of being in the presence of God. We just wanted to have a feast that provides a foretaste of that day."

They would go on to talk about the life, death, and resurrection of Jesus as God's invitation to a feast. Other people might answer the same question by talking about the hidden goodness of God's creation found in the ingredients of the food as an indication of God's goodness and generosity—all pointing to the generosity of the cross. This situation created organic opportunities to share the gospel. It provoked the curiosity of the guests who didn't know Christ, but it had an even greater impact on the friends, coworkers, and neighbors who didn't believe in Jesus but had accepted an invitation to participate in The *With* Collective. These people had assumed that Christianity was a stodgy religion of joyless people, but they instead encountered a joyful feast of extravagant love that provided a taste of the kingdom.

How did The *With* Collective participate in God's mission?

Stewardship. They displayed the creativity of God through flaky pastries, perfectly marinated meats, and salads that nourished the body *and* stimulated the taste buds. Through their hospitality, they displayed God's hospitality.

Service. They displayed the love of Christ by sacrificing their time and money for those who were homeless. They embodied the love of Christ by sharing more than a mere cash donation; they shared their homes and invited others into their daily lives.

Spoken Word. They told people about how God, through the work of Christ, is inviting us to a great cosmic feast and inviting us to live and flourish with him forever.

Hustle Phoenix

If you find yourself at a coffee shop in Phoenix, Arizona, there's a good chance you will see a large bald man who looks like an NFL linebacker or a Terry Crews impersonator. He will likely be sitting across from someone, sipping hot chocolate, and passionately casting a vision with his unmistakably bold and raspy voice. If he's alone, he will likely be holding a book within a few inches of his face, and it will be a book about theology, entrepreneurship, or poverty. Ironically, this man, who is known for his poor eyesight, has some of the best vision we've ever seen. He sees all of life through the lens of the biblical story, he sees God as the ultimate entrepreneur, and he sees all people as created in God's image. He sees examples of idolatry and injustice that are often overlooked by others. He has a vision for restorative entrepreneurship to extend shalom to underserved communities. His name is Oye Waddell.

Though Oye currently lives in Phoenix, he spent his childhood in urban, inner-city Los Angeles in a neighborhood that was teeming with creativity and talent but was economically depressed. Lacking the opportunities of those in wealthier communities, dozens of his friends turned to economic crimes, such as selling crack cocaine.

Over the years, Oye realized that some of the best natural entrepreneurs are in underserved urban communities. They have the God-given skills of entrepreneurs but lack key resources needed to create sustainable businesses that benefit the broader community. So Oye launched an organization called Hustle Phoenix that is focused on helping urban entrepreneurs launch sustainable businesses by connecting them to (1) intellectual capital, offered in education and skill development; (2) social capital, offered in mentoring by mature entrepreneurs; and (3) financial capital, offered in introductions to potential investors.

For the last five years, Oye has been working hard to serve urban entrepreneurs in the Phoenix area, providing entrepreneurial training and helping launch a wide array of businesses that are filling the city with good products and services, providing jobs, and answering people's prayers for God to provide their daily bread.

How does Oye participate in God's mission?

Stewardship. Few people are as creative and persistent in pursuing justice as Oye Waddell. The hard work he's done to provide intellectual, social, and financial capital for these entrepreneurs displays the creativity and persistence of God, who will one day bring full justice. With each hint of restoration that God brings through Hustle Phoenix, he's providing a glimpse of the restoration he will one day bring to all creation.

Service. Few people know how much Oye has sacrificed for the sake of these entrepreneurs. He has a broad network of connections that he could easily use to launch himself high in the world of business. Instead of finding investors for his own ventures, he's raised hundreds of thousands of dollars of investment for other people's businesses, even as he has worked multiple jobs to provide for his family. When people see the hundreds of thousands of hours and dollars that Oye has poured out for the community, they catch a glimpse of the generosity and self-giving love of Christ.

Spoken Word. When people ask why Oye engages in restorative entrepreneurship and pursues justice for these communities, he's able to tell them about the God who will one day restore all things and perfectly establish justice on the earth. When they ask why he spends so much of his education, connections, time, and capital for the flourishing of others' businesses, he's able to tell them about the generosity of Christ, who gave his whole life to reconcile them to God and restore the world.

The Music of Mission

The music of mission is made through the blending of three movements: stewardship, service, and the spoken word. Each of these is a response to God's action and an invitation to join his mission. We distort his mission if one of these movements is emphasized to the exclusion of the others. Just as symphonies are incomplete when one of their movements is missing, our participation in mission is incomplete when we ignore one of these three elements of mission. The mission of God consists of intentional engagement in good work, tangible service, and the verbal proclamation of the gospel in every context. In the following chapters, we look more carefully at each of the three movements in the symphony.

4

STEWARDSHIP

Displaying the Glory of the Father
through the Work of Our Hands

The world desperately needs to behold the glory of God—his wisdom, goodness, creativity, love, and provision. And God has chosen to display these things through our daily work. When we speak of work playing a substantial role in God's mission, we're not just referring to the work of church-based ministries or mission agencies; we're referring to the varied activities of daily life, such as mopping floors, leading staff meetings, repairing printers, making bread, and sending emails. As Steven Garber says, "Vocation is integral, not incidental, to the *missio Dei.*"[1] Through our work we perform a beautiful melody about the glory of God in the various auditoriums of daily life—our homes, offices, and the public square.

However, many people don't see how their work fits within God's mission. They wonder if their work really matters and may suspect that it is merely something they must do to finance the truly important things in life. One person who has helped me feel the weight of these questions more than anyone else is Joe.

---

1. Steven Garber, *Visions of Vocation: Common Grace for the Common Good* (Downers Grove, IL: InterVarsity, 2014), 155.

Turkish Basketball and the Glory of God

Just like his name, Joe's appearance is average in almost every way. If you met him on the street and saw his height, weight, build, and demeanor, you would never guess that he was one of the best basketball players in the world.

Despite being only 6'0" tall and not very fast or strong, Joe is a master of the game, with the delicate attention to detail that you see in the sketches of an architect or the deft movements of a surgeon. Seeing the ball roll off his fingertips with perfect backspin and swish through the net, you know you are in the presence of someone who really knows what he's doing.

When I first met Joe, he was playing in the Turkish Basketball League, and I was attempting a career as a basketball scout. I was pleased to find a follower of Christ who was living in a predominantly Muslim country and who was also involved with sports. At that time we were both trying to figure out how sports fit within God's mission. We had great conversations together about the article "Delighting in God's Good Gift of Competition and Sport" and books like *Creation Regained*.[2] However, Joe told me about a time in his life when he couldn't see the connection between his work and the mission of God at all.

I once saw Joe play in an unforgettable game. He was the leader of a small, underfunded team from a rural town in western Turkey. They were playing the perennial champion team from the big city of Istanbul, which was stacked with former NBA players. Nobody thought Joe's team had a shot at winning. But Joe didn't back down; he played a masterful game, handling the ball with skill and creativity. He passed with such precision that he enabled his teammates to score with ease. His shots were so accurate that the repeated sound of the ball hitting nothing but net began to take on an almost musical beauty. He was the leading scorer in the game but not in a selfish way. He generously shared the ball with his teammates in a way that elevated their performance and helped them play their best.

The game came down to the final seven seconds, and Joe's team was down by two points. Of course, the ball was in Joe's hands to take the last shot. They inbounded the ball to Joe, and as he dribbled up the court, he was trapped by two giants, both of whom seemed to be at least 6'7" tall. Somehow he

---

2. Michael W. Goheen, "Delighting in God's Good Gift of Competition and Sport," in *Engaging the Culture: Christians at Work in Education*, ed. Richard Edlin and Jill Ireland (Sydney, Australia: National Institute for Christian Education, 2006), 173–86. This article was originally given as a keynote address at the Christian Society for Kinesiology and Leisure Studies Annual Conference in Ancaster, Ontario, on June 5, 2003. It can be found online here: http://missionworldview.com/wp-content/uploads/2011/07/Gods-Good-Gift-of-Athletics.pdf. Albert M. Wolters, *Creation Regained: Biblical Basics for a Reformational Worldview*, 2nd ed. (Grand Rapids: Eerdmans, 2005).

managed to squeeze through them as time dwindled. He rushed up the court as the clock kept ticking: five, four, three, two, one.

Falling away, about thirty feet from the basket, he launched a three-point shot. And again, it was nothing but net.

The crowd erupted in celebration. Strangers hugged one another. The community from that small town in Turkey was bursting with joy on that thrilling Thursday evening. Most people who see games like this experience a deep, unexplainable joy, a sense that there's something inherently good in a moment like that. When we see human greatness, we often sense that we are getting a small taste of the way the world should be.

But we don't always know how to make sense of the goodness and beauty that we encounter in the world. Many of us struggle to make sense of the meaning behind the good work we see. Something deep inside of us declares that there's an inherent goodness to the well-ordered business plan, the abundant garden, compassionate nursing, and wise parenting. But how does such goodness fit within God's mission? Joe struggled with that question for several years before I met him. He wondered, What's the merit in spending so much time playing basketball?

What would you have said to Joe? How would you have encouraged him? Imagine meeting him during his season of big vocational questions, and imagine him asking for your advice. Imagine the morning after a big game, like the one I just described. Hours after the cheers have faded and the crowd has shuffled out of the stadium, Joe is sitting in front of you, taking bites of a flaky Turkish pastry called *borek*, passing you the salt, and tossing hard questions at you from across the table.

He's trying to reconcile the joy he feels when playing basketball with his commitment to Christ. He begins to wonder aloud if this game of basketball fits within God's mission at all. He wonders if he should quit playing basketball—the craft that he has mastered over many years—and go be a pastor or a missionary or start a nonprofit organization.

As he sips his black Turkish coffee, he hits you with a series of questions: "Does basketball even matter to God?" "Isn't this just a simple game? How does it help anyone?" "Am I wasting my life?" "How does this game fit within God's mission?" What would you say to this conflicted craftsperson?

Does My Work Matter?

Joe isn't the only person to ask these questions. The world is filled with accountants who can't reconcile crunching numbers with the biblical story, janitors who want to wipe the slate clean and start a new career, contractors who want to build a more meaningful life, and salespeople who wonder if they should shift their focus from sales commissions to the Great Commission. They are all asking Joe's questions: Does my work matter? Does it fit within God's mission?

Before answering these questions with the Bible and discussing the important role of work within the mission of God, I want to address four insufficient answers we might give to people who are struggling to understand why work matters in the kingdom of God. Each of these insufficient answers bears a glimmer of truth, but ultimately none do what's necessary: see work itself in the light of the biblical story.

Work matters when it's fulfilling. Many think that work matters because it gives a sense of joy and fulfillment. They therefore assume that the greatest vocational quest is to find enjoyable work. While it's true that enjoying your work can be an indicator that you are doing something you were created to do, it's an insufficient answer to why work matters. Work in a fallen world will always have challenges and struggles that aren't enjoyable. Work is painful because the invasive weeds of sin have crept into every area of life, filling every occupation and vocation with thorns and thistles. Many of us fall into the trap of bouncing from job to job in search of Eden, trying to find a back door into that world we know we were meant for. To long for this type of joyful and fruitful work is right and good. We should try our best to experience glimpses of it in this world. But we need to remember that no job is a sufficient savior; mere work cannot satisfy our deepest needs. The day is coming when God will restore all things and we will experience the joy of complete fruitfulness. But until Christ returns, we need a better answer for why work matters.

Work matters because it pays the bills. Some of us take a pragmatic approach to the question of meaningful work. We see it as a means of making money that will help us fulfill our seemingly more important responsibilities, such as putting food on the table for our family, giving money to the church, or sharing with those in need. Although this is a good place to start, it fails to see the inherent value in the work itself. This mentality puts us in danger of appraising the value of the work by the numbers on the paycheck, of equating wealth with fruitfulness. People with this perspective are usually responsible and generous but lack a bigger vision of how the actual fruits of their labor—such as good insurance policies, efficient logistics planning, or clean bathrooms—fit within God's mission.

Work matters when it's focused on "spiritual things." Some of us value the work of pastors, missionaries, or nonprofits above all other types of work, seeing so-called sacred work as the only valuable work. The work of the pastor, missionary, and nonprofit leader are important, but to rank "spiritual" work above "secular" work is a dangerous heresy—it denies the goodness of God's creation and functionally tears out the pages of the first and last two chapters of the Bible (Gen. 1–2; Rev. 21–22). To divide work into these artificial categories is to tell a story of our world and our creator that begins with sin (Gen. 3) and ends in heaven (Rev. 21). That's simply *not* the way God's story goes!

Work matters because it's a platform for evangelism. Many of us see the value of work solely in the opportunities it provides to evangelize our coworkers. Evangelism in the workplace is important, and sadly, it often gets downplayed. However, if we believe evangelism to be the only valuable aspect of our work, the quality of our work itself will inevitably suffer. We will be tempted to see the nonevangelistic moments as a waste of time and will struggle to stay motivated and focused on the task at hand. This will result in poor work, which will diminish our witness. As I once heard someone say, "Your work will never be a platform for evangelism until it's first more than a platform for evangelism."

All of these approaches to work have some merit, but they are all insufficient answers to how and why work has meaning. God called humanity to work before he called us to do anything else! Stewardship, the act of working within God's world, is the first music we perform in the symphony of mission, intended to harmonize with our service and spoken word to bring the message of the gospel to the ears of the world. Therefore, this chapter will help us reflect on stewardship and how to bring missional intentionality to our work, whatever that work may be.

Work in Biblical Perspective

Work matters because it's the first task God gives to his people. God created humanity in his own image and blessed them with the opportunity to display his glory, goodness, wisdom, and strength through the work of their hands. As God's image, we're called to imitate his work through our work and so to provide the world with a picture of what God is like. This is an important way to participate in God's mission. When our work is done well, we provide the world with a small, incomplete but beautiful portrait of what God is like.

The biblical concept of glory can be a little hard to understand. In the Old Testament, the Hebrew word for "glory" is *kavod*, which refers to something weighty. It was used to describe the greatness or gravitas of someone important: their power, splendor, and renown. *Kavod* came to be translated by the Greek word *doxa*, which refers to personal honor and majesty. Perhaps Gerhard von Rad captures the heart of it when he says that glory is that which makes someone "impressive and demands recognition."[3] God's glory is his majestic and magnificent character on display in the world. It is uniquely impressive, and it demands recognition by his creatures in praise, submission, awe, wonder, and worship. Throughout Scripture we see that God is on a mission to fill the world with the knowledge of his glory (Ps. 96:3; Hab. 2:14). He reveals his glory through the brilliance of his creation (Num. 14:21; Ps. 72:19; Isa. 6:3) and especially through the pinnacle of his creation: humanity.

We humans were created for God's glory (Isa. 43:7; 1 Cor. 10:31) and have the unique task of displaying God's character through the way we live in the world (Matt. 5:16; 1 Pet. 2:12). There are many ways we humans can glorify God (including in our rest, relationships, prayer, and quality of character), but this chapter will focus on how our *work* displays the glory of God.

Work here refers to human stewardship of God's world in every area of life, not employment alone but all human activity that's productive and positively affects creation. Work includes the jobs that provide our paychecks, but it also includes parenting, gardening, art making, volunteering, home repair, and a host of other important activities that aren't typically rewarded financially.

The call to display God's glory through our work can be found throughout Scripture, but in this chapter we will focus on Genesis 1–2, the story of creation. These pages tell the story of the God who created everything and declared that it was good. However, the creation of human beings goes beyond "good" and moves God to assess the world as "very good." We are the crown of his creation, distinct from all plants and animals because we have a unique identity and calling as his gift to us.

Our distinctiveness in creation comes from being made in the image of God. This means that something about the way we are made is like God, able to embody his glory in the world. But it also means that we are able to see and understand his glory. Because we can love, we can comprehend God's love; because we can speak and hear, we can understand what it means for God to speak and hear. As Wilhelm Vischer puts it, "Man is the eye of the whole body of creation which God will cause to see His glory."[4] We have

---

3. Gerhard von Rad, "Kavod in the OT," in *Theological Dictionary of the New Testament*, ed. Gerhard Kittel, ed. and trans. Geoffrey W. Bromiley (Grand Rapids: Eerdmans, 1964), 2:238, s.v. "δόξα."

4. Wilhelm Vischer, *Das Christuszeugnis des A.T.* (Zollikon-Zurich: Evangelische Verlag, 1934), 1:59–60, quoted in Karl Barth, *Church Dogmatics*, vol. 3, *The Doctrine of Creation*,

the unique dignity and responsibility of putting God's glory on display, carrying a higher status than the rest of creation. We are not gods, not in any way equal to God, but we do provide a creaturely snapshot of the divine, a glimpse of what God is like. And we can recognize and respond to his glory in thanksgiving, praise, and love.

However, human beings were not just given a distinct identity as image-bearers; we were also given a distinct calling. We were explicitly called to work, to take care of everything else God created. Image-bearing isn't a static or passive activity; it is a verb not a noun. We aren't portraits hung on a celestial wall but living monuments of God, sent into the world to work.

We see the explicit call to work and its relationship to image-bearing in Genesis 1:26–28:

> Then God said, "Let us make mankind in our image, in our likeness, so that they may rule over the fish in the sea and the birds in the sky, over the livestock and all the wild animals, and over all the creatures that move along the ground." So God created mankind in his own image, in the image of God he created them; male and female he created them. God blessed them and said to them, "Be fruitful and increase in number; fill the earth and subdue it. Rule over the fish in the sea and the birds in the sky and over every living creature that moves on the ground."

God gave humans the explicit calling to "rule" and "subdue" the earth. These words provide the divine invitation, blessing, and authorization for humans to cultivate God's world responsibly and reverently, making it more fruitful and productive. Essentially, God calls humanity to sink their hands into the soil of the earth, harness the strength of an ox, and turn a mound of dirt into life-sustaining rows of zucchini, tomatoes, and basil.

Both the process of working and the products that result from work display the glory of God. Our work imitates God's work; our products display the deep goodness of God's productivity. God sent his people on a mission to dig deep into the crust of the earth to discover its hidden potential and transform metals into saxophones, surgical instruments, and skyscrapers. The wisdom of the farmer dramatizes the wisdom of God. The sound of the oboe amplifies the brilliant potential that God has joyfully embedded in creation and generously invites us to discover. Detail-oriented managers display the intricacy of God's sovereign rule, investigative journalists dramatize the vast knowledge of God, and good police officers provide a

---

ed. Geoffrey W. Bromiley and Thomas F. Torrance, trans. J. W. Edwards, O. Bussey, and Harold Knight (Peabody, MA: Hendrickson, 2010), 194 (3.1).

glimpse of God's protection. Our good work imitates and magnifies God's own good work.

However, the call to work isn't a license to be flippant or reckless in our relationship with the earth. Certainly it is not a license to trash the place. Those who use Genesis 1 to justify environmental degradation have distorted its meaning. They have likely fallen prey to the humanist spirit that seeks domination over nature. To truly understand the nature of the words *rule* and *subdue*, we have to read them in the context of Genesis 2:15, which says, "The LORD God took the man and put him in the Garden of Eden to work it and take care of it." God has made a beautiful home where he can dwell with humanity. Imagine being invited to live in a beautiful home with someone, only to take the opportunity to wreck it! God commissioned Adam and all of humanity to be the gardeners of his world. Rather than relating to the earth as if it were an all-you-can-eat buffet strictly for enjoyment, we should care for God's creation with the patience and skill of dedicated farmers. We aren't called to leave the world alone, nor are we called to recklessly scorch it. We're called to care for it as stewards who work on behalf of its true owner by employing both innovative fruitfulness and reverent preservation to make it flourish. We're called to create and sustain, because we bear the image of the creator and sustainer of all things.

Our call to work is first seen in Genesis 1–2 in the perfect flourishing of God's good creation. While work is certainly affected by the reality of sin in Genesis 3, the stewardship mandate isn't revoked. We see it throughout Scripture. It's reiterated after the flood (Gen. 9), celebrated in the Psalms (Ps. 8), reflected on in the wisdom literature (Prov. 31), fulfilled in the life of Christ (Heb. 2:5–18), and commanded to Christ's followers in the New Testament epistles (Col. 3:23). The book of Revelation paints a final picture of human work being incorporated into the renewed creation (Rev. 21:24–27). Furthermore, Paul frequently calls the church to glorify God in all of life, and this certainly includes our work (1 Cor. 10:31; Col. 3:16).

Theologians often refer to the biblical call to work as the "cultural mandate," because as we work together in community to provide for our needs and for the needs of one another, we develop patterns of cultural life together. So this mandate is viewed as an invitation for humans to cultivate culture from the raw material of the world. However, this formation of culture through work, relationships, and customs should be done in a stewardly way, so in this book we refer to these verses as the "stewardship mandate."

The word *stewardship* acknowledges that the world belongs to God. He has entrusted his human image-bearers with responsibility over the creation. We are to develop its potential as we lovingly care for it. And we are accountable as stewards for carrying out the task we've been given by our master. The concept of stewardship highlights, on the one hand, that we can't do whatever we want with the creation; we've been given a specific job to do. But, on the other hand, it makes clear that *everything* we do—not merely the applause-winning acts of public culture—is part of this mandate. Stewardship isn't about changing the world; it's about changing diapers, light bulbs, and the oil in your car. All these things are involved in developing and caring for God's world.

We're called to engage God's world with faithfulness in all aspects of life—family, education, business, government, art, and sports—with a humble desire to serve our neighbors and display the glory of God. We are responsible, however, for dramatizing the grace, provision, knowledge, communication, and compassion of God in our daily activities.

What follows are four ways in which good human work puts God on display.

Good Work Is a Portrait of God's Character

Humanity is a self-portrait by God. By filling the world with humans and human activity like architecture, art, and agriculture, God is filling the world with little portraits of himself.

We are not divine or equal to God, just as a picture of a person isn't the same thing as that person. However, a picture does *represent* the real thing. A picture of someone can give a small sense of what that person is like. When we live in the way God intended, we give the world a snapshot of God. But, of course, when we live in ways that are *contrary* to God's design for us, we distort the image of God—like a toddler scribbling on a wedding album.

If our missional task is to display the character of God, we should reflect what God is like! And one of the many things we learn about God from Scripture is that he is a worker. Genesis 1:1 doesn't say, "In the beginning God was relaxing in a hammock." Or, "In the beginning God made humans as his servants because he didn't like to work." Rather it says, "In the beginning God created the heavens and the earth." And then he puts in a good week of work to get the job done. The very first thing that God reveals about himself is that he's a creator and a worker.

What could display the inherent goodness of work more clearly than the fact that God *chooses* to work and that it's the first thing God reveals about himself in Scripture? Figuratively speaking, when we first encounter the God of the Bible, we see a God in work boots and overalls not a Hawaiian shirt and flip-flops. God delights in getting his hands dirty in the soil of the earth. He works for six days, takes a break, and then invites us to follow his pattern.

When we encounter good work, we are often compelled to think about the worker who has done it. A well-designed bicycle reveals something about its designing engineer; a superb meal gives us a glimpse into the mind of the chef who prepared it. The masterpiece of God's creation shows us (at least in part) what God is like. When we look at the world through the lens of the biblical story, we see that God is a worker and that his work is good. So what *kind* of worker is he?

God is the *great architect* who perfectly designed the world with function and beauty. His brilliant design includes balanced ecosystems with usable and renewable material.

God is the *interior designer* who created the full spectrum of colors and painted them across the mountains and flowers and people. His sketchbook isn't a moleskin-covered journal but the Arizona sky, where each night he sovereignly stuns us with another orange and purple sunset. God didn't just choose the best colors for those sunsets; he actually decided what colors should exist. The color orange was *his* idea.

God is the *great auditor* and *quality control manager* who watches over every inch of creation and declares, "It is good!"

God is the *great entrepreneur* whose enterprise is sustainable and constantly filled with goods, like acorns, and services, like shade trees.

God is the *farmer before all farmers* whose original work is behind every morsel of food we've ever enjoyed and who employs billions of microbes in the soil to cultivate sweet blackberries and giant pumpkins.

God is the *great landscaper* who not only fills the world with evergreen trees, shrubs, and stones but carefully separates and organizes them to make the world delightful.

God is the *pioneer of the hospitality industry* who perfectly prepared a place for human flourishing.

God is the *administrative assistant* who supports our work, not by keeping our calendar but by ordaining and ordering time itself.

God is the *great janitor* who mops the earth with the generosity of his raindrops.

Then we turn the page and begin to see, from Genesis to Revelation, that God is a great worker. He's the great security guard who promises to protect his people, the doctor who heals us, the nurse who comforts us, the maintenance man who sustains the earth, the server who washes our feet, the teacher who is the source of all knowledge, and the general contractor who will one day renovate and restore all of creation. God is glorious and majestic and holy and good—and God is a worker.[5]

Don't we want people to know this God, the giver of all good gifts and the creator of all good things? Telling the world about this God is clearly one of the most important aspects of mission, but the question is, How does the world come to see the invisible God? How do they come to know that God is a creator, protector, rescuer, and restorer?

God has embedded living analogies of his glory in the glory of his creation. By looking at the masterpiece he has made, we can catch a glimpse of what God is like. This is true for all of creation, but it's especially true for humans, the bearers of his image.

We were made to be workers so that we could reflect the image of the ultimate worker. Returning to Genesis 1:26–28, we see that humans were given the unique task of stewarding God's world and the unique identity of being made in his "likeness" and in his "image." Most Christians have at least a vague understanding of what those terms mean. Theologians debate the specific definition of God's image, but most agree that something about humanity is fundamentally similar to God and displays what God is like. The language in Genesis is comparable to that used by ancient kings who placed statues and emblems in the cities that were under their reign. These "images" represented the king's rule, reminding the people what the king was like. In a similar way, God fills the earth with image-bearers who are like statues that signify the reign of God and provide a glimpse of his likeness. All our human activity—the work of our hands—has the potential to magnify the action and character of God. Good work, when done God's way, helps the world behold the majesty of God.

God's self-portraits aren't confined to one particular gallery or photo album but are scattered among all the fields of human activity. They can be found on construction sites with hammer in hand, behind websites with beautifully crafted graphics, in trucks that deliver important goods over dangerous mountain roads, and in classrooms where the wisdom and order of God is magnified through algebra. Pictures of God can be found in the living room, where one person picks up toys for the tenth time that day and another (smaller) person stacks LEGOs for the first time in her life.

When work is done well, it draws us in. Human excellence is inherently attractive. Good books fill us with wonder, good counselors bring

---

5. Herman Bavinck develops this from Scripture in a section on the names of God. He speaks of God being named by human body parts, emotions, actions, and finally professions and offices. He says, "God is often called by names which indicate a certain office, profession, or relation among men." He lists a number of these professions and relations in Scripture. See *Doctrine of God*, trans. William Hendriksen (Grand Rapids: Baker, 1951), 87.

us comfort, and well-designed roads bring a measure of peace. All these things functionally help us, but we also find them pleasing and admirable, even when we aren't receiving a direct benefit. I believe this is because whenever we encounter good work, we actually catch a glimpse of God's glory.

But humanity has disfigured the image of God in us, and our work bears the wounds of our rebellion. And so, central to the mission of the church is the summons to demonstrate what it means to be restored to our true and full humanity. We're meant to show what it is to be renewed in the image of God by displaying the glory of God in the work of our hands. We are to say with our lives, "This is what God always intended for human life together in community. We are a living embodiment of God's design for human flourishing. See God and come and join us."

Here are a few examples of how the glory of God is displayed through the work of human hands.

Andy, a portrait of God's faithfulness. God never breaks his promises, never lies, and constantly moves toward his people with steadfast love that is as dependable as tomorrow morning's sunrise. You can count on God. In a world where most people quit their jobs every few years, there's something admirable about those who faithfully work at the same place for decades. Andy has worked at the same insurance office, in the same neighborhood, serving many of the same people, for over thirty years. The way he faithfully engages his work each day gives us a glimpse of the faithful God who always shows up for his people. When we engage in our work with faithfulness and trustworthiness, we have the wonderful opportunity to give the world a glimpse of a faithful and trustworthy God.

Jamie, a portrait of God's order. Through her well-ordered budgets, well-designed timesheets, and easily interpreted emails, Jamie lifts up the God of order. She's a project manager and administrative assistant whose efficient processes can turn an hour's worth of work into a fifteen-minute task. Her coworkers describe her attention to detail as "absolutely impeccable." They say that she "creates order out of chaos." Their admiration for Jamie is ultimately an admiration for the reflection of God that's displayed through her work. Through her skilled project management and administrative competence, Jamie has given her coworkers a glimpse of the God who orders the world in such intricate detail. Through her clearly defined timelines, she displays the God who created the very concept of time. The God who created the laws of physics that keep our world from falling into disarray is magnified by people like Jamie who keep the office from devolving into chaos.

Joe, a portrait of God's wisdom and knowledge. We often find ourselves amazed when we encounter a brilliant mind that contains a deep well of knowledge about a particular subject. It's even more impressive when such people have wisdom and know how to apply their knowledge. Our friend Joe is a successful entrepreneur, restaurateur, and housing developer. Even in his fifties, after all his successes, he's still one of the most intentional learners I know, always asking questions, reading books, and taking trips to learn more. He's one of the wisest and most knowledgeable businessmen you'll ever meet. He's likely to ask other people questions in conversation, but if you are able to slip in a question for him, he will answer wisely and knowledgeably on topics as diverse as sustainable farming, business start-ups, Lebanese cuisine, coffee roasting, and urban planning. It's easy to find yourself in awe of his vast knowledge. But he's the first one to point out that any wisdom he has comes from God, the Source of all knowledge. All the libraries in the world cannot contain what God knows, but when humans develop a deep knowledge of their field of work and cultivate wisdom over time, they point to the God who knows all things.

How about you? What do people see when they encounter your work? If your work is a commentary on the character of God, what does it communicate? Does your work show a God who is faithful, excellent, and marked by sacrificial love? Or does it (unconsciously, of course) portray a God who is uninterested in this physical world or selfish or untrustworthy? The witness of the church has greatly diminished over the past few decades because so many Christians don't take work seriously. For the most part, I don't think this is because most of us have bad intentions. The problem is we don't see our normal human activity as sacred. We have placed a higher value on so-called spiritual things, like church attendance, evangelism, pastoral work, and prayer, and our everyday activities—from yard work to office work—are engaged without much enthusiasm. And we claim to be "on fire" for God and for spiritual things! To be on fire for God is good, but when we show little care for his world, including the social, vocational, economic, aesthetic, and physical aspects of life, our "fire" for God can send our witness to the world up in smoke. We simply can't afford to ignore things that are important to God and to the neighbors to whom we seek to bear witness.

The work of your hands communicates something to the world about God. What does your work say? Is it in harmony with the great symphony of God's mission, making beautiful music to the nations? Or is it merely making noise and so distorting the music of the gospel? God is the good worker who is inviting you to work with diligence and wisdom as his image-bearer to give the world a glimpse of what he is really like.

Good Work Is a Magnifying Glass for God's Creation

When I was in my early twenties, I spent most of my time with a group of friends who could best be described as Reformed theology groupies. We engaged in smug theological diatribes online and talked about old Puritan preachers like they were members of our fantasy football team. Our veneration of Reformed theologians often had us tossing around silly questions like, Who is your favorite preacher?

Most people would say Charles Spurgeon, Jonathan Edwards, John Calvin, or Martin Luther, even though most of us hadn't actually read their works; we were just repeating stories we had picked up from others. One day I asked this question to an older man named Ken, who had been a missionary in a Muslim country for decades, and he gave an answer that I never could have anticipated. He said, "A maple tree. My favorite preacher is a maple tree." I rolled my eyes at his hippyesque answer. I thought he either was blowing me off or just wasn't very smart; either way, I wasn't impressed.

Several years later, when I actually decided to read John Calvin, I read a sentence that immediately reminded me of Ken's answer. It said, "There is not one little blade of grass, there is no color in this world that is not intended to make men rejoice."[6] I couldn't hear it from Ken at the time, but John Calvin got my attention. God's creation is the faithful preacher that's constantly showing us something about God. Psalm 19:1 says, "The heavens declare the glory of God; the skies proclaim the work of his hands." Paul, in Romans 1:20, says something very similar: "God's invisible qualities—his eternal power and divine nature—have been clearly seen, being understood from what has been made, so that people are without excuse." In other words, God shows the world what he is like through his creation. Flowers and fish, sand and sunsets, grass and goats—all of these are evangelists whose very existence says something about God's glory.

Our work has the potential to amplify the voice of creation and its preaching about God's glory. Good work that cultivates and develops the raw material of creation draws the world into a deeper experience of wonder. It displays how wonderful creation really is. As people see the glory of God's world, they catch glimpses of the glory of the creator; as they encounter the beautiful, good, and intricate things God has created, they experience something of the beauty, goodness, and wisdom of God. When someone discovers the potential of medicine in a simple flower, they discover the hidden brilliance of God's creation. Each person involved in the process

6. John Calvin, "Sermon no. 10 on 1 Corinthians," 698, quoted in William J. Bouwsma, *John Calvin: A Sixteenth Century Portrait* (Oxford: Oxford University Press, 1989), 134–35.

of transforming that flower into medicine and delivering it to the world—from the manufacturers to the truckers, the quality control specialists to the marketers—plays a part in magnifying the hidden goodness of creation. Abraham Kuyper says,

> Eden is planted, but humankind will cultivate it—that is the fundamental law of creation. Which is to say: creation was fashioned by God, fashioned with life that surges and glows in its bosom, fashioned with powers that lie dormant in its womb. Yet lying there, it displayed only half its beauty. Now, however, God crowns it with humanity. They awaken its life, arouse its powers, and with human hands bring to light the glory that lay locked in its depths but had not yet shone on its countenance.[7]

When the powers and glory of creation's potential are finally unlocked and displayed, God's own glory is seen all the more.

Perhaps the best way to illustrate this is to ask a question that might at first seem heretical. Reread Genesis 1 and ask, What did God *not* create? You might first think, "Nothing! God is the creator of all things." But perhaps there is another answer. In the beginning God didn't create pancakes. Oh, he could have—he could have made everything that would ever fill the earth. Instead, he displayed hospitality and restraint, choosing to unfold his creation through the work of human hands. He left pancakes for *us* to do. He filled the world with uncultivated potential and then invited humans to find the treasures embedded in the soil, trees, and water.

When God created Adam and Eve, he didn't invite them to sit down to prefabricated tables already loaded with buttery pancakes and fresh-squeezed orange juice. He didn't make the world with prebuilt houses, sheds full of shovels, or iPhones preloaded with phone numbers of predetermined friends. He showed restraint in the first days of creation by not making everything that would ever be made or every person that would ever be born. He allowed us to join in his work and invited us to cultivate the potential that he hid within the raw material of the world.

Consider something as simple as maple syrup. It's a wonderful thing but not an obvious thing. In the depths of a maple tree, God placed a gift—one that lay hidden for millennia—that would one day partner with pancakes to claim Saturday mornings as sacred. For thousands of years he waited for some person to hammer a tap into a tree, experiment with boiling temperatures,

---

7. Abraham Kuyper, "Rooted and Grounded: The Church as Organism and Institution," in *On the Church: Collected Works in Public Theology* (Bellingham, WA: Lexham Press, 2016), 51. This is from Abraham Kuyper's inaugural sermon at Nieuwe Kerk, Amsterdam, August 10, 1870.

and take what he made good and display its potential for more goodness. By *not* creating pancakes and maple syrup on the first day of creation, God invited us to search for that delectable combination, to extend his creativity by the good work of our human hands.

From deep inside the seemingly mundane stuff of the earth, God calls us to discover and develop the potentials of his creation. And when we do this work well, we display the mysterious heights of his glory. Consider the hospital building in which you were born, the scalpel that removed your mother's cancer, the oven that you used to cook your Thanksgiving meal, and the engine in your first car. All these things are made of steel, which God hid inside some seemingly insignificant rocks. God hid a pharmacy in the forest, embedding the pain-relieving and even lifesaving potential of a medicine like aspirin in the bark of a willow tree. As James K. A. Smith says,

> When God calls creation into being, he announces that it's very good, but he doesn't announce that it's finished! Creation doesn't come into existence ready-made with schools, art museums, and farms; those are all begging to be unpacked. But unfurling that potential is going to take work—and that work is the labor of culture, of cultivation, of unpacking. Indeed, creation is itself a call and invitation; the riches and potential of God's good creation are entrusted to his image bearers. That is our calling and commission.[8]

Creating something good by cultivating God's world is called culture making, and it's an important part of the human vocation. When we discover and unfold the inherent goodness in the things we make, we fill the world with things that evoke awe and wonder, and our work becomes a magnifying glass that provides a clearer picture of God's majestic creation. When humans experience wonder and delight as they encounter good culture—whether it's a symphony, a baseball game, or a sandwich—they are experiencing an amplified image of God's good handiwork. Our work can give people a glimpse of the majesty of God's creation and a sense that there is something greater than themselves in this world.

Consider something as simple as sand. When children sink their hands into it to make a sand castle, they discover the way God made sand to work with water and how it binds together with a little bit of pressure from our hands. Because we've seen hundreds of sand castles, we may not think much about them. But something as simple as a sand castle is uniquely human. You'll never stumble upon a seagull who's passing the time by making a sand castle. Through the work of a seven-year-old child, we see the image

8. James K. A. Smith, *Letters to a Young Calvinist* (Grand Rapids: Brazos, 2010), 109.

of God—the great creator—and furthermore, the great potential he has buried in sand.

From something as simple as beach sand, we discovered how to make the sidewalks for our streets and the stucco for our walls; silicon (also from sand) is used in the semiconductors in our computers and cell phones. Glass also comes from sand. When humans discovered the potential of glass, we made more than just stained glass windows. We made other holy instruments, such as wine glasses for weddings, aquariums where even landlubbers can admire the beauties of corals and sea fans, eyeglasses to help the over-fifty crowd read their favorite novels, and microscopes and telescopes to help us discover even more of the hidden riches of God's good creation.

All good work is a lens to help us focus on the beauty, goodness, wisdom, and splendor of God's world. But all of our work, good as it may be, depends on the prior work of God, the raw material that God has embedded in creation:

> For a Christian, the mind is important because God is important. Who, after all, made the world of nature, and then made possible the development of sciences through which we find out more about nature? Who formed the universe of human interactions, and so provided the raw material of politics, economics, sociology, and history? Who is the source of harmony, form, and narrative pattern, and so lies behind all artistic and literary possibilities? Who created the human mind in such a way that it could grasp the realities of nature, of human interactions, of beauty, and so made possible the theories on such matters by philosophers and psychologists? Who, moment by moment, sustains the natural world, the world of human interactions, and the harmonies of existence? Who, moment by moment, maintains the connections between what is in our minds and what is in the world beyond our minds? The answer in every case is the same. God did it, and God does it.[9]

God is behind all of our good work. He gave us the raw material for all of culture—from the grain of sand that becomes a microchip to the grain of wheat that becomes your toast. He knows the potential in every blade of grass and could easily speak into existence the very things that take centuries for us to discover. But he shows restraint, allowing his human image-bearers to discover what he has hidden.

Your work is a lens to bring into focus the creative work of God. In the kitchen, your crepe recipe magnifies the brilliance of the God who made eggs, milk, and flour to harmonize with blueberries and cream. As a structural

9. Mark A. Noll, *The Scandal of the Evangelical Mind* (Grand Rapids: Eerdmans, 1994), 51.

engineer, your work ensures that a building will stand for decades, magnifying the God who created physics. When you make up a simple song to help your child remember an important truth, you are magnifying the God who created the simple gift of melody and the complex mysteries of neuroscience. Culture making, the daily work of the human vocation, isn't peripheral activity that distracts us from the mission of God. Rather, it allows us to make visible the glory and grace of the invisible God to a watching world.

Good Work Displays God's Loving Provision

I have a lot of books—far too many! But they function for me as a set of tools the way a carpenter has his tools. In the same way a carpenter needs a hammer for certain jobs and a screwdriver for others, I need different books for different jobs. The problem comes when I cannot find the book I need. Having a lot of books can simply lead to clutter and the loss of otherwise valuable space. I need good shelves laid out in a way that makes my books readily available for my use.

So I invited Alex, a young carpenter in our congregation, to come and build some bookshelves for me. We talked about the best way to lay out and build the shelves. Then he spent a number of days at our home working away in my office. When he finished, his carpentry skills were on full display. Those shelves provided the room I needed. I couldn't wait to rearrange my books and put them on the shelves.

But then Alex said something that took me by surprise: "I can't charge you for my work. After all, you're a pastor. This work will enable you to use your books to benefit me. So I would like to offer this work as a gift." I appreciated the gesture, but I firmly resisted and used the opportunity to help him understand something about work in God's economy.

I said, "God has given different gifts to people so they can use those gifts to love and serve one another. He didn't give you the gift of preaching and teaching, but he gave those gifts to me so I could love and serve you. He certainly didn't give *me* the gift of using tools—I don't know which end of a hammer to hold—but he obviously gave *you* that gift so you could love and serve me. You have loved and served me by building these bookshelves, which will enable me, in turn, to serve and love you. That's the way our work is supposed to work. In fact, that is how all work is supposed to work.

"God has designed community so that in good work that loves and serves our neighbor we can take care of our needs and those of our families. I get paid to preach and teach. You get paid to use your carpentry skills. God has made each of us with many needs but only a few gifts. We must use those gifts to serve and love one another. And in the process, you can take care of your needs. So if you really want to live within God's designed economy, you will take this check to fully pay for your work."

Alex had been schooled in the Western economy, which says work is about looking out for yourself—the gifts and abilities God has given you are yours so that you can make good money and take care of yourself. This attitude takes one creational aspect of work (making money to care for your needs) and makes it the whole point of work. So when Alex suddenly found himself doing a job for someone he cared about and recognized that this work would benefit him, he wasn't so sure he should be paid. But work was *designed* to be this way.

When I think of my own gifts and abilities, I realize I have very few. Thankfully they have been needed by others, and through them I have been able to provide for the needs of my family. But I'm well aware of my utter dependence on others to fix my car or my plumbing, make shelves for my books, or move my piano. And that is only the beginning: I also need food and the food industry that has developed to take food from the farmer's field to the supermarket. As we continue to think about these things, we become more aware of just how dependent on one another we really are.

The contemporary testimony *Our World Belongs to God* puts it this way:

> Our work is a calling from God.
> We work for more than wages
> and manage for more than profit
> so that mutual respect
> and the just use of goods and skills
> may shape the workplace.
> *While we earn or profit,*
> *we love our neighbors by providing*
> *useful products and services.*
> In our global economy
> we advocate meaningful work
> and fair wages for all.
> Out of the Lord's generosity to us,
> we give freely and gladly
> of our money and time.[10]

So much work in the twenty-first century, especially in the world of business, is driven solely by profit. Profit is a good part of God's design: one who

---

10. *Our World Belongs to God: A Contemporary Testimony*, par. 48 (testimony, adopted by Synod 2008 of the Christian Reformed Church; italics mine), http://missionworldview.com /wp-content/uploads/2011/07/Our-World-Belongs-to-God-2008.pdf.

does not work for a profit will not last long. But profit is not what should first motivate a Christian in his or her work. Our motive should be to love our neighbor by providing useful products and services.

God could have made each of us completely self-sufficient, but he didn't. He formed human beings to live in community and parceled out his gifts so we would be dependent on one another. Good work is one way to love our neighbor—by providing what they need.

Good Work Is a Preview of God's Kingdom

Dave was clearly puzzled. He looked me in the eye and said, "Are you telling me that croissants go to heaven?" Dave was an architecture student at Arizona State University and was thinking about a career change. "I don't want to waste my life," he said. "I want to devote my life to eternal things." He went on to ask me if I thought he should become a pastor, a missionary, or a nonprofit leader—jobs that he thought really mattered in God's economy.

So I leaned in, looked him in the eye, and said, "Do you want me to tell you about some eternal things? Some occupations that have an eternal impact?" He emphatically said, "Yes!" So I told him he should consider a career in baking pastries, filling out tax returns, landscaping, or designing buildings, because our work today might just be incorporated into the worship of God for all eternity and has the potential to provide a glimpse of the kingdom.

The fourth way our work participates in the mission of God is that it provides a preview of God's kingdom. One day Jesus will return to renew and restore all of creation to the perfect flourishing for which it was intended. All death, sin, pain, and brokenness will be banished, and we will live in a perfect world—the way things were supposed to be.

Revelation 21:1–5 describes the future destiny of creation, what life will be like after Jesus returns and fully establishes his kingdom. God will evict sin, Satan, and death. The earth and all that was broken in it will be mended. Rather than feeling like we are far from God, we will experience his presence palpably. Social strife will be replaced by an eternal feast. The physical pain that we experience in arthritic knees, root canals, and cancer will be replaced by physical wholeness that exceeds that of the healthiest Olympic athlete. The groaning creation will experience liberation. Heaven and earth, now torn apart by sin, will be stitched back together through the work of Christ.

The prophets use rich analogies to describe what we will experience when God renews and restores all things. For example, they describe the peace of the kingdom with images of weapons repurposed as farming tools (Isa. 2:1–4; Mic. 4:1–4). They describe the safety and security of the kingdom with images of wolves snuggling with lambs for nap time, vegetarian lions, and babies play-ing hide-and-seek with cobras (Isa. 11:6–9). These are rich images from their day that describe for us what the restoration of the kingdom will look like.

Can you imagine a world of such deep and broad flourishing? Sin has so deeply stained and distorted our world that it's hard for us to picture what's to come, but I think picturing the kingdom is what Jesus is inviting us to do when he tells us to pray for his kingdom to come on earth, to be *here* as it is in heaven. He is inviting us to imagine life as it was supposed to be and then to pray for and work toward displaying bits of the kingdom here on earth—a preview of what is to come fully when he returns. Our work may be an enacted prayer for the coming of the kingdom.

A few years ago, I was discussing the imagery of God turning swords into plowshares with my friend Warren. We started discussing what language Isaiah might have used in our day to show us what it will be like when God restores all things. Here's what we came up with:

Strip clubs would be repurposed into museums that celebrate the dignity of women.

Healthy, refreshing water would flow from the perfect pipes of Flint, Michigan.

Aleppo, Syria, would be the ultimate vacation destination, so safe that people would nap in the streets.

Prisons would be repurposed into first-class elementary schools.

Every afternoon we would gather around to watch a dunk contest among people who used to be in wheelchairs.

We would take classes from those who retain the gifts of autism but no longer suffer from its pain and frustration.

The purpose of the IRS would be to explain, in great detail, all the bless-ings you have in life.

But our imaginations should do more than encourage us with this sort of harmless daydreaming; they should shape our engagement with the world as it is right now. Our work—not just our employment but all aspects of human culture—can be a preview of what the fullness of the kingdom will be like. We don't *build* the kingdom; that job is exclusively reserved for God. But we can live in such a way that our lives provide a glimpse of what the kingdom of God will be like.

At the movies we often have to watch previews of coming attractions for about ten minutes—if we're lucky. Sometimes they drag on for much longer.

Those previews don't provide us with the full experience of the movie, but they do provide a snapshot of what the movie is all about and whether it's worth watching. A preview is meant to generate desire for the real thing coming in the future.

Good work has the potential to provide our world with a preview of the coming kingdom. When hardworking landscapers use careful pruning techniques to reveal the elegance of high-reaching aspen trees, they help us to catch a glimpse of the tree of life. Artists who provide momentary encounters with breathtaking combinations of colors provide previews of the brilliant creator of colors and giver of breath. Insurance agents who write timely checks to help restore homes ripped apart by hurricanes provide a foretaste of God's restoration of this ravaged earth. Teachers who skillfully captivate the imaginations of students—keeping them on the edge of their seats—point to a day when we will sit before the throne, learning from the ultimate creator of photosynthesis, algebra, and the adjectives of every language.

Every adjective is a precious gift from God, but all of them together cannot adequately describe the glory of God and the beauty of his kingdom. The English word *amazing*, its Turkish equivalent *muhteşem*, and the Chinese word 驚人, combined with all of the superlatives from every other language, fail to describe the glorious destiny of creation. Fortunately, God uses more than words to entice us to his kingdom. Instead of sending invitations in well-written prose, God sends well-crafted people whose good work provides a glimpse of what's to come.

What about the Twisting Impact of Idolatry?

Much of this chapter has focused on Genesis 1–2 and God's original plan for humanity, but some may object to such an emphasis, reminding us that we live in a world steeped in idolatry and far from the original paradise of Eden. Idolatry certainly has the power to utterly twist our work. In fact, Mike has attended to this very issue in his reflection on the way our global economy is one of the most powerful idolatrous currents at work in our world today.[11] However, in writing one must always choose what to emphasize in terms of the space given.

The Bible tells the story of God's mission to save, heal, and restore the creation. Salvation is always *creation regained*. That is, the whole goal of

11. Michael W. Goheen and Erin G. Glanville, *The Gospel and Globalization: Exploring the Religious Roots of Globalization* (Vancouver: Regent College Press and Geneva Society, 2009). The whole text of this book can now be found on www.missionworldview.com.

God's mission, centered on the work of Jesus Christ, is to restore the creation to what it was meant to be. The emphasis on Genesis 1–2 here is to excite readers' imaginations with a glimpse of what work was meant to be. Only when we begin to see this original intent will we be able to imagine what our own work—if done in joyful obedience to the Lord who gave it to us—could look like in our present broken world.

But there is a twofold problem in the evangelical community that must be overcome if we are to get there. First, salvation is, among evangelicals, not usually considered in terms of the restoration and recovery of creation. It is normally believed to be only a return to a personal relationship with God: the individual person is saved from the guilt and power of sin. And sometimes salvation is understood to be otherworldly: we are saved to leave this earth and go to heaven. These misunderstandings hinder a good vision of what work could look like here and now.

But a second problem is that, generally, evangelicals have an impoverished view of creation. "Creation" too often means either "the nonhuman part of the world" or "what God did in the beginning." So when Paul speaks of "things taught by demons," it is hard for us to imagine that he is talking about those who are undermining the goodness of creation (1 Tim. 4:1–5). Our imaginations are often not fired with the images of what God's good world is supposed to be and what it *could* be, because we are bound by a poor doctrine of creation.

And so this chapter stresses what good work might have looked like when God made the world the way it was supposed to be. Hopefully these images will challenge you to ask what work can look like today as God is restoring the world.

Gardening in Babylon

Some may be thinking that our work shouldn't be compared to the idyllic act of gardening in Eden. Rather, since sin has infected all of life, our work more resembles toil in a cosmic sweatshop. It's true that Genesis 3 speaks of a fundamental change in the nature of work as a consequence of the fall, but the call to be gardeners in God's world has never been revoked. God still calls us to reflect his image through our work and provides the grace to accomplish much, despite the reality that sin and idolatry poison every area of life.

It's hard to imagine a more hostile work environment for exiled Israel than Babylon, a foreign land rife with injustice and idolatry. They were living as refugees under a hostile government and in a completely pagan culture. So what does God tell them to do? He gives them essentially the same command he gave to Adam and Eve in the garden: plant gardens, build houses, and start families (Jer. 29:4–7). By giving them this command, he's reaffirming the stewardship movement, even in Babylon, not for the sake of only his own people but for the flourishing of the idolatrous city surrounding them. In other words, Israel was called to garden in Babylon, to fill the city with beautiful and beneficial things, to plant an oasis of God in the desert of idolatry.

We are called to do the same thing: to seek the flourishing of our cities as we grow God's gardens of grace in the midst of a world of idolatry, injustice, and sin. Lest we think these instructions were just for the exiles, we see the apostle Peter using the imagery of the Babylonian exile when he says, "Beloved, I urge you as sojourners and exiles to abstain from the passions of the flesh, which wage war against your soul. Keep your conduct among the Gentiles honorable, so that when they speak against you as evildoers, they may see your good deeds and glorify God on the day of visitation" (1 Pet. 2:11–12 ESV). Just as God's people displayed the uniqueness of God among the nations in Babylon and in the early church, so we are called to seek the shalom of the cities and towns we live in and to glorify God through good works in our own place and time.

The Good Contractor

Several years ago, my wife and I bought a new house. Our favorite part of the house was the open floor plan where the kitchen and living room flowed into each other, an effect that had been created by the previous owners when they had removed a wall between the two rooms before flipping the house and selling it to us.

But after living in the house for about a year, we noticed a crack in the ceiling where that wall used to be. We only noticed the crack because it was right above our daughter's favorite place to play. I assumed it was only a cosmetic problem but took precautions and asked a friend who works in construction to come and take a look. He climbed into the attic and came back down looking a bit pale. The former owners had removed a load-bearing wall without bracing it correctly! The entire weight of the front of the house was resting on a thin beam directly above my daughter's toy box. Later, we found out that rather than hiring a competent builder, the former owners had made a fake invoice on the letterhead of a real contractor and then hired an amateur handyman to take out the wall. This saved them a few thousand dollars—but could have cost our daughter her life.

Several contractors came, and all gave the same advice: "You are not safe! The beam could give way at any moment." However, one of those contractors went the extra mile. His name was John, and after looking at our situation, he said, "Your house isn't safe, and I cannot leave here in good conscience without doing something about it. Right now I am going to build you a temporary wall. You don't have to pay me for the labor or the materials. You don't have to hire me for the permanent job. But I cannot leave this house knowing that your family is in danger." He took a few hours to build a temporary wall, which pointed to the character of our God as a great protector and place maker. A few weeks later, we hired him to repair the ceiling and replace the beam. His work was excellent. The craftsmanship, timeliness, professionalism, and posture of John's service helped us see a glimpse of God.

We have already discussed how good work can (1) provide a portrait of God's character, (2) be a lens to focus our view of the brilliance of his creation, (3) help us love our neighbor by providing useful services and products, and (4) provide a preview of the kingdom. John's work did all of these things. Through his work, we saw God's character. Our God is the protector of his people, and John provided us with a living analogy of God as he, through great sacrifice to himself, protected our daughter from the weight of the roof. His work, when we observed it closely, also demonstrated the brilliance of creation in its quality and care. He took the raw materials of wood and nails and rearranged them into a strong beam that held the weight of our roof. God hid the potential of protection and shelter in the wood of a tree, and John magnified the goodness of that material by cultivating it into a new piece of our home. Moreover, he offered a valuable service for us that we could not have provided for ourselves. It takes insight and skill to do his work, and we were dependent on it. By making our home safe, he provided us a small glimpse of what life might be like when God renews all of creation and we finally dwell in perfect safety.

As John was working, I struck up a conversation with him. It soon became apparent that he was (and is) a follower of Christ. He winsomely connected his good work to his relationship with God. His work was so excellent and sacrificial that he had instant credibility with me. If I were not already a follower of Christ, I imagine that I would have been very receptive to hearing about him from someone like John.

Imagine if our cities were filled with excellent work like this. Imagine if the most creative and most excellent work in every industry emerged from groups of people working in the name of Jesus. C. S. Lewis talks about how the world will see the beauty of the gospel not by reading excellent books *about* Christianity but by reading excellent books by Christians on other subjects, such as geology, astronomy, botany, and politics.[12] The world would be intrigued if the best books on every major subject were written by Christians. And I believe this extends beyond writing books to every area of life. It's possible for the glory of God to be displayed through the excellent work of our hands, even though Christians are not necessarily more skilled than those who don't follow Christ. Through common grace, God is working through the good work of humans, whether they acknowledge him or not. But followers of Christ who have truly been shaped by the biblical story should have a greater degree of meaning in their work. They should be filled with awe and wonder toward God and his generous gifts of creation. This should fuel deeper joy and commitment to good work than can be found anywhere else in the world.

Imagine if the city were filled with followers of Christ who carried out their daily tasks with a sense of wonder that inspired them to produce the most excellent work in each industry. If the best plumbers subdued the smell of sewage for God's glory, they might encounter the fragrance of Christ. Consider what it would be like if a unique group of policy makers didn't bow their knees to the ideology of a particular party but instead bowed their knees to Christ and washed the feet of their constituents with nuanced policy, deep integrity, sincere humility, civil discourse, and the refusal to be swayed by special interests. Imagine if the finest buildings, menus, and signs were designed by those who had clearly encountered the Designer of all things. Imagine if you couldn't walk a single block without stumbling upon the grace of God embedded in the smoothly paved roads and sidewalks. Imagine if our cities were adorned with the beautiful work of those who adore the name of Jesus. Our neighbors would behold the character of God on every corner, discover the brilliance of creation in every industry, and see a preview of the kingdom on every street.

Conclusion

This chapter began with the story of Joe, a professional basketball player who at one point in life struggled to see how his work fit within God's mission. He immersed himself in the biblical story and eventually came to see his work as a means of displaying God's character, as a way to magnify creation, and as a foretaste of the kingdom. He knew that his crossover displayed the creativity of God. He knew that developing a jump shot was, for him, cultivating the potential that God had hidden within the laws of physics and the muscles

12. C. S. Lewis, *God in the Dock* (Grand Rapids: Eerdmans, 2014), 91.

of his hands. With every last-second shot at the end of a game, Joe provided a preview of the joy we will all experience in the restoration of all creation at the end of history. He came to see every basketball court as an arena for God's glory. Commenting on Psalm 135:13, John Calvin says, "The whole world is a theatre for the display of the divine goodness, wisdom, justice, and power, but the Church is the orchestra."[13] Our work might not happen on a basketball court, but every inch of this world is a showplace for God's glory, an opportunity to either display or distort the music of the gospel. Whether it's a living room or a boardroom, whether we're sitting at a desk or standing at an intersection, the places where we work are all concert halls for the symphony of mission, full of opportunities to display the glory of God through the work of our hands.

---

13. John Calvin, *Commentary on the Psalms*, trans. James Anderson (Edinburgh: Calvin Translation Society, 1839), 5:178.

5

SERVICE

Displaying the Love of Christ
by Washing the Feet of the World

Hamid sat across the table from me, the sound of a Turkish football game on TV amplified by our silence. Our typical laughter had been replaced by nervous smiles and clenched teeth. We avoided looking each other in the eye as we shoveled chunks of *tavuk doner* into our mouths, followed by sips of Turkish tea. Eating gave our mouths something to do instead of talking. We just sat there. Thousands of times we had sat like this, enjoying each other's conversation. This time we both felt tense and frustrated, with nothing to say.

He was my closest friend in Turkey, the person who had taught me how to speak Turkish and whose friendship had motivated me to plunge deeply into the language. Our friendship was so close that we referred to each other as *kardesim*, "my brother." The friendship had been forged over thousands of cups of tea. We'd been there with each other in the big moments of life. He was the first friend to greet my wife and me after my daughter was born. I was there when he was deciding if he should propose to the woman who is now his wife. He was there for me when my wife almost died in a Turkish hospital. We went to soccer games together, dreamed of cofounding a nonprofit organization, and talked about almost everything.

On most nights conversation came easily, but that night our laughter had been chased away by tension. It was a Tuesday, the night we would typically meet up to chat about everything from foreign policy to football. However, over the past several weeks, our discussions had turned to the weightier questions of life and to the nature of God. Our discussions about Jesus had started with the parables and his miracles. We had pondered the meaning of those stories together and shared a sense of wonder about the uniqueness of Jesus. However, the discussion had soon turned to the two topics about which we strongly disagreed: the cross and the resurrection. He considered these events fiction; I considered them the most significant events in history, the climax of the true story of the world. Only our strong friendship allowed us to set aside pretense and to speak with sincerity and candor on topics such as these.

For the past several Tuesday nights we had met up at a café in downtown Ankara to talk about the Gospels. We had printed out stories and discussed them each week. It was risky for him as a Muslim to carry around a manila folder of Gospel stories, but Hamid had always wanted to read them. Curiosity had turned into affection with each new story we discussed. Each week it had seemed like Hamid was becoming increasingly interested in Jesus. But this night was different. We had come to the end of the book—the cross and the resurrection.

He looked me in the eye and told me that he had enjoyed virtually everything we had discussed but was disturbed by the ending. As a Muslim, he couldn't understand how the Messiah could be publicly shamed through the horrific act of crucifixion. It seemed like nonsense to him. So he proposed that we just find commonality in our shared affection for the life of Jesus and his teaching and in the agreement that there's only one God. He wanted to set aside discussions about the suffering love of Jesus. But I couldn't let the subject go. These were the very events that defined the life of Jesus, his teaching, and the nature of the one God.

I told him I wanted to continue reading the Gospels together and having these discussions. But I also told him that the cross and resurrection were central. To remove those mighty acts of God from the story would be to deny and distort the message. Being a good friend, he gave me time to explain the importance and beauty of the cross. He was patient and attentive but remained unconvinced. So after about fifteen minutes of trying to recite the arguments from every apologetics book I'd ever read and giving a minisermon about the significance of the cross, I just sat there with him in silence in that smoke-filled café.

My mind drifted a bit. I started to recall the hundreds of similar conversations I'd had with Muslims and others who rejected the cross. I started to wonder if there was something missing in my communication of the gospel. Was there a better way to explain?

Then Hamid said something I will never forget—a clue to the very question I had been pondering. He said, "Do you remember when we read Luke 6, where Jesus commands people to sacrificially love their enemies? That was my favorite part!" He continued, "How many Christians have read these words? Because if so many Christians view Muslims as their enemy, wouldn't they be obligated to do good things for them? If they really believed these words, they would be building schools in Afghanistan, welcoming Muslim refugees at the airport, and inviting every Muslim they know to join them for dinner." And then with seriousness in his voice he looked at me and said, "Jim, you should go back to America and teach Christians about this. If they really believed Jesus, it would change the world!"

That was the day a Muslim commissioned me to preach the gospel to Christians. Amid the irony, I sensed that there was something profound about what he was saying, a connection between the sacrificial love of Christians and the perceived credibility of the cross. However, I wouldn't make that connection until some five years later when I was staring at the business end of a semiautomatic rifle.

The Cross and a Peacemaking Presence

Now back in the United States, I was sitting in my house and scrolling through Facebook. One friend had posted a picture of a cheeseburger, another of their newborn baby. There was a sports debate, a Churchill quote, a yoga pose. Then I saw something that deeply disturbed me, a Facebook article about an upcoming rally. A group of armed bikers was organizing an event outside of a local mosque where they would bring weapons, burn copies of the Qur'an, draw lewd pictures of Muhammad, and scream obscenities at people as they entered to pray. The particular mosque they had chosen was in a neighborhood with the largest percentage of refugees in the state. These people had been displaced from their homes and families and were trying their best to navigate the challenges of living in a new culture. All of them had experienced some form of suffering and danger: torture, natural disasters, ethnic cleansing, war. When I looked at the Facebook event for this rally, I saw that hundreds of people had already signed up to tell these globally homeless people to go back home.

I remembered the words of Hamid and how he had challenged me to call Christians to obey the words of Christ. So in an act of overstated slacktivism, I expressed my disgust on Facebook. It was a well-worded mini-rant that made me feel better about myself.

Then I closed my computer to pray, not the bold prayers of faith but the deflated prayers of a disheartened disciple. I had a sense that Jesus's name was about to get dragged through the mud once again and that violence was imminent. I was especially concerned because I had friends who attended that mosque and I didn't want them hurt. I also imagined how horrible it would make Christians feel if someone surrounded our church with guns, ripped up the Bible, and slandered Jesus. The thought was awful. I felt helpless.

After logging back onto Facebook a few hours later, I saw that several people had commented on my post, and I was struck by one comment in particular. Erin, a woman from my church, thought we should *do* something about the rally, that it wasn't enough to make a Facebook post. Since this was happening in our city, we were implicated. We needed to respond.

Honestly, I was reluctant and afraid, but I knew she was right. Her post prompted me to reach out to Adam Estle, the executive director of Evangelicals for Middle East Understanding, and to our mutual friend, the president of the mosque. We met for dinner and dreamed up a little plan. With only about twenty-four hours notice, Adam and I invited followers of Christ from around the city to join us at the mosque to be a prayerful presence in a place of hostility.

We didn't go there to protest or even counterprotest (as the media suggested). Our aim was to create a physical barrier of protection with our bodies and a spiritual wall of protection through our prayers. We committed to being a calming, quiet, friendly, peaceful, and prayerful presence. We wanted our response to be marked with the fruit of the Spirit: love, joy, peace, patience, kindness, goodness, faithfulness, gentleness, and self-control (Gal. 5:22–23).

Our strategy was to arrive early so that we could fill the sidewalk in front of the mosque, thus forcing the hostile protesters to the other side of the street. We also wanted to be the first people our Muslim neighbors would see when they exited the mosque, so they'd be greeted by followers of Christ holding out hands of friendship rather than by protesters holding handguns.

But the main reason we were lined up on the sidewalk was to turn our bodies into a physical barrier of protection for our Muslim neighbors. We wanted to dramatize the cross. We stood between the masked men with guns (a *lot* of guns!) and our Muslim friends because Jesus stood for us. Because Jesus had absorbed our death to give us life, we were willing to absorb bullets to defend the lives of our neighbors. He put himself in harm's way for us, so as his disciples, we were compelled to put ourselves in harm's way for our Muslim neighbors. There wouldn't be a single bullet that would pierce the body of a Muslim unless it went through the body of a Christian first.

We didn't organize the Love Your Neighbor Rally with heroic moxie but with trembling hands and nervous prayers for protection. Two types of people participated: those who were afraid and those who didn't really understand the danger. I didn't expect many people to show up.

With each hour that passed there were new waves of hostility posted on social media. Almost all local and national media outlets were covering the event and using sensational language that seemed to make things worse. The organizers of the protest were calling people to bring as many weapons as they could carry on their motorcycles—and to be ready to use them. ISIS was tweeting ominous threats about blood being spilled in the streets, local businesses were closing shop, and (to make matters worse) it was the hottest day of the year. It was not hard to find a reason to stay home that day.

People from our group started arriving around 5:00 p.m. At first, there were just a few of us, and we didn't really know what to do. We were awkward, not accustomed to being at a protest. My fears of a low turnout seemed confirmed. But then, at about 5:20 p.m., we saw one of the most beautiful things I've ever seen in my life: *hundreds* of Christians began to stream down the street in groups of five or ten, putting themselves in danger in order to love their Muslim neighbors. There were soon as many Christians assembled to be a peaceful presence as there were protesters: more than two hundred Christians from about fifteen local churches. There were also a number of people from other backgrounds who had been invited by their Christian friends. We had decided to wear blue shirts (a calming color), and as I saw that flood of blue shirts coming down the street, I began to imagine them as God's tears: tears of sorrow as he wept over this broken city and tears of joy to see his people unified in sacrificial love.

When everyone had arrived, we spread out on the sidewalk along the front of the mosque. We stayed calm, prayed, sang some worship songs, and had great conversations. Almost everyone held up signs that had been made by Josh Harp, a pastor at Via Church, which said "love your neighbor" on one side and explained our purpose on the other side. We asked people to avoid yelling, chanting, or bringing signs with antagonistic slogans. We asked them instead to pray, to tell stories of positive friendships with Muslims, to describe calmly what we were doing, and to explain how Jesus was our motivation.

On the other side of the street were more than two hundred protesters. Many of them were masked, wore bulletproof vests, and carried pistols, knives, and semiautomatic weapons. They were from many backgrounds, including atheism and neo-Nazism. A few even claimed to be Christians. Their signs and chants said some of the most vulgar things you could imagine—I won't repeat them here. They burned Qur'ans and held up indecent pictures drawn ahead of time at a "Draw Muhammad" contest they'd held before coming to the protest.

Though our first job there was to pray for and be a human shield for our Muslim friends, we also encouraged our people to pray for and try to reach out to the protesting bikers. After all, they were created in God's image too, and behind their masks and bulletproof vests were genuine fear and pain that needed the healing of the gospel. We reminded one another that we weren't there to be *against* anybody, because our enemy is not flesh and blood but the spiritual powers that produce such hatred: sin, idolatry, Satan, and demons.

Throughout the protest we sent a handful of blue shirts over to the protesters' side of the street. Some in our group had brought ice cold water on that blistering hot day to share with the protesters. We looked for the loudest and angriest people there and tried to engage them in conversation. It was clear they wanted to be heard, so we thought maybe we could help de-escalate the situation by simply listening.

As we listened, we realized that there was real fear under all that anger. It grew out of thousands of hours of being discipled by sensationalist YouTube videos and talk radio shows. They were genuinely afraid. However, almost none of them (except a handful of people who had served in the military) had met an actual Muslim. Many of the veterans were struggling with PTSD, and some had lost limbs in Iraq or best friends in Afghanistan. The most formative years of their adult lives had been spent learning to view Muslims as the enemy. Now they felt rage when they heard a few words of Arabic conversation at a grocery store. So we listened, and kept on listening. Several of our conversations with the protesters ended in tears, prayer, and a deep sense of longing for God to mend this hemorrhaging world.

I remember so much from that night: our Muslim friends who handled everything with such poise, the hard work of police officers, a petite nineteen-year-old girl in a blue shirt who showed kindness to a furious three-hundred-pound protester who was wearing a bulletproof vest and was armed with an AR-15. I remember the many conversations about Christ we had with the nonbelievers who joined our group, with our Muslim friends, and with the protesters. But what I remember most vividly is our times of prayer. It seemed like each time the protesters got louder, we prayed more fervently and the Spirit extinguished the waves of hostility. Standing in the most hostile street in the city that night, we worshiped God and experienced a real sense of the presence of Christ.

Throughout the night, we saw groups of protesters walk away in a contemplative manner. Some of them turned their "F—— Islam" shirts inside out. Some even seemed to have a change of heart and sought out the leaders of the mosque to apologize. By the end of the night, there hadn't been one shot fired, one punch thrown, or one person arrested. We called on the Prince of Peace for the welfare of the city—*and he showed up.*

The next morning, I woke up and started to thank God for what had happened the night before. I was grateful to be no longer standing in front of masked men with guns, but I actually felt saddened that it was all over. I assumed that the beautiful night of the church's unification in missional peacemaking was just going to drift into our memories and ultimately be forgotten. But when I checked my email, I realized that something bigger was going on.

Waiting for me were dozens of emails, Facebook messages, tweets, and voicemails from Muslims around the world expressing their gratitude for the many Christians who had shown love by forming a human shield in front of that mosque. The messages came from Pakistan, Saudi Arabia, Indonesia, Turkey, and Afghanistan as well as many different cities within the United States. I wondered how they had heard about the events of that night and then realized that a Muslim man had snapped a picture that beautifully captured an image of the sacrificial love that existed all across the city and had shared the picture on social media. The picture was of four people from Missio Dei Communities (a local church in the Phoenix area), and the caption said, "It is reported that more Christians showed up to stand in solidarity with the #PHxMosque this evening than protesters." This photo was shared 6,079 times on Facebook and probably just as many times on Twitter, mostly by Muslims.

Many news reports had been written by local and international media, some of them even quoting us as we pointed to the cross as our motivation. For example, *Vice News* quoted me as saying, "One of the main reasons we set up here on this sidewalk right now is to create a physical barrier between the mosque and our Muslim friends and potential violence and hostility. . . . If they suffer, we suffer with them. To stand in between the potential pain and danger they are in in the same way that Jesus stood in between it for us."[1]

In the months that followed we had dozens of opportunities to speak to groups of Muslims and have coffee with Muslim friends. In almost all of those instances we were asked the question, Why did you do it? In those moments we were able to share how we had been reconciled to the God of peace and were therefore compelled to be peacemakers. We were able to proclaim the self-giving love of Christ that was displayed on the cross. We shared the gospel with thousands of Muslims.

That season helped me realize that the sacrificial love of Christians—when we suffer for the sake of others—is the best apologetic for the cross. Now I've spent a lot of time learning apologetic arguments for the Christian faith.

1. Troy Farah, "Here's What Happened at the Anti-Islam Protest," *Vice News*, May 30, 2015, https://news.vice.com/article/heres-what-happened-at-the-anti-islam-protest-and-draw -muhammad-contest-in-arizona/.

I don't regret the time spent, but I wish I had spent as much time and effort dreaming up ways to love my neighbors—especially my old friend Hamid. He had heard the gospel so many times that he could recite it better than most preachers. But I genuinely wonder if he ever saw the beauty of the cross through the sacrificial love of Christians.

Sacrificial Love of Christ Displayed in Sacrificial Service

The second missional mandate, the service movement in the symphony of mission, displays the sacrificial love of Christ through lives of selfless service. As we generously give our lives to serve others, we imitate and display the generous love of Christ and his work on the cross. The service movement harmonizes with the other sounds of mission—stewardship (cultural engagement) and the spoken word (evangelism)—to become the music of the gospel to a world that needs to hear it.

When as followers of Christ we generously share our time, money, knowledge, possessions, homes, and lives, we dramatize the generous sacrificial love of Christ that was displayed on the cross. This chapter will explain the biblical call to participate in this aspect of God's mission. Sacrificial love is a recurring theme throughout the biblical story, but here we will focus mostly on Jesus's parable of the good Samaritan. The service movement is the call to love our neighbors in a sacrificial, creative, and systemic way. This chapter includes examples of this kind of love in action to encourage readers to cultivate the same kind of love in their own lives.

The heart of the biblical story is love. Love originates with God, who cares so deeply for his creation that he launched a rescue mission to redeem it from its slavery to sin, Satan, the curse, and death. Unfortunately, the word *love* in the English language seems to have been emptied of much of its meaning. In North America we generally use the word to describe strong affections, usually for people: I love my children; I love my wife. But it can also be used to express affection for slightly less important things, like nachos or ice cream. When the same word can be used to describe both the covenantal commitment of marriage and one's snack food preferences, the result can be confusing. Furthermore, in the English language *love* is often used in cliché ways. It brings to mind hippies with tambourines, Valentine's Day cards, romantic comedies, and the self-help aisle of the bookstore. How many modern-day commercial brands use the word *love* in their slogans?

NBA: "I love this game."

McDonald's: "I'm Lovin' It."

Revlon: "Love is on."

Subaru: "Love. It's what makes a Subaru, a Subaru."

It is too easy to read the cheap sentimentality of modern Western culture into the biblical use of the word *love*. So we need to work a little harder to understand what the Bible means when it refers to love.

God is the very definition of love, the fountain from whom all love flows. His love is such a core aspect of his character that Scripture can simply say, "God is love" (1 John 4:8, 16). His love isn't just an abstract principle. It's defined not by a cosmic dictionary that God sent from heaven but in the form of a human body—his Son—sent to live and die among us. To see Christ is to see love. Jesus's life was marked by deep affections and tangible generosity for a world hemorrhaging from idolatry, corruption, and injustice. He touched the untouchables, healed the sick, feasted with the outsiders, delivered the demonically oppressed, defended the most vulnerable, and washed the feet of his disciples. The ultimate demonstration of God's love comes through the death of Jesus, who entered into the full pain of humanity and sacrificed himself to reconcile even his enemies to God (John 3:16; 1 John 4:10). The love of God definitely includes deep emotion, but it culminates in sacrificial service. Love is affection manifested through generosity.

Love is marked by service, not sentimentality. Jesus describes his mission of service when he says, "Whoever would be great among you must be your servant, and whoever would be first among you must be slave of all. For even the Son of Man came not to be served but to serve, and to give his life as a ransom for many" (Mark 10:43–45 ESV). Jesus is inviting his disciples to participate in the true greatness of self-giving service. Paul promotes the same thing when he tells those in the Philippian church to "look not only to [your] own interests, but also to the interests of others" (Phil. 2:3 ESV). We are to imitate Christ, who "emptied himself, by taking the form of a servant" (2:7 ESV).

To serve someone is to take one's own time, money, ability, knowledge, home, and possessions and to invest them in another person's flourishing. This is the type of love we see in Christ, who washes the disciples' feet and whose own feet are nailed to the cross. He brings salvation, displays God's love through a life of humble service, and then calls his disciples to be a foot-washing community of service.

Few themes in Scripture are so prevalent and explicit as the call for God's people to display the love of Christ by serving others. Jesus, echoing the Torah, said that the greatest commandment is to love God with everything and to love our neighbors as ourselves (Lev. 19:17–18; Deut. 6:4–5; Matt. 22:35–40).

Loving God and loving our neighbors cannot be separated. To claim to love God while refusing to love our neighbors is to lie about the character of God with our lives (1 John 4:20–21). That's why the church is to be known as the community of mutual love (1 Pet. 1:22; 1 John 4:12). The first fruit of the Spirit is love (Gal. 5:22), and the scope of our love should be so broad that it embraces even our enemies (Luke 6:27–36).

Just as the love of God is marked by practical generosity and service, so should the love of God's people be marked. The sacrificial love of Christ displays the love of the Father; when we engage the world in sacrificial service, we display the love of Christ.

When we choose to mow our neighbor's lawn, buy groceries for a struggling family, open our homes to foster children, spend our Saturday helping a friend move, or take the hardest assignment at work, we're functioning as a living analogy of the self-giving love of God. Once we've experienced the costly grace of the gospel, we're compelled to imitate Jesus and to give ourselves to others in a manner that costs us.

The Good Samaritan

One of the best examples of the nature of love and service is in the parable of the good Samaritan (Luke 10:25–37). Jesus tells this story in response to a Jewish expert in the law who tests Jesus with a question in an attempt to discredit him. The Jewish expert asks Jesus what he must do to inherit eternal life. But Jesus turns the question back on the law expert, challenging him to state what *he* thinks is the answer. He responds correctly by quoting from Deuteronomy 6:5 to say that the highest goal of God's people is to love God with everything they have. Then, perhaps demonstrating that he has been paying attention to Jesus's teaching, the man also quotes Leviticus 18:5, which commands God's people to love their neighbors as themselves. Jesus affirms these answers.

Up until this point, the interaction has been fairly safe and noncontroversial. Most Jewish people would agree about the centrality of loving God and loving one's neighbors. However, the law expert is testing Jesus (Luke 10:25), so he follows up with another, more difficult question: "Who is my neighbor?" This isn't innocent; his motivation is to "justify himself," to prove that his own life is marked by love and justice. Based on the way Jesus tells this story— making a Samaritan its hero—he seems to be responding to a nationalistic ideology that limits the definition of *neighbor* to ethnic Jews. Rather than giving a short, precise definition of the word *neighbor*, Jesus tells a story that a Jewish nationalist would have considered scandalous and subversive.

The story starts with a man (presumably Jewish) who is mugged on the dangerous road from Jerusalem to Jericho. The thieves beat him up, steal his possessions, and leave him badly hurt on the side of the road. Unless he gets some help, he's probably going to die.

Fortunately, a Jewish priest is traveling on the same road. As a priest, he should know God and should understand God's commands to show mercy. But instead of helping his neighbor, the priest walks to the other side of the road and lets the traveler continue to stain the ground with his blood. The second person to come along is a Levite, a member of the holiest tribe within Israel, a family set apart for ministry in the temple. Surely he will understand the heart of God and show compassion to his neighbor! But he doesn't and instead hurries past the wounded traveler.

Finally, someone does stop to help. It is a Samaritan—an object of hatred to the Jewish people—who is compassionate toward the wounded traveler. He tends to the suffering man's wounds with oil to ease the pain and wine to prevent infection. Then the Samaritan loads him onto his own animal and moves him to safety. Once he arrives in town, the Samaritan continues to care for the assault victim by opening his wallet, giving the innkeeper two days' wages, and telling him to spare no expense in caring for the wounded man. He promises to return to town in a few days and pay any further costs.

After telling this parable, Jesus says, "Which of these three, do you think, proved to be a neighbor to the man who fell among the robbers?" The law expert, perhaps unwilling even to utter the word *Samaritan*, says, "The one who showed him mercy." Then Jesus tells him and the listening crowd of Jewish people, "Go and do likewise." In other words, if they really want to love their neighbor, they need to follow the example of this Samaritan.

There are many implications we can draw from this story about what it means to sacrificially love our neighbors. The focus in this chapter is on three characteristics of love: that it is to be sacrificial, creative, and systemic.

Sacrificial Love

Love is costly. Real love is not found in the cute sentimentality of Hallmark cards or YouTube kitten videos. It's the mess of childbirth, the burnt arms of firefighters, the scars from dogs' teeth on the arms of a civil rights leader, and the sore knees of a factory worker who has punched the clock for forty years to put food on the table. Love is ultimately expressed through sacrifice.

The story of the good Samaritan shows us a picture of the sacrificial nature of love. Consider the cost of the Samaritan's actions.

He gave money. The Samaritan used his expensive oil and wine to provide relief for the traveler. In order to make bandages for the wounds, he likely tore strips of cloth from his own clothes. Furthermore, he spent at least two days' wages to pay for the traveler's room, board, and medical costs—and then he promised to pay for future medical expenses.

He sacrificed his own physical comfort. The Samaritan had brought the oil and wine for his own refreshment, but he shared them with the wounded traveler instead of using them for himself. By placing the body of the traveler on his own animal, the Samaritan likely had to complete his journey on foot.

He offered time. Taking responsibility for the wounded man cost the Samaritan a considerable amount of time, both in the time it took to care for his wounds and in forcing a slower pace of travel.

He jeopardized his own safety. The wounds of the Jewish man testify to the danger of the Jericho road. By looking after the wounded man, the Samaritan made himself less mobile and thus more vulnerable to the attacks of robbers.

He risked his own reputation. By so closely associating himself with this Jewish man and staying with him in a Jewish village, the Samaritan was transgressing the social divisions between Jews and Samaritans. This likely caused Jewish people to look at him with suspicion and his fellow Samaritans to see him as a traitor.

The Samaritan displays the costly nature of love. It's generous and sacrificial. The command to love our neighbors as ourselves invites us to audit our lives and identify the things we use to care for ourselves—time, money, possessions, abilities, physical energy—to find ways to use them for the flourishing of our neighbors. This type of costly love isn't an act of heroism. It doesn't come from mustering up enough courage or toughness to do our duty. Jesus is the fountain from whom all love flows. Only when we have marinated in the love of Christ, experienced union with him, and been gripped by the mercy of the cross can we joyfully pursue lives of sacrificial love.

There has never been such beautiful and terrifying love as when the soil beneath Jesus's cross was stained red. Compelled by his love, Jesus reconciled a lost, wounded, and sinful humanity by giving himself on the cross. The exalted creator of all things was humiliated, tortured, and murdered by the humans he had created, by the hands he had given them, on a cross made from a tree he had spoken into being. The one who should have been exalted above all was humiliated and publicly shamed as his crucified body was displayed for all to see. The one who breathed life into the lungs of humanity struggled to pull life-sustaining air into his own collapsed lungs.

The healing hands of Jesus were wounded by the nails of the cross, but by those same wounds, God healed a wounded and sinful world. "He committed no sin, neither was deceit found in his mouth. When he was reviled, he did not revile in return; when he suffered, he did not threaten, but continued entrusting himself to him who judges justly. He himself bore our sins in his body on the tree, that we might die to sin and live to righteousness. By his wounds you have been healed. For you were straying like sheep, but have now returned to the Shepherd and Overseer of your souls" (1 Pet. 2:22–25 ESV). Echoing the words of Isaiah 53, Peter points to Jesus as the long-awaited Messiah who heals us by being wounded, returns lost sheep to the good Shepherd, and makes sinful humans righteous. Jesus's suffering was motivated by his love, and that love was demonstrated through self-giving generosity.

We are saved by the grace of God through trusting in the work of Christ. The cross accomplished what we could not accomplish, and this should cause us to overflow with gratitude and joy. However, our relationship to the cross should go beyond the enjoyment of God's generosity; it should also be manifested through our own generosity.

The cross is the path that leads us to God, and it's also the path that leads us to our neighbors. Peter describes the suffering of Christ as our only means for salvation, but he also declares that Christ's suffering is the example for how we are to live: "To this you were called, because Christ suffered for you, leaving you an example, that you should follow in his steps" (1 Pet. 2:21). For all the mystery that's often associated with the idea of God's "calling," Peter makes it clear that we are called to at least one thing: self-giving love. It's the path that Jesus walked, and if we follow him, it is our path too.

Robert Gelinas, a pastor at Colorado Community Church, comments on this passage by comparing the cross to footprints intentionally left in the snow to be followed by others: "The death of Jesus is to be your path. When Christ took our place on the cross, he absorbed our pain, and now the church, as a cross-formed community, is to be a pain-absorbing people."[2] The community that is gathered by the cross is called to display the same generosity and self-sacrificing love.

Why is the church, the "cross-formed community," called to a life of sacrificial love? It's certainly not because our sacrifice accomplishes our salvation. That would diminish the work of Christ. Instead, our sacrifice comes from gratitude for the sufficiency of Christ's sacrifice and our desire to dramatize the love of God to the world. It's simply too good not to share with others! People need to hear the good news in words, but they also need to see it lived out.

As we give our time, money, effort, and abilities for the flourishing of others, we create an echo of divine love, a street performance that is homage to

2. Robert Gelinas, *Living Sacrifice: The Cross as a Way of Life* (Denver: Wolgemuth & Associates, 2015), 37.

the drama of the cross. The apostle Paul describes the ministry of the church as feeble jars of clay that carry the treasure of Christ to a needy world (2 Cor. 4:7). Through our suffering, our breaking, and our sacrificial lives as Christ's followers, we make visible the light of God's glory to a blind world. We are the wrapping paper for the gospel that must be torn apart to reveal the gift.

What does it look like to dramatize the cross to a watching world? Over the years, many people have displayed the sacrificial love of Christ through their generous lives. Here are a few of them.

Roy and his truck. People buy trucks for many reasons, whether for work, camping, or off-roading or as a status symbol. My friend Roy is the only person I've met who chose to buy a truck partly because he wanted to help people move. Most people dread picking up a phone and hearing a friend ask them to wake up early on Saturday morning and haul junk around town. But Roy has a completely different perspective, one that has been shaped by the cross. He's a strong guy, a skilled driver, and is spatially oriented. In other words, his gifts and abilities make him the perfect friend to help people move. For the more than twenty years I have known him, he has helped me move more than a dozen times, and I'm not the only one. He makes himself available for coworkers, neighbors, and even people he has never met. He sacrifices his time, energy, and money to wash the feet of his neighbors by helping them move. Many people have remarked on the distinctiveness of his character and what would compel him to do such things, and these remarks give Roy an opportunity to point to the distinctiveness of Christ, who came to serve and not to be served.

Teena's tables. Teena worked as a server at a local restaurant. A few years ago her coworker's girlfriend suddenly died. This man was obviously devastated and needed to take some time off work. So in the spirit of sacrificial love, Teena offered to cover his shift. Along with the pain of losing his girlfriend, her friend was also in financial trouble, living paycheck to paycheck. He couldn't afford to take much time off. He knew he needed to pick up more shifts to make up for the lost hours. But when he returned to work, he was shocked to find out that even though Teena had worked all those hours on his behalf, every dime she made during those weeks was being paid to *him*. Teena's sacrificial love was a living commentary on what 2 Corinthians 8:9 says about Jesus: "Though he was rich, yet for your sake he became poor, so that you through his poverty might become rich." Teena didn't have a lot of discretionary income (her husband was in medical school), but she did have the wealth of the gospel. Knowing that Christ had worked on her behalf, she was able to work generously on behalf of another person.

John's chair. Our friend John cuts hair for a living. When the financial crisis of 2007 hit the United States, he saw how many people were out of work. He knew that people were working hard to find new jobs and often didn't have money to make ends meet, so he decided to give free haircuts to anyone who was on their way to an interview. Because John was seated with Christ who had loved him and given himself for him, he could open up a seat in his salon and so dramatize the generosity of the gospel.

Imagine if sacrificial love like this were the distinguishing mark of the church. Rather than being focused on self-preservation or self-interest, what if we were a people marked by self-sacrifice? Imagine if people with special needs weren't pushed to the margins but were treated like royalty in the church. Imagine if we were known as the people who cleared out the man cave to welcome the stranger, providing a home for the homeless and refuge for refugees. Imagine if there were no longer a need for a foster care system because there were so many open beds available in Christian homes. What if Christians were known as the people who lived simple lives so they could give away piles of money? Every town would be filled with hospitals, microenterprises, community gardens, and drug-rehabilitation facilities. And as money generously poured out of the pockets of Christians, people around us would be reminded of the blood that poured out of the veins of Christ.

Creative Love

The world is filled with innovation and creativity. Some of these innovations— like solar panels, technologies that detect cancer, and beautiful paintings— contribute to the common good. Others seem frivolous—like banana slicers or prosthetic testicles for dogs. And some innovations are far worse than frivolous—when, for example, people abuse their God-given talents to create evil things, such as chemical weapons, designer drugs, and iPhone apps that help people commit adultery.

It's rare to combine the words *creativity* and *love*. But creative love is exactly what Jesus is calling us to through the story of the good Samaritan and his command to love our neighbors as ourselves. We are called to be entrepreneurs of blessing, inventors of neighborly kindness, and artists of shalom—employing our whole minds, including our imaginations, in loving God and our neighbors.

Creativity is a characteristic of the love we see in the life of Jesus and in the parable of the good Samaritan. We see this creativity in the way Jesus answers the law expert's question about the identity of the neighbors God wants us to love. The clear answer is that Jesus calls us to love all people. Jesus could have said this plainly and explicitly in just a few sentences. Or he could have told a story in which a Jewish person rescues a wounded Samaritan. Both approaches would have made the point. Instead, Jesus told the story in a creative way. He made the Samaritan—the religious, political, and ethnic Other—the hero of the story, thus affirming the value of the unconsidered Others in our world and showing that they have dignity as image-bearers and should be treated with respect.

We also see the call to creativity in Jesus's command to "love your neighbor as yourself." At first glance this might seem like a sweet and harmless command. However, it's actually a call for creative love. This passage isn't just calling us to be nice people; it's calling us to audit our lives, identify the resources we use to love and bless ourselves, and then reimagine them as instruments of love for our neighbors. John Calvin expresses this clearly when he says that "all the gifts we possess have been bestowed by God and entrusted to us on condition that they be distributed for our neighbors' benefit."[3]

In order to love your neighbor as yourself, you must first answer the question, How do I love myself? You will probably come up with many answers. You may have bought a home, earned an education, grilled steaks on Sunday afternoons, pursued life-giving friendships, grown a garden, ridden a bicycle, or saved money. We all have an array of good things that we use for our own benefit, such as relationships, education, training, possessions, skills, and personality traits. However, the uniqueness of the kingdom is that we are called to view these things as the raw materials of love and to repurpose them for the sake of others.

Over the past decade, some of the churches in the Surge Network have been dreaming up creative ways to reimagine simple gifts—from rusty shovels to spare bedrooms, bicycles to baked goods—as instruments of love. We've taken simple things and tried to see them and use them as resources that God has given for the flourishing of our neighbors. Let us tell you a few of these stories.

Uber and Lyft as Vehicles of Love

For several years I've met with other followers of Christ from throughout the city for breakfast at the Crêpe Bar (my favorite local restaurant) to dream about ways to love our neighbors. One morning we asked a simple question

---

3. John Calvin, *Institutes of the Christian Religion*, trans. Ford Lewis Battles, ed. John T. McNeill (Philadelphia: Westminster, 2006), 695 (3.7.5).

that has resulted in thousands of dollars leveraged for the good of the city and in hundreds of deep conversations with strangers: "How can I use my Toyota Corolla as an instrument of love?"

Several of us signed up to become Uber and Lyft drivers for the common good. Our first priority was to serve these passengers as God's instruments of protection by providing safe rides, but we also saw our times with the passengers as opportunities for creative love. We decided to give away all the money we made from these rides.

So far we've given thousands of dollars to important nonprofits that serve our city. However, we didn't just make unilateral decisions about where to donate the money. We invited the passengers into the process and asked them to vote among three options, such as homeless shelters, entrepreneurial training initiatives, or refugee resettlement programs. Whichever organization had the most votes at the end of the week would receive the donation. The passengers typically responded with wonder and delight, awakened from the monotony of just another Uber ride to suddenly discuss how to make our city a better place.

The donations of money were good, but they were not the most important acts of love. The primary way we loved our neighbors was by asking deep questions and providing warm conversations in a society that's increasingly lonely because of the distance caused by technology. After each passenger voted, we asked why they voted for that particular nonprofit. This question helped us cut through the trivial chitchat and steer into conversations about what is most concerning in the world.

Humans were created to be known. It's one of humanity's most fundamental needs. As drivers we viewed our role as serving others by asking good questions and really listening. We wanted to provide a space where people could feel truly heard. You may be skeptical about how much depth of conversation can happen in an Uber ride, but the reality is that some people go through an entire day without anyone genuinely listening to them and asking good questions. Countless rides ended in tears as passengers talked about the heavy burdens that they had been waiting for someone to ask about. We were often able to pray for these passengers.

Of course, not all our conversations ended in tears! Many conversations were imaginative and whimsical yet somehow provocative. We came to see the simple act of asking questions as a means of loving our neighbors, even by asking playful questions to get people thinking about important things: "If you could have anyone from history as your Uber driver, who would you choose?" Or "What's one thing you've learned from your work that everyone in the world should know?" These questions often turned into deep discussions about life as we pondered what's broken about the world and what the ultimate solution might be. Many times a week these conversations were guided by the Spirit into discussions about the creative and sacrificial love of Christ as the good news that counters the world's bad news.

The Tempe Bike Gang

During yet another Friday morning breakfast, someone mentioned a recent news story about a huge gang of bikers that had swarmed a car, pulled a passenger out, and brutally attacked him—almost killing him in the process. We were disturbed. We prayed. We also started to ask a strange question: "How can we reimagine the mob mentality for the common good?" One of us had the idea to start something called the Tempe Bike Gang, a mob of people on bicycles who would cruise around the city doing random acts of blessing. We joked about this being the hipster version of the Sons of Anarchy, but our conviction that we should move forward with this increased even as we laughed about its absurdity.

If you were on the streets of Tempe in March 2014, you may have seen a strange mob of more than twenty bicyclists swarming through the parks, cruising through alleys, and clogging the bike lanes. You may have seen us dismount every fifteen minutes or so to engage in some act of generous love. We picked up dog poop at the local dog park. We stopped in front of a house to give out an "Awesome Front Yard" award to unsuspecting residents with a beautiful garden. We jumped on board a minibus to give the driver a one-hundred-dollar tip. We gave out more than thirty thank-you notes to coffee-shop baristas to honor their excellent work. If you saw us, you may even have been compelled to join us, just like the handful of strangers out riding their bikes around town who *did* decide to join our mob—as if they had heard the voice of Jesus say, "Come, follow me!" through our silly acts of vigilante love.

These simple expressions of creative love display the self-giving love of Christ by finding ways to shift our resources outward. It's not complicated; we just need to slow down, think, pray, and reflect on deliberate ways we can use our skills, possessions, resources, time, and imagination to serve our neighbors.

Among the many words associated with Christians, what if *creative* and *love* were at the top of the list? What if we displayed the creativity of the Father and the sacrificial love of Christ by being a people filled with simple innovations of blessing? What if Christians were known as innovators of good? What if we were just as serious and deliberate about inventive love as Elon Musk, Steve Jobs, or Thomas Edison were with their innovations?

Systemic Love

Marcos is an architect who worked on designing a bridge in Reno, Nevada. He struggled to see how this activity had any value. He wondered if his time might be better spent doing something "important," like working for a nonprofit or doing missions. He didn't want to waste his life on what he perceived as frivolous; instead, he wanted to love God and his neighbor. He didn't want to design lighting fixtures for a bridge that would merely cut down commute times. In frustration he said, "How can I love the people of Reno if I never even see them? I've only been there a few times, and most of my work is done from my desk in Arizona. I'd be better off moving there and just being a good neighbor." I challenged him to consider how the fruit of his work either diminished or enhanced the life of the people in the city. All of a sudden, with wide eyes, he pulled out his phone and started typing some numbers into the calculator.

He realized that the bridge he was working on would save drivers hundreds of thousands of hours of driving time each year. Time that would otherwise be wasted in traffic could instead be spent with friends and family—making good art, reading good books, or engaging in good work. This bridge would redeem thousands of hours for the city! I heard a new excitement take hold with this new understanding of meaning in his work. Marcos realized that he could participate in the service movement through his daily work: washing the feet of the world with systemic love.

Most people in the West, like Marcos, associate the command "love your neighbor" with personal acts of kindness—making a meal, listening to a neighbor's worries, helping someone move, or volunteering at a homeless shelter. These are all good ways to participate in God's mission. But the parable of the good Samaritan shows us that love has another dimension. Love can be individual and personal, but it can also be systemic.

We see an example of systemic love when we look closely at the parable of the good Samaritan. After personally caring for the wounded man, it would have been easy for the Samaritan to drop him off in the center of the village and expect someone else to play their part. After all, he had already exerted exceptional physical and emotional effort to care for this dying man, risking his own life and reputation to bring him to safety. He had certainly done more than the religious leaders who had passed by their bleeding Jewish brother. Few of us would condemn the Samaritan for playing his part and then moving on to his final destination.

But the Samaritan's love was both personal and systemic. He created a system that continued to provide for the wounded man even after he'd gone:

"The next day he took out two denarii and gave them to the innkeeper. 'Look after him,' he said, 'and when I return, I will reimburse you for any extra expense you may have'" (Luke 10:35). Innkeepers in Jesus's day were not expected to provide medical care, but the good Samaritan negotiated, organized, and financed a system to provide food, water, housing, medical care, and protection for his wounded neighbor. This is part of what it means to display the love of Christ and wash the feet of the world.

The call to love doesn't end when someone leaves our field of vision. Love isn't out of sight, out of mind. We are called to follow the example of the good Samaritan and seek the flourishing of our neighbors by positively contributing to the systems that affect their lives. For example, we love our neighbors when we start businesses that provide jobs, vote for good policies, organize responsible supply chains, or make donations to organizations that do good in the world.

Wendell Berry, a highly esteemed author and farmer, has identified how much of the suffering we face today comes from harmful systems rather than harmful individuals. He says, "We have the ancient and long-enduring cultural imperative of neighborly love and work. This becomes ever more important as hardly imaginable suffering is imposed upon all creatures by industrial tools and industrial weapons. If we are to continue, in our only world, with any hope of thriving in it, we will have to expect neighborly behavior of sciences, of industries, and of governments, just as we expect it of our citizens in their neighborhoods."[4] Berry's words encourage us not to disconnect the call to love our neighbor from our contribution to the systems that affect the lives of our neighbors. Our employment, civic engagement, financial investments, and the other systems in which we participate can be means of either loving our neighbors or letting them suffer on the modern-day Jericho roads.

The call to systemic love is found throughout the biblical story. In creation we see that God provides us with food, water, and air, which sustain our physical lives through an intricately tuned ecosystem (Ps. 104). After the fall we see that God institutes law, which functions to protect God's creation from the harsh realities of a world filled with sin and pain, to establish systemic patterns of mercy and justice.

We also see examples of systemic love in the life of Christ. He announces salvation to the world, not by personally traveling to each town but by forming a community of people (the church) who are indwelled by the Holy Spirit and compelled to proclaim and demonstrate the good news. The church is the systemic means God uses to extend the blessing of the gospel to the ends

---

4. Wendell Berry, *Our Only World* (Berkley: Counterpoint, 2015), 156.

of the earth. Once the church became established, it wasn't just a group of people who were organically "doing life" together; rather, they created structures and systems. For example, in Acts 6 we see the apostles creating a system of food distribution to serve the poor, combat systemic racism, and provide more time for preaching the gospel.

There are many ways we can love our neighbors by engaging in systems and processes. Examples include culture making and responsive justice.

Culture Making

God's people are called to feed the hungry, but how should they do it? If you had one neighbor who was starving, you could cook and bring her a meal every day; this intimate form of service would display the love of Christ. But it's not the only way. What if you started a business and hired your neighbor to work in it? In doing this, you would be creating a system that alleviated her hunger in a more sustainable way, a system not dependent on your extra income but generated through the revenues of your business. "Give someone a fish and you feed them for a day; teach someone to fish and you feed them for a lifetime," the old proverb goes. Another approach would be to start an urban farm. Many people are hungry because they have limited access to food, perhaps because of environmental conditions or unjust laws. An urban farm would create a system of soil stewardship to turn a vacant field into an abundant feast. This farm wouldn't provide access to food for just a single hungry person but could provide food for hundreds, even thousands, of people.

As Martin Luther says,

> When you pray for "daily bread" you are praying for everything that contributes to you having and enjoying your daily bread. . . . You must open up and expand your thinking, so that it reaches not only as far as the flour bin and baking oven but also out over the broad fields, the farmlands, and the entire country that produces, processes, and conveys to us our daily bread in all kinds of nourishment. . . . God could easily give you grain and fruit without your plowing and planting, but he does not want to do so.[5]

In other words, agriculture is the main way that God feeds the hungry. Our loving Father provides our daily bread, not by making biscuits fall from the sky but by calling farmers and bakers to cultivate loaves of grace from the soil of the earth.

5. Samuel Janzow, ed. *Luther's Large Catechism: A Contemporary Translation with Study Questions* (St. Louis: Concordia, 1988), 90.

The same is true for other forms of culture making. Construction, insurance, aviation, law enforcement, plumbing, youth sports, farmers markets—these are all means of God's provision, systems that contribute to the flourishing of our neighbors. As we participate in these kinds of activities, we are actually participating in systemic love and being conduits of God's provision. Even though we aren't physically present with each of our neighbors all the time, we are obeying God's call to love them.

Responsive Justice

Systems and institutions can be channels of shalom, but they can also be pipelines of pain and suffering. One of the ways we can love our neighbors is by seeking to change the systems, structures, and cultural norms that harm them. Sometimes this means that we are called to pursue good public policy that contributes to the flourishing of our neighbors and all aspects of creation. Laws cannot change hearts, but they can be instruments of God's grace to protect our neighbors from the full effects of idolatry, injury, and injustice.

For example, the practice of redlining, which existed until the 1970s, prevented African Americans from buying homes in certain neighborhoods that were exclusively reserved for white people who were trying to "protect their home value." As the home values increased, white families amassed wealth that they were able to pass down to their families for generations. This created an economic disadvantage for African American families that has had a ripple effect for generations. Those who challenged and overturned this policy all played a part in loving their neighbors by pursuing justice: academic institutions researched redlining; white homeowners advocated for change; politicians created better policies; and nonprofit organizations provided low-interest home loans for African American homeowners.

Our commitment to systemic justice shouldn't be limited to political engagement but should also include working against the unjust policies or systems of any community, including our companies, our families, and voluntary organizations we're associated with. In the previous section, the ways in which our daily work can be an act of loving our neighbors was discussed, but our work can also be a means of harming our neighbors. Think of the many organizations whose revenues increase with the increase of abortions or of the pharmaceutical companies who continue to sell products that do more harm than good. When systems become disordered and contribute to the suffering rather than the flourishing of others, injustice is the result. Just as the proactive work of culture making is an act of systemic love, so is loving our neighbors by challenging the systems that harm them and vandalize God's world.

Our concern for justice should be ultimately rooted in God's character; he is a God of justice (Ps. 146:5–9; Isa. 30:18; Jer. 9:23–24). His passion for justice is seen through the many commands for justice and mercy we see in Scripture (Deut. 10:17–20; Mic. 6:8; James 1:27). These commands often come as admonitions to care for the most vulnerable. Deuteronomy 10:17–18 describes God as completely just, showing "no partiality" and accepting "no bribes." It describes God as actively defending the cause of the fatherless, widow, and foreigner. Since God is an advocate for the vulnerable, he commands his people to "love those who are foreigners, for you yourselves were foreigners in Egypt" (10:19).

In the Old Testament we see a special emphasis on what some have called "the quartet of the vulnerable": widows, orphans, immigrants, and the poor (Deut. 24:19–22; Zech. 7:10). We see special concern for vulnerable groups in the New Testament as well; for example, in the book of James we read that pure and faultless religion is to "look after orphans and widows in their distress and to keep oneself from being polluted by the world" (1:27). These vulnerable groups had little social influence and power and were in danger of manipulation, exploitation, and oppression.

In the Old and New Testaments the frequent uses of the Hebrew word *tsedaqah* and the Greek word *dikaiosunē* reveal that justice is a central concern. Both words are typically translated as "righteousness," which many in the West associate with living morally upright lives as individuals. But these words are actually closely associated with the concept of justice: "When most modern people see the word 'righteousness' in the Bible, they tend to think of it in terms of private morality, such as sexual chastity or diligence in prayer and Bible study. But in the Bible, *tzadeqah* refers to day-to-day living in which a person conducts all relationships in family and society with fairness, generosity and equity."[6] Therefore, when Jesus says that we are to "seek first his kingdom and his righteousness [*dikaiosunē*]" (Matt. 6:33), he's calling us to trust God and to devote our lives to the right relationships of kingdom justice. Furthermore, in Matthew 23:23 Jesus condemns the Pharisees for their hypocrisy in neglecting "the more important matters of the law—justice, mercy and faithfulness." So passionate is Jesus about justice and mercy that he equates meeting the needs of the most vulnerable with giving food, water, shelter, and clothing to Jesus himself (Matt. 25:31–46).

6. Timothy Keller, "What Is Biblical Justice?," *Relevant*, August 23, 2012, https://relevant magazine.com/god/practical-faith/what-biblical-justice.

Ultimately, pursuing justice is an act of love. Loving our neighbors, especially the most vulnerable, means challenging and changing the systems, practices, laws, and policies that bring them harm. Martin Luther King Jr. describes this by inviting us to imagine what should have happened after the Samaritan in Luke 10 helped his Jewish neighbor. He says, "On the one hand we are called to play the good Samaritan on life's roadside; but that will be only an initial act. One day we must come to see that the whole Jericho road must be transformed so that men and women will not be constantly beaten and robbed as they make their journey on life's highway."[7] He challenges us to love our neighbors both by personally caring for their immediate needs and by working to improve the broader systems that affect their lives. Love goes beyond stopping the bleeding; it includes pursuing the kind of justice that prevents bleeding in the first place. Love is about having just, well-enforced laws associated with the Jericho road. It's about addressing the racism that kept Samaritans and Jews apart. It's about improving the lighting along the road to prevent crime. It's about raising funds to start the first Good Samaritan Hospital for injured travelers. Or as Lesslie Newbigin, who spoke with Martin Luther King Jr. at a rally that initiated the civil rights movement, says, "It is not enough to deploy Good Samaritans around the place; we must also guard the road."[8]

We might not live in a first-century Middle Eastern village, but it's important to remember that a Jericho road runs through every city, industry, and issue where we live. Metaphorically speaking, all of us travel along the Jericho road and stumble upon wounded travelers. What do you see around you? Do you see Somali refugees? Our friend Joel did, and after realizing how much trauma they had experienced, he offered his services as a counselor for free. Do you see children in need of a home? Our friend Dennae not only adopted two children but also started an organization to help birth parents reunite with their children. Do you see people struggling to pay their bills? Our friend Jeff did and chose to pay his employees considerably higher wages than the industry standards as a result.

When pursuing justice, we must pay attention to the local contexts, to our cities, our industries, and the issues that affect those immediately around us. Seeking justice isn't about expressing outrage over every issue on social media. It's not about making a good point, but it's about making a difference. It's about seeing the wounded neighbors in *our* stretch of the Jericho road.

7. Martin Luther King Jr., "Beyond Vietnam: A Time to Break Silence," *Common Dreams*, January 15, 2004, https://www.commondreams.org/views04/0115-13.htm/.

8. Lesslie Newbigin, "The Churches and the CASA," *National Christian Council Review* 93 (1973): 546.

Robbed by Jean Valjean

The world should see the love of Christ through the sacrificial, creative, and systemic love of his people. At this point you might be wondering if the service movement is a death sentence, a burden too heavy to bear, or perhaps a call to a life of dreary asceticism. Actually it's quite the opposite. True, we are called to die to ourselves and to take up our cross as we seek to follow Jesus. However, there is a deep and inexplicable joy in the experience of suffering love. This is the kind of joy that Jesus felt on his way to the cross (Heb. 12:2), and it is the kind of joy we have access to as we share in the fellowship of Christ's sufferings (Phil. 3:9–11). As we pour ourselves out for others, we find that the place of pain is where we meet with God. There's a mysterious relationship between the act of loving others and our own experience of God's love (1 John 4:11–12). We don't earn God's love by loving others, but something about the experience of sacrificial love gives us an experiential encounter of God's love for us. Just like a friend who has a favorite place to hang out, Jesus loves to spend time in places of pain. Friends often have favorite activities, like watching movies, drinking good coffee, or playing basketball; Jesus has favorite activities as well. He loves to wash feet, and he's inviting us to join him, to experience the joy of giving ourselves away for the sake of others.

In 2012 I met with Jesus in the place of pain. In the span of a few short weeks, my daughter was diagnosed with autism and my wife with a genetic defect that gave her a 90 percent chance of getting breast cancer. On top of all that, the work we had been doing with Central Asian Muslims had drawn the attention of nationalists from one of the Central Asian countries; they were sending me death threats with explicit details about my family. That season was brutally tough, and there was a low-grade bitterness in me. My mind was occupied with strategies to fix these things. I borrowed a gun to protect myself and my family from the nationalists. I stayed up late googling treatments for autism and diets to prevent breast cancer.

Just when I thought things couldn't get worse, we returned home from lunch one afternoon to find that something was wrong in our house. Someone had broken in, ransacked our living room, and taken thousands of dollars worth of possessions. While I was still taking in what had happened, I realized that the blinds on the back door were still swinging—the burglars had either just left the house or were still in there. Without thinking twice, I grabbed a shovel and ran through the house in a rage, yelling shameful obscenities and hoping for a chance to hit one of them across the chin with my muddy shovel. But they were nowhere to be found.

My heart boiled with anger, not just because of the robbery and the possessions we lost but because over the past few months, my daughter's future, my wife's health, and our safety and future dreams had been stolen as well. Among the thousands of dollars worth of possessions they had taken was a hard drive that contained all our family pictures. It felt like they had robbed us of our memories of the past—and like God was stealing our future.

A few weeks after the robbery I started to realize how toxic my heart had become; it was filled with prideful entitlement and a longing for vengeance. But I began to see that God didn't owe me anything and that I should be grateful we weren't home when this happened. I started to realize that my rage was connected to my vision of the good life. I wanted a fruitful and enjoyable life without suffering. However, I started to reflect on both the biblical call to die to myself and to find my life in losing it. This was an opportunity to see if that was really true.

I started to focus my energies on serving Jenny, Elliana, and others. As a discipline to remind my heart about the love of Christ, I started to do hidden acts of service for others. This ended up being one of the richest seasons of my life in experiencing the love of God. During those days I broke into tears at unexpected moments, gripped by the love of God I was experiencing while I focused on others.

Along with reading Scripture at that time, I was also reading *Les Misérables*. I found myself crushed when I read about Jean Valjean's encounter with the bishop. In the story, Valjean is cold, hungry, and in need. He finds mercy and respite in the home of a Catholic bishop who gives him food and shelter. How does Valjean return the favor? He steals some valuable possessions from the bishop's home. Eventually Valjean is caught by the police, who take him to the bishop's home to ask the bishop if the items in Valjean's possession belong to him. Of course, if the bishop confirms the theft, Valjean will be sent away to prison. But in a moment of great compassion and mercy, the bishop tells the police that the stolen items had been a gift to Valjean. Through love, the bishop turns an enemy into a brother, and the experience changes the trajectory of Valjean's life.

Until I read that section of *Les Misérables*, I had still been daydreaming about catching those thieves and slapping their faces with the blunt end of my shovel. Now, though, I was deeply convicted of my sin. I knew that my heart wasn't right; I needed to explore what it meant to forgive and to love my enemies. So we began to pray for them. My wife in her wisdom also suggested that we make a sign to express our forgiveness to those who had robbed our home.

Honestly, we doubted that anyone would see it. But we posted it on the outside of our house as a discipline of love, praying that our hearts would live up to our words. We kept it taped to the wall that faced the busy street for about three days and then took it down. We continued to pray God's blessing over these enemies and eventually began genuinely to desire their good. We began to wonder about their stories and what had compelled them to break into someone else's home.

About two weeks later, I was working on my front gardens when a man sheepishly approached me. He was acting kind of strange, making small talk even though it was obvious that something was on his mind. Eventually he broke through the small talk, pulled out an iPad, and told me he had found it in my yard and wanted to give it to me. It was the iPad that had been stolen from my house.

Without his saying it, we both understood that he was the person who had broken into my home and that he had come to make amends. I was looking into the eyes of the man who had broken my window, rummaged through my bedroom drawers, and stolen thousands of dollars from me. If I had seen him a few weeks earlier, I would have hit him with a shovel. But the Spirit was at work in that moment, reminding me of the joy of the cross and the example of self-giving love I had recently read about in *Les Misérables*. In words that surprised me even as they were coming out of my own mouth, I told him to keep the iPad, that it was a gift.

His eyes filled with tears, and he started to share his life story with me. His cousin lived in the house right across the street from the wall where we had posted our forgiveness sign. He'd been staying with that cousin for a while and had to look at our sign every day as he left the house. Most of our stuff had already been sold, and the iPad was all that was left. He told me that there were warrants out for his arrest and that he was on his way to turn himself in but wanted to stop at my house first. For a whole hour, I stood in my front yard in deep, meaningful conversation with a man who, just a few weeks earlier, had smashed my kitchen window and rummaged through my closets.

Based on the questions he was asking, it was evident that he had read my journal, which had been stuffed into one of the backpacks he stole. It contained my written prayers, reflections on Scripture, and struggles with sin. I would have been mortified if I had known that those words would eventually be read by someone else. But somehow, by the strange grace of God, these words had provoked questions in him about the gospel. It's hard to describe that incredible conversation. We made plans to meet up when he got out of jail and to turn my front yard into a community garden. Then we said our goodbyes, and he was on his way to the police station.

There are many things about that encounter that remain fuzzy in my mind and many questions that are yet unanswered. I'm not sure if that conversation was a moment of conversion for him or if he was just curious about his neighbor's God who compelled people to make strange posters. Also, I forgot to ask his last name and therefore haven't been able to find him. (If you ever meet an Andre who tells you a story like this, please let him know I'm looking for him.) But in spite of how many things were unclear about that incredible morning, I'm certain of one thing: Jesus was there. As I loved Andre and got lost in my desire for his flourishing, I encountered the presence of Christ. The joy that came from loving my enemy-turned-brother was greater than the amusement found in a million iPads.

Even though, unfortunately, my love for others doesn't always match the love I had for Andre on that day, I am convinced that this kind of self-giving love is where true joy and abundant life are found. The grain of creation runs contrary to the logic of this world. The world says to look out for yourself and your own people. It tells you to live a life of consumerism and self-protection, to spend your life obtaining stuff and experiences. It tells families to hide and protect themselves instead of engaging the world. It tells churches to focus on their own growth and prosperity. It tells nations to put themselves first. But this mentality is a lie that contradicts Jesus's call to "seek first the kingdom." This mentality creates an illusion of satisfaction, but it is ultimately empty. Those who constantly look inward eventually become spiritual cannibals, trying to sustain their own lives by consuming their neighbors'. The self-serving life is filled with the cancers of anger, jealousy, and cynicism. It eventually metastasizes into dehumanizing violence and implosion. True joy can't be found in selfishness and self-preservation.

We find our lives only by losing them, we receive by giving, and we feast by sharing our bread. As we kneel to wash the feet of our neighbors—sacrificially, creatively, and systemically—we find a friend there waiting for us. Jesus, our king, is also scrubbing toes. It doesn't make the task less grimy, but it does give us the incomparable joy of union with Christ. By choosing self-giving love over self-preservation and selfish ambition, we have the privilege of dramatizing the cross to a world that needs to know the good news.

6

THE SPOKEN WORD

Displaying the Power of the Holy Spirit
by Opening Our Mouths

On a warm spring day in 1822, a crowd gathered in the streets of Vienna, waiting to enter the concert hall where a German composer by the name of Ludwig van Beethoven was preparing to unveil his final symphony, which would change forever what the world knew about that musical form.

As the audience found their seats, they expected to be delighted and surprised by the arrangement of the bright sounds of the flutes, the rich tones of the bassoons, the crash of cymbals. They could not have guessed what they were about to hear. In the final movement of his last symphony, Beethoven chose an instrument that had never been used in symphonies until that day.

It was the human voice.

Beethoven's Ninth was the first symphony in which a composer incorporated human voices, the world's very first choral symphony. Classical music would never be the same again. The symphony had always been about storytelling, but after the Ninth the story became clearer as humans began to sing their lyrics to the world.

As momentous as Symphony no. 9 was, it pales in comparison to the day when the human voice was added to the symphony of God's mission. It was a warm spring day in the year AD 33 when a large crowd gathered in the streets of Jerusalem. On that day, Jesus's disciples were in Jerusalem to celebrate the Jewish Feast of Weeks, also known as the Feast of Harvest, because it celebrated the grain harvest and the abundance of God's provision. It was a covenant renewal ceremony for God's people to remind themselves of their identity as God's people and to recommit their lives to Yahweh. Because the temple was central to the celebration of the Feast of Harvest, Jewish people from all over the known world had to make a long pilgrimage to the city of Jerusalem.

The disciples probably heard dozens of foreign languages as they walked through the streets. The presence of people from Mesopotamia, Egypt, and Cappadocia might have reminded them of Jesus's commission to bring the gospel to all nations (Luke 24:46–48; Acts 1:7–8). However, Jesus had given them explicit instructions to wait there for the Spirit to come upon them and empower them for that mission.

The disciples were still in Jerusalem, watching and waiting, praying with patience. And then God, the great conductor, added the human voice to his symphony of mission. Amid flames of fire and the sound of a rushing wind, the disciples began speaking in different languages, proclaiming the mighty deeds of God with words that could be understood by all the language groups gathered in Jerusalem. At the sound of this strange commotion, a large crowd began to form around the disciples. Some people thought the disciples were drunk—until they started to hear the gospel proclaimed in their own language. As this was happening, Peter stood up to proclaim the gospel to this multinational audience. He narrated Israel's history, showing how Jesus is the true Messiah and that whoever calls on the name of the Lord will be saved. At least three thousand people responded to Peter's message and were baptized on that one day.

Since that day, the mission of God's people has included proactive, verbal proclamation of the gospel. God's people are still called to display the uniqueness of our God through the way we live, work, and worship. However, since the coming of the Spirit, we're also empowered to invite people to join the family through the work of Christ, and for that, we need words. The book of Acts is the story of how God's people were empowered by the Spirit to verbally proclaim the gospel, starting in Jerusalem and extending to the ends of the earth. Until Pentecost, mission had been centered on one nation and one place. But with the sending of the Spirit, God's people were called to take the good news to all nations and all places. Just as Beethoven added the words of the Ode to Joy to his ninth symphony, God gave the lyrics of the gospel to the church so that they could sing the good news of great joy to the nations.

The Final Movement

The third movement in the symphony of mission is what we call the spoken word movement. It's about joining the Spirit's work of pointing people to Christ by opening our mouths to proclaim the gospel. God is not only glorious and loving; he's also inviting people to be reconciled to himself through the life, death, and resurrection of Jesus. The people of the church are called to be his ambassadors, proclaiming the gospel of peace to a conflicted world. This chapter describes how to participate intentionally in this movement and provides a few examples of how we can effectively open our mouths and sing the gospel to the nations.

Some people see the book of Acts as a history of the early church's mission to spread the gospel, but it's better described as a history of the Spirit's powerful missional work through an obscure and often confused group of disciples. The advancement of the gospel is driven, empowered, and led by the Spirit, not by human ingenuity or strength. In the symphony of God's mission, the Spirit takes the lead.

In the book of Acts and the Gospel of John the Spirit is tied to the effective witness of the church (Acts 1:8; John 15:26–27). The Spirit is the ultimate missionary who reveals the character of God, convicts people of sin, and brings people to repentance and faith in Jesus. However, the Spirit sings the gospel through the vocal cords of the church. He's the choir director who guides the many voices of the church to harmonize and bear verbal witness to Jesus.

The verbal proclamation of the gospel was a high priority for the church because faith comes by hearing God's Word proclaimed by God's people (Rom. 10:13–15). It was such a priority that the church appointed specific people to do the work of evangelism (Eph. 4:11; 2 Tim. 4:5). In his letters Paul implies that the gospel was spreading through the verbal witness of the church (Phil 1:14; 1 Thess. 1:7–8). Both Paul and Peter describe the church's missional identity with language that implies the church is the messenger of the gospel. Paul says that the church has been given a ministry of reconciliation and that God makes an appeal of reconciliation through the *words* of his people (2 Cor. 5:18–20). Peter describes the church as a holy priesthood called to proclaim verbally God's mighty acts (1 Pet. 2:9).

It's clear that the verbal proclamation of the gospel is a vital aspect of God's mission, but one thing that can be puzzling about the New Testament is the lack of direct commands for ordinary believers to verbally share the gospel. Why do we see only a few verses in the epistles that command the ordinary believer to do evangelism? The reason is most likely that the church was so unique and distinct in character that people would ask *them* about their faith.

The church's communal generosity, fruitful work, loving families, hopeful suffering, and courageous public life set them apart from their neighbors and provoked questions wherever they went.

Imagine if you were to start dressing up like a clown each day. How difficult would it be for you to bring up conversations about your clown costume? It would be easy. You wouldn't need to do a thing. People would ask you questions about your strange attire everywhere you went. As you walked your dog in the morning, your neighbor would ask why you were dressed for Halloween. Your coworkers would inquire about your colorful wig in the moments before a meeting, and even your local barista would have some comment. The question isn't whether or not you would be able to strike up a conversation about your clown suit; the question is whether or not you would have a good explanation for it. This is probably what Peter means when he calls God's people always to be "prepared to make a defense to anyone who asks you for a reason for the hope that is in you; yet do it with gentleness and respect" (1 Pet. 3:15–16 ESV).

God's people are called to stand out, not because we're wearing silly costumes but because we are putting on the unique clothing of Christ's character (Col. 3:12–14). In a world of greed and consumerism, God's people are called to wear the garments of generosity. In a sexualized world, we should stand apart as people with strong marriages and deep friendships. In a world of "me first," we should display the gospel by sacrificially seeking the flourishing of the most vulnerable in society. If we truly lived like that, we would stand out as unique and distinct and would point to the healing for which the world is groaning. The lives of early Christians were of such a unique character that people inevitably asked questions about their faith. That's why the epistles emphasize the importance of having Christlike character that's in step with the gospel and of being ready to give an answer to those who have questions about the peculiar lifestyle and unique God (Col. 4:5–6; 1 Pet. 3:15).

If the church truly displayed the unique character of Christ, was fully engaged in fruitful cultural work (stewardship movement), and sacrificially loved others (service movement), we would have no shortage of opportunities to proclaim the gospel to our neighbors with the spoken word. The question is whether we would be ready to answer their questions.

Three Major Shifts

We need to be prepared to bear witness to Jesus with words in a way that harmonizes with the stewardship and service movements. Three major shifts in concepts and practices are proposed here that will help the church in North America to proclaim the gospel in the twenty-first century, most of them from the missional rhythms in the book of Acts.

1. *From generic to craft.* Like Paul in Athens, we need to present the gospel in thoughtful and contextual ways to be more like craftspeople than mass producers.
2. *From manipulative marketing to gospel storytelling.* Rather than giving cheap gospel presentations that promise heaven in exchange for a prayer, we need to proclaim the events of the gospel story.
3. *From reading a script to listening to the Spirit.* The spoken word movement isn't just a conversation with our neighbors; it's also rooted in a constant conversation with God through prayer. The human voice needs to be directed and tuned by the Spirit to make the beautiful music of the gospel.

From Generic to Craft

Take a moment and think of your favorite living band or musician. Now imagine that they are in town and you have an opportunity to hear their music, but you have to choose the format. You could (a) listen to their music on an MP3 player, (b) attend a live concert, or (c) have a live performance at your house with your closest friends.

The answer is obvious for most people: *c.* Most of us would choose to hear our favorite band in the intimacy of our own living room and among our closest friends, wouldn't we? But why is this? It's certainly not in the hope of hearing better quality music, since a professionally mastered MP3 has a significantly higher quality of sound than what you would generate in your living room. And your home pales in comparison to a professionally designed concert venue with its tens of thousands of dollars worth of equipment.

So why would we choose the personal over the polished? Because we are relational creatures who find value not only in the end product but also in the process, in the experience of nearness. To know that your favorite musician is making music for *your* friends in that specific place and time carries a deeper meaning than any performance, however good, recorded for the nameless masses. We would choose the living room because there's something profoundly beautiful and personal about a specific, small audience. Whether in locally roasted coffee, handmade furniture, artisan bread, or a quick trim in an old-fashioned barbershop, there has been a surging interest in local craftsmanship over the past several years. People prefer their local breweries to Budweiser, heirloom tomatoes from the farmers market to Walmart's frozen veggie mix, and underground hip-hop to homogenized pop songs on the radio. It's an emphasis on local over global, quality over quantity, and excellence over efficiency.

This craftsmanship movement isn't a condemnation of manufacturing and mass production as much as it's a corrective, an attempt to swing the pendulum the other way. We need both craftsmanship and standardized production. Without the standardized production of things such as nuts and bolts, medical equipment, and building materials, the world would be a substantially more expensive and potentially more dangerous place. There's an important balance to strike between craft and mass production.

But when it comes to the verbal proclamation of the gospel, our imaginations have been shaped more by the industrial revolution and the triumph of mass production than by a craft mind-set. Many of us think the goal of evangelism is to boil down the gospel into a few generic points and then mass-produce it, distributing it to as many people as possible. A lot of good has come from the wide distribution of tracts, videos, and other types of gospel presentations that are intended to reach the masses. However, there's a need for the pendulum to swing back toward craft evangelism. Theologians call this contextualization, and this approach appears throughout the book of Acts.

Wherever the apostles went, they proclaimed the unchanging events of the gospel, especially the centrality of Jesus and his resurrection. They called all people, no matter their background, to repent and believe in Jesus. However, their approach changed with their audiences (1 Cor. 9:20–23). When the apostles spoke to Jewish audiences, they reframed Israel's story with Jesus as the hero. They showed how the deep longings and expectations of Israel had been fulfilled through Christ. They described Jesus as Israel's true Messiah and king, the sacrificial lamb who atoned for their sins, their ultimate high priest, and the true seed of Abraham who brought God's blessing. They spoke of the reign of God breaking into history through Jesus's resurrection. They would often quote Scripture and use imagery familiar to Jewish people to paint a portrait of Jesus that affirmed the goodness of the Jewish story while challenging their idolatry. Most of all, they showed how all of Israel's Scriptures ultimately pointed to Jesus.

However, when Paul spoke to a non-Jewish audience, he took a different approach. He appealed to the concerns of their culture, showing them how Jesus is the answer to the questions they were asking. He called them to turn from the empty idols of Greece and Rome to find life in the living God. But he used the stories, symbols, and vernacular of his audience. Consider, for example, what happened when Barnabas and Paul entered the city of Lystra, a gentile community immersed in Greek mythology, which looked to the pagan gods for health, agricultural abundance, fertility, and everything they thought was part of an abundant life (Acts 14:8–23). Upon arriving there, the apostles heal a crippled man who had never walked. In awe of this miracle, the people of the city begin to proclaim that Paul and Barnabas are incarnations of the Greek gods Zeus and Hermes. In response, the apostles passionately narrate the Lyconians' cultural story, affirming their longing for divine power to bring health and abundance. But Paul and Barnabas insist that the power for healing and the abundant crops come from Yahweh not from the Greek gods—and they presumably go on to point to the resurrected Jesus as the *true* story of how God became incarnate on this earth.

We see this again in Acts 17 when Paul enters the Areopagus in Athens, a place for philosophical and religious debate. He shows how the answers to the philosophers' deepest questions are in the resurrected Jesus. He retells their cultural story in a Jesus-centered way, even quoting (what appears to be) a hymn dedicated to Zeus, written by Epimenides of Crete, and a poem called "Phainomena" by the Stoic poet Aratus. Paul was such a craft evangelist that he mastered Greek poetry and philosophy, using common Greek vernacular and literary references to point to Jesus. He even found an altar devoted to an unknown god and used that opportunity to announce that the unknowable God could in fact be known through Jesus.

Throughout the book of Acts we see Paul and the other apostles doing evangelism as craftspeople, carefully and prayerfully choosing words best fitted to proclaim the good news to specific people in particular places. Furthermore, rather than giving us one standardized narrative, the first-century church left us with four Gospels, each telling the narrative of Christ's life for different cultural audiences. These are well-written, carefully crafted, Spirit-inspired accounts of the gospel tailored to the needs of differing audiences.

What if we approached evangelism with the same sense of craftsmanship and focused our attention on specific groups of people? While the gospel remains rooted in the events of Jesus's life, death, and resurrection, our language, metaphors, and methods should be contextualized to explain their significance to the specific audiences we encounter. What if we thought less about the mass production of the gospel and thought more about how we can beautifully and intentionally speak to small, specific groups of people?

What might this look like? Rather than writing a generic pamphlet to be distributed to thousands, an accountant might write a personalized theological reflection on accounting to share with her coworkers. Imagine someone who chooses to go to the same restaurant each week, befriending the staff, anonymously paying for another customer's meal as a reenactment of God's grace, and looking for opportunities to tell his server about the lavish grace of God. Imagine a father who gives his children a handwritten prayer for each day of the week. Imagine a boss who chooses to serve his staff each week by personally cleaning the bathrooms, looking for an opportunity to tell them about the King, who washed feet and came to serve. Imagine a musician who, instead of trying to write the next big song, writes a very particular song for a small group of high school friends, showing how their time together is a gift from God. Just as someone slowly and deliberately learns how to roast coffee, build furniture, or paint a picture, we should pursue rich ways of communicating the gospel that include language, symbols, and images that resonate with a particular group of people at a particular point in time.

This approach to evangelism is marked by four characteristics.

It is specific. God has sovereignly placed each of us among a small and specific group of people. Therefore, we should reflect on what images, analogies, stories, and questions can be a bridge to the people of our particular context. We need to ask God how Jesus is the answer to the questions and issues of "my volleyball team," "my neighbors on Palm Lane," or "the other accountants at my office." We should see tremendous value in thinking small scale and discerning the questions that the people we know best are asking.

It is costly. Following in the way of Jesus, who poured himself out on the cross, we should joyfully give our time, skills, training, finances, and friendship to love our neighbors. One of the ways we love them is by putting in the time to get to know people and listen to them. Furthermore, we should be willing to spend time praying and reflecting on how to communicate the gospel with intentionality rather than flippancy, not viewing it as a waste of time to spend many hours articulating the good news to just a few people.

It is prayerful. Even though we are emphasizing focus, intentionality, and craft, we must remember that people will come to understand the gospel only through the work of the Holy Spirit. The same Spirit that hovered over creation and empowered artisans to make the tabernacle (Exod. 28; 35) can also paint a portrait of Jesus through our craft evangelism.

It is of high quality. If the gospel is truly beautiful, shouldn't we communicate it with beauty and intentionality? Our methods indicate what we believe about our message, and sadly, they often communicate that the gospel is a Kroger-brand salvation certificate rather than the true story of the world. The gospel is free, but it is not cheap. Its cost was the life of Christ. The gospel is the world's greatest message, an incomparable treasure; our approach to evangelism should indicate that we are offering something of tremendous value.

The hard thing about craft evangelism is that it can't be prescribed in a few easy steps. There is no generic script. Our words must come from listening well to both the Spirit and our neighbors.

In the early 2000s I was a part of a small community of friends who chose to live in the international neighborhood near Arizona State University. One of our missional rhythms was to eat at the same Middle Eastern restaurant each week. Eventually we became good friends with Mohammed, the owner of the restaurant. Nearly every day someone from the group would drop by the restaurant to drink tea and spend time with him. We talked about everything—family, business, international relations, food. One of the things Mohammed was most proud of was his hummus, which he was convinced was the best in town.

To honor Mohammed's good work and to show him a glimpse of God's glory, a few of us spent some time writing a short essay that paid homage to his excellent hummus and to the God who had created the human creator of that hummus. The essay was both a gesture of honor and a redemptive analogy that pointed to God's creativity and generosity. It declared, "God, the First Chef, gave the gift of garbanzo beans to satisfy our taste buds and sustain our lives. Hummus points to a God who cares for more than efficiency and functionality; he also cares about making the world hospitable and delectable." The essay went on to point to Jesus as the face of God's hospitality, the one who is calling a world to come feast with him.

An essay about hummus may seem like a silly gesture to most people, but it was quite meaningful to Mohammed. He was honored that someone took the time to think deeply about his work and express appreciation. The essay was craft evangelism that honored the work of a craftsman. The three hours it took to write the essay sparked many conversations that eventually led to a fuller explanation of the gospel and an appeal to respond to God's generosity in Christ.

From Manipulative Marketing to Gospel Storytelling

A few years ago I ended each day by checking the mailbox. I would pull into my driveway, pop out of my car, and plunge my hand into a pile of junk mail. I was expecting delivery of a book by Orhan Pamuk, my favorite Turkish author, who writes riveting fiction about life in Anatolia. His stories draw me into a different world—the Ottoman Empire of 1517. Each day as I drove home from work, I was hoping for the arrival of good news: that a good story had arrived in the mail.

However, for about five straight days I was disappointed. The mailbox was full of coupons. Coupons are fine, but they are not really good news.

Sometimes they come in handy, but they never grip our hearts or imaginations. Behind every coupon there's somebody trying to sell something, and there's always a catch, even when the coupon says "free."

Unfortunately, many people approach evangelism as if they were scattering coupons rather than bringing good news. We treat Jesus like he's the free coupon that gets people to heaven and like we just need to stuff him into as many mailboxes as possible. Even if people on the receiving end think he might be beneficial to them, they also suspect that there's a catch.

The gospel is not a coupon for heaven; it's the true story of the world. It's not just a captivating story to occupy your mind for a few hours, like a good Orhan Pamuk novel; it's the ultimate story that gives meaning to our whole lives. It doesn't just provide us with a pleasant evening; it provides deep and eternal joy. Most good stories help us know more about the world, but the gospel story introduces us to the God who *made* the world. Only this message makes sense of all of life.

Jesus, the hero of the story, is an unparalleled character, the answer to the world's deepest questions. As we read the Gospels, his unique personality radiates from the pages, showing us the true face of God and of humanity while unmasking the villains of sin, Satan, and death. He assassinates death with the weapon of a crucified body. He liberates us from the tyranny of sin. He thwarts the cosmic terrorist by falling on the bomb of idolatry. His heroism is filled with riveting plot twists that invite our full attention as he empowers the weak, finds the lost, sees the unseen, and turns enemies into brothers.

Jesus isn't a coupon for free admission to heaven. He's the main character, the true protagonist, in the drama of life. His story isn't a work of fiction intended to entertain a passive audience. It calls us to jump into the pages through repentance and faith so that we enter into his story and into real life.

Sadly, many Christians think that God wants us to distribute coupons of salvation or give a high-pressure sales pitch and close the deal by any means necessary. However, when we observe the pattern of evangelism in the book of Acts, we see passionate storytellers bringing the good news of the true story of the whole earth. We see Jesus and the apostles pointing to simple things like birds, crops, Greek poetry, and childbirth as echoes and analogies to the gospel. These analogies show the deep meaning behind the simple things of daily life. They are bold and persuasive. But they are not manipulative, because they are compelled by love rather than personal gain. They tell of God being the creator of all things, of sin tarnishing God's good work, and of Jesus rescuing the mangled world. They don't treat Jesus as a product to be peddled but as a God to be known. As we open our mouths to proclaim the gospel, we should follow the example of the apostles and learn how to tell the gospel story. There are many ways to do this, but three are emphasized here: to renarrate the world's story, to remember our personal stories, and to retell Jesus's stories.

RENARRATING THE WORLD'S STORY

As we look at the book of Acts, we see that the apostles were Spirit-empowered storytellers who addressed people's particular questions and concerns by renarrating their local cultural story in light of the biblical story. They pointed to the goodness of creation as a generous gift from God and showed how the pains of the world point to our need for God to rescue it and us. They showed people how the everyday stuff of life was an echo of the gospel.

If we want to follow the apostles and learn how to renarrate the world's story, we might be wise to learn from the passionate and knowledgeable tour guides at the Motown Museum in Detroit. If there's one word that captures the flavor of a Motown tour, it is *reenchantment*. The gifted guides there help you imagine what it must have been like to watch the Temptations practice dance moves or to see Marvin Gaye sitting on the floor scribbling lyrics on a yellow notepad. They help you reimagine the significance of everything in the museum.

For example, in one corner of one room there's a small desk—most people would never notice it—once used by Diana Ross. Our tour guides told us the riveting story about how Diana Ross used to be Motown's secretary and spent her days behind the desk, answering the phones. One day a backup singer for another band didn't show up, and the band needed someone to stand in for the sound check. They looked around the room and saw Diana Ross. The tour guides told us that when Ross jumped up and belted out her powerful vocals, everyone just stopped dead in their tracks. The producers put a contract on that dusty desk the same day, a contract that launched the career of one of the greatest R & B vocalists of all time. Right there and then, a guide jumped onto that desk and started singing some of Ross's greatest hits. That dusty old desk, one you'd find at any thrift store, was suddenly filled with wonder and meaning because of beautiful, passionate, enchanting storytelling.

What can we learn about telling the gospel story from the guides at the Motown Museum? Well, in some ways, involvement in the spoken word movement is like being a cosmic tour guide. We help people see the deep meaning and wonder behind even the simplest things by being narrators of life.

The whole earth is filled with wonders—from photosynthesis to farming, sandboxes to skyscrapers—but most people miss them. These incredible things provide glimpses of God's glory, fragments of his story. But most

people have never heard the true story that gives these glimpses and fragments
their real context, the story that shows the true meaning of all life. We get
the privilege of being tour guides to help people see the Grand Canyon as a
portrait of God's majesty, a smooth cup of coffee as an echo of the goodness
of creation, arthritis as evidence of a sin-gripped world, marriage as a drama
of Christ's love, and a renovated house as a foretaste of the coming restoration of all things. Habakkuk 2:14 tells of the day when the whole earth will
be filled with the knowledge of God's glory "as the waters cover the sea." As
God's tour guides, we get to participate in that aspect of God's mission by
showing how the places where we live, work, and play are already brimming
with God's glory.

Evangelism is the process of reenchantment, which shows the deep meaning
that can be found in the simple stuff of life, rather than a high-pressured sales
pitch. Just like tour guides at a museum who explain the deeper meaning of
monuments and help people understand the story behind each exhibit, we
tell the larger story that makes sense of life. The good, inspiring, and beautiful things people encounter in the world are monuments of God's creational
goodness. The evil, pain, and suffering of this world are monuments of the
reality of sin, Satan, and death. Every act of sacrifice, heroism, or restoration
serves as a monument of the gospel. We get the privilege of drawing people's
attention to these monuments and telling the grand story to which they point.

Monuments of God's Creation

As cosmic tour guides, we get to draw people's attention to the gifts from
God that bear witness to the joy, beauty, splendor, goodness, and righteousness
of the Giver. Architecture, friendship, woodworking, well-written computer
code, and cozy cabins are all monuments of God's goodness. We shouldn't
berate people for enjoying these things but should build upon their enjoyment of God's world to show them how every good gift in this world comes
from God.

The neighborhoods in North Tempe are known to care about placemaking,
urban gardening, and craft. So the Tempe Bike Gang (see chap. 5) decided to
give out placemaker awards to people who had creative and beautiful front
yards filled with plants and gardens that showed hospitality. Most of the homeowners were grateful for—but a bit puzzled by—this strange act of honor.

As our relationships with these people developed, we were able to ask
them why they loved good architecture, urban gardens, and walkable neighborhoods. These conversations created opportunities to point them to God,
the great placemaker, whose image they were reflecting. The best of urban
placemaking is an echo of the placemaking Jesus himself does for us; he's

preparing a place where we will live with God and one another in safety and community in the beauty of a restored creation.

Monuments of the Fall

What do the following have in common: a manipulative coworker, another news story of political incompetence, the threat of nuclear war, and the common cold? Every one of these things reminds us that our world is broken and needs to be healed.

We can serve people by drawing attention to the ways sin is twisting and wounding the world. It's easy to look away, change the subject, or just ignore the pain of others. However, all that's broken in this world points to the reality of idolatry, injury, and injustice. When we engage in discussions about the complexity of the world's problems, we help people see how desperate we all are and see the inadequacy of our false saviors. Only the Spirit can convict us of sin and show us Christ, but the Spirit will often use the brokenness of the world to open up discussions about the consequences of human rebellion.

When we ask why there's so much pain, fear, and injustice in the world, we realize that the problem is too big for us. We need a savior big enough to address not just the sin "out there" in the world but also the sin that has metastasized in our own hearts.

I once asked someone to name one thing he would "disinvent" if he had the opportunity. He said he would disinvent Facebook. When I asked him why, he talked about how everyone using Facebook acts "fake." Eventually our conversation drifted toward Genesis 3 and how Adam and Eve were ashamed and hid their nakedness with fig leaves. I was able to share how I think of Facebook as the fig leaf of the twenty-first century, a cover-up that people wear to hide their true selves from others. I pointed to Christ as the one who dealt with our shame on the cross, allowing us to be completely known and fully loved by God. This conversation was possible only because I kept asking questions that helped us go deeper in our exploration of the brokenness of the world rather than keeping the conversation at a surface level.

Several medical professionals I've known speak of Jesus as the wounded healer, the one who became the answer to our pain by entering our pain. There are no cheap answers for why people suffer, but physical pain bears witness to a reality we've never known: that the human body is a masterpiece that was made for flourishing but has been distorted by suffering. These medical professionals describe Jesus as the one able to empathize with a suffering world as the one who endured the wretched pain of the cross. Even though we don't understand why we suffer, in Jesus we see a God who came to suffer with us. We find our healing from his wounds. The resurrected body of

Jesus is a preview of the day when arthritic hands will carve sculptures, the paralyzed will break-dance, and cancer will be a distant memory.

A pastor friend who is an effective evangelist once went to get his hair cut. The hairdresser was gay, and both men recognized a degree of awkwardness in the silence between them. Finally our friend asked the hairdresser what kind of world he would like to live in. He described a world of harmony between humanity and nature—he loved the outdoors and was terribly disturbed at the way humanity was trashing the planet. Our friend then asked him if he knew that the Christian faith is all about such harmony. The hairdresser responded with an astonished "No!"

"Yes," our friend went on to say, "God made a world in which humanity was given the task to care for the world, but because of our rebellion, we now use it up for our own selfish benefit. The Bible tells a story, centered on Jesus, about how God is healing that relationship. One day, when God completes his work, the relationship between humanity and the nonhuman creation will be restored."

The hairdresser was stunned. He said, "I have always heard Christians say that going to heaven when we die is what matters and that we don't have to be concerned for this world." Our friend said that some misguided people do believe that, but it is not the story of the Bible. The hairdresser was in church the next Sunday, saying to his partner, "You've got to hear this preacher who has good news."

Monuments of Redemption

The human heart is drawn to stories of heroism and sacrifice, because they're an echo of our savior. Full-grown men with thick beards may be moved to tears when they see an injured player win the game with his last-second shot. Long lines curl around movie theaters to see the latest Marvel film. Few people are admired as much as the 9/11 first responders.

While our small stories of heroism and sacrifice point to insufficient saviors, they also serve as echoes of Christ, the one who rescued the world through his sacrificial love. That's why we believe we should amplify these stories. They are living monuments to the gospel. As cosmic tour guides, we can celebrate these stories, ask good questions to help people explore why they are so drawn to them, and respectfully tell people about the bigger story to which all stories of sacrifice and heroism point.

When I talk about the self-giving love of Christ, I often tell the story of Dr. Ebru, the tiny Muslim woman who saved my wife's life. She was my wife's doctor in Turkey, and she delivered our daughter, Elliana. However, she was more than a doctor to us; she became an echo of God's own hospitality and self-giving love. Most doctors try to move through their list of patients as quickly as possible, but Dr. Ebru took the time to get to know us. She also gave us her personal cell phone number in case we needed anything. As it turned out, her cell phone number ended up being more than a convenience for our family; it was a lifesaver.

The labor and delivery for our daughter's birth lasted less than six hours, and there were no complications. However, six weeks later, on a cool spring evening in Ankara, my wife began to hemorrhage. Then, when she simply tried to reach for a jacket, she fell to the ground unconscious. Within minutes I was holding my infant daughter in one arm and my bleeding, unconscious wife in the other. Confused and in panic, I grabbed Jenny's cell phone and called Dr. Ebru. Before I could finish my sentence, she said, "Get to the hospital right away!"

As I hung up, my friend Mark arrived. Together we carried my wife's limp body down the stairs and into a taxi. Within ten minutes we were at Guvenlik Hospital and were greeted calmly by Dr. Ebru. She rushed Jenny to surgery and ushered me into the waiting room. For more than four hours I held my daughter in my arms there, wondering if I would ever hear my wife's laugh again, if my daughter would ever know her mother. My worried prayers were at last interrupted by an exhausted nurse who came to say that my wife was OK, that Dr. Ebru had saved her life.

As we walked together to the recovery room, the nurse told me that Jenny could have died or had severe brain damage if she had lost any more blood. However, Dr. Ebru had stepped in, rushed Jenny into surgery, and spent those long hours performing the procedure that would save her life. All this happened after Dr. Ebru had already worked a twelve-hour shift delivering babies. My phone call had come at midnight when she was already in bed. She could easily have ignored that call, knowing that she needed—and deserved!—sleep. But she responded and, at great cost to herself, had saved my wife's life.

When I share that story with my friends, they are often moved to tears. Why? I believe it's because the beauty of sacrificial love is an echo of the sacrificial love of Christ. Telling that story has led to literally hundreds of conversations about the love of God in Christ. I tell people that a small Muslim woman—who doesn't believe in the cross—is one of the best biblical commentaries I've ever read. I tell them that what Dr. Ebru did for my wife, Christ does for the world.

The goodness of creation, the devastating effects of the fall, and the beautiful stories of redemption all provide echoes of the gospel. Our role is to listen for the echoes and then tell the world. Our role is to look for the monuments of creation, the fall, and redemption and then, as cosmic tour guides, explain the deep meaning behind them.

Removed from the dynamics of real conversation, these examples might seem a little trite. But they are not meant to be a script—they are intended to provide only a few short examples to spark the imagination. Ultimately, each person needs to look at the context in which God has placed him or her and ask, What are the questions that people around *me* are asking to which Jesus is the answer? How can I renarrate the experiences of *my* context in light of the biblical story?

REMEMBERING OUR PERSONAL STORIES

The book of Acts describes the missional identity of the church with the word *witness*. This is courtroom language to describe someone who testifies about what they have seen and heard. The apostles were witnesses of the life, death, and resurrection of Christ. Their mission was to tell the world what they had seen with their own eyes.

How about us? Are we witnesses to the events of the gospel? True, we haven't seen the risen Lord Jesus with our own eyes. However, we still play the role of witness, because even though we didn't see the actual event, the impact of the resurrection has powerfully transformed our lives. We bear witness by adding our voices to the testimony of the apostles. They bore witness to the actual events of the life, death, and resurrection of Jesus. We bear witness to the impact of those events in our own lives. We introduce the big story of the gospel by fleshing it out with our own smaller stories about how the gospel has shaped our lives.

The simplest way we can share the good news in words is by telling people our personal stories and the ways Jesus has rescued us. A beautiful example of this comes in Jesus's tender encounter with the Samaritan woman at the well. He reveals himself as the living water who satisfies our thirst and as the Messiah who gives access to the Father—access not based on social status but simply on knowing Christ. Many people are familiar with this scene from John, but what happens next is often overlooked. The Samaritan woman immediately heads back to her town and shares her testimony. What was the result? "Many of the Samaritans from that town believed in him [Jesus] because of the woman's testimony, 'He told me everything I ever did'" (John 4:39). God used this woman as his instrument of revival in that Samaritan village. As a woman in that culture, she didn't have power or status; as someone who had been divorced multiple times, her reputation was tarnished. She wasn't educated or experienced. She didn't even know that much about Jesus because, after all, she'd had only a short encounter with him.

But she did have a story about her personal encounter with the Messiah and how he had transformed her life. The same is true for us. In order to participate in the spoken word movement, all we need to know is the story of how God has worked in our lives. As our friend Tom Shrader used to say, "If you know enough to believe the gospel, you know enough to share the gospel." While it's not enough just to tell people about our personal experiences, our stories can be on-ramps to the gospel story and bear witness to the present power of the gospel.

RETELLING JESUS'S STORIES

Another way to tell the gospel story is retelling the stories about Jesus found in the Gospels. This isn't very difficult. You just immerse yourself in the Gospels and prayerfully identify the stories that connect with the questions, concerns, and struggles that people are wrestling with in your particular context. Then spend time just drinking in those stories, reading them over and over again. Let them seep into your heart and flavor your prayer life. Read and reflect on them until they are such a part of your life that they just seem to naturally spill into every conversation.

Spend some time learning these stories—not memorizing them but *learning* them—so that you can easily retell them in casual conversation. Then prayerfully look for opportunities to tell them to people. You don't have to be awkward or formal. Simply ask someone you're talking with if you can tell them a story, or ask them if they have ever heard the story about _____.

For people struggling with questions about life and death, you may want to tell the story of Jesus raising Lazarus from the dead and of his claim to be the resurrection and the life. You can point to Jesus's power over death and disease. You might want to ask what it would have been like to see Jesus perform that miracle firsthand. It might even be appropriate to talk about how Jesus wept over the death of Lazarus and how, through Jesus, God enters into the pain and brokenness of this world. Jesus conquered death, but he also weeps with us over the dreadful reality of the pain it causes. These conversations could naturally lead to a discussion about Jesus's death, resurrection, and future restoration, when he will wipe away the tears from the eyes of a weeping world.

Jesus's parable of the good Samaritan in Luke 10 (see chap. 5) is another powerful story to tell several types of people. You can bring it up to those who are seeking to do good in the world. You can affirm their volunteer work, generosity, or efforts for public justice and then simply ask if they've heard where the phrase *good Samaritan* came from. When I've told this story, it has led to conversations about why humanity feels the impulse to do good in the world and to discussions about the generosity of God in Christ and the unique nature of Jesus's love, which calls us to love and respect even our enemies, not just those whom we perceive as worthy. These discussions often lead to opportunities to discuss how Christ loves us and died for us when we were his enemies and hostile toward him. This parable is a great story also to bring up among those critical of the hypocrisy and racism of many so-called Christian leaders. It's important to show them that Jesus also sees and rejects such hypocrisy and that he is drawn to those who are overlooked and oppressed in the world.

Some Christians don't think telling Jesus's stories is a legitimate evangelistic practice because they've been trained to think that real evangelism is a systematic explanation of how to get "saved." They think they're being unbiblical unless they're quoting from Romans or Galatians and then offering people an opportunity to pray the sinner's prayer. (The irony is that the sinner's prayer isn't found anywhere in the Bible.) The primary evangelistic tool of the early church was simply the four Gospels, the contextual retellings of Jesus's life, death, and resurrection. Romans and Galatians weren't given so that we could clip a few sentences out, detach them from their contexts, rearrange them into a list of neat principles, and then try to slip them as quickly as possible into every conversation.

We do, however, need to be careful when it comes to telling Jesus's stories. Just as people lift verses from the full narrative context of Romans and Galatians, we run the risk of extracting Gospel stories from the full story of the gospel. We can be tempted to use Jesus's stories to affirm whatever ideology or idolatry our audience already believes, using them as prooftexts for what people want to hear. It's a wise practice to build upon common ground and to affirm what is good in the life of whomever you're talking with, but it's also important to know that we haven't gone far enough until we have proclaimed the death and resurrection of Jesus and invited people to repent of their old lives and believe in Christ. You don't have to say everything in every conversation. Just as Jesus didn't explain everything to his disciples in one sitting, it's often wise for us simply to share these stories, provide people time to reflect on them, and then keep inviting them to go deeper.

When we tell Jesus's stories, we use our words to draw people into the Gospels, knowing that as they see the face of Christ, they will begin to see the glory of the Father and hear the Spirit's invitation to repent and believe. John 1:18 says, "No one has ever seen God, but the one and only Son, who is himself God and is in closest relationship with the Father, has made him known." Our goal in telling these stories isn't to entertain, inspire, or provide people with a few helpful principles for life. It's to show them the glory of God in the face of Christ.

From Reading a Script to Listening to the Spirit

WHAT IS THE GOSPEL?

If the symphony of mission includes a missional choir that sings the words of the gospel to the nations, then the question may arise, What are the lyrics? What words must be included when we announce the good news? But the Bible doesn't give us a comprehensive script for proclaiming the gospel. Instead, it tells about Christ-followers rooted in the biblical story, who understood their own culture and relied on the Holy Spirit to help them proclaim Christ as the answer to the particular questions of their cultural contexts. From Peter's expositions of the Old Testament to Paul's explanation of the unknown God, from the Gospel of John (describing Jesus as the Word) to the Gospel of Matthew (describing Jesus as the son of David and Lord), the gospel is proclaimed in a wide variety of ways in Scripture.

However, there are some common themes, especially among the various summaries of the gospel provided for us in the New Testament. The first proclamation of the gospel by Jesus is that the kingdom of God has arrived in him (Mark 1:14–15). Paul offers a different yet clear and decisive definition of the gospel in 1 Corinthians 15:1–5: "Now I would remind you, brothers, of the gospel I preached to you . . . : that Christ died for our sins in accordance with the Scriptures, that he was buried, that he was raised on the third day in accordance with the Scriptures, and that he appeared to Cephas, then to the twelve" (ESV). In this passage there are at least three intertwined characteristics of proclaiming the gospel: the gospel is centered on Jesus; it announces the good news of God's reign as the climax of a long story; and it is a message of salvation.

THE GOSPEL IS CENTERED ON JESUS

When we proclaim the gospel, we are announcing real historical events. This may seem obvious, but many gospel presentations reduce the gospel to abstract ideas or principles about how to be saved. Even the historical events are reduced to theories about those events. In the New Testament, however, the focus is on concrete events. Christ's life, death, resurrection, and exaltation and the outpouring of the Spirit are the real historical events through which God saves and brings his kingdom. Mark introduces his Gospel as "the beginning of the good news about Jesus the Messiah . . ." (1:1). That little phrase implies that the whole gospel story is the good news about Jesus the Messiah. While the gospel has to do with the whole story of Jesus, his death and resurrection clearly occupy the central and dominant place. Jesus died for our sins to reconcile the world to God, and the resurrection is the firstfruits of the new creation (1 Cor. 15:20–24).

THE GOSPEL IS GOOD NEWS THAT IS THE CLIMAX OF A LONG STORY

In the first century God's people were longing for the day when God's presence would return to Israel and restore all that was broken. Their story was looking for its climax, for the Messiah to return and make things right. When Paul says that the gospel of Jesus is "according to the Scriptures," he's saying that the gospel fulfills Israel's longing for God to restore all that's broken and to begin his reign over the whole world.

The word *gospel* literally means "good news." God's people in the first century expectantly read passages like Isaiah 52, which speaks of the good news of God's reign as king, as bringing peace, joy, and salvation. They were looking forward to a day when the redemptive work of God would come to its climactic fulfillment, when idolatry, injustice, and pain would be cast away by God. When Jesus proclaims that the kingdom has come, he's proclaiming that the long-awaited good news of God's restoration has come, and it has come through himself.

To North Americans, the ideas of a king and kingdom seem foreign, the stuff of fantasies not salvation. But when Jesus proclaims the coming of the kingdom, he is making a specific announcement about the world's last days: "The day of God's reign is here!" This message dominates Paul's writings as well. With Christ we have reached the fullness of times (Gal. 4:4; Eph. 1:10); the "day of salvation" is here (2 Cor. 6:2); the "new creation" has come (2 Cor. 5:17); the "culmination of the ages" (1 Cor. 10:11) and the "later times" (1 Tim. 4:1) are upon us; and we share now in the inheritance of the kingdom (Col. 1:13–14). The gospel announces that God's kingdom is breaking into the world through Christ to restore and renew all that's broken. While it's true that God's restoration is both "already" and "not yet"—that it has been inaugurated through the first coming of Christ but waits to be completed upon his return—we should remember that when we proclaim the gospel, Christ is the good news who rescues us from the bad news of idolatry, death, brokenness, and injustice.

THE GOSPEL IS A MESSAGE OF SALVATION

God could have dealt with sin by destroying the world and starting over. Instead he chose to renew creation and rescue his rebellious image-bearers. The gospel is about Christ accomplishing the goal of the whole biblical story: the restoration of all things, with human beings at the heart of that restoration. It is the demonstration of God's power to save, redeem, reconcile, heal, and liberate. God is restoring his good creation from the horrific impact of human rebellion, and his restoration extends to all of his good creation. This isn't to say that everyone will be saved, because one enters the kingdom only by repenting from the old life and placing faith in Christ. Jesus is the exclusive source of salvation: "Salvation is found in no one else, for there is no other name under heaven given to mankind by which we must be saved" (Acts 4:12). For those who trust in Christ, God's power to save includes many blessings and gifts: forgiveness, a new relationship with God, justification, the Spirit's renewing power, peace. But it also comes with demands for living faith, true repentance, costly obedience, and sacrificial love.

When we announce the gospel, we tell the story of Jesus's birth, life, teaching, death, resurrection, and ascension. This message is the good news of a comprehensive salvation. God's mission to restore creation and rescue humanity from sin, Satan, and death is accomplished through Christ, the one true hero. When we proclaim the gospel, we are announcing that there's an answer to the brokenness of this fallen world, an answer to the sin that enslaves and distorts. In Christ, God is breaking into history and dealing with the sin, brokenness, and perversion that torment us all.

Speaking by Listening

While several biblical passages give us a rough outline of the types of things to include in our proclamation of the gospel, the Bible certainly doesn't give a script for every situation. We must learn to speak the language of the gospel by relying on the Spirit. Learning how to share the gospel is like learning a new language. A good teacher doesn't just provide the language learner with a list of phrases to repeat verbatim. Rather, the teacher immerses the student in the language and provides the student with the ability to respond dynamically to each particular situation.

While I lived in Turkey, I spent six months learning Turkish. Since my biggest struggle was with pronunciation, my language teacher advised me to focus on listening rather than speaking. The problem didn't have anything to do with the mechanics of my mouth; I wasn't hearing the words accurately.

By focusing on listening to native speakers pronounce the words rather than trying harder to pronounce them myself, I was able to overcome my difficulties. When we struggle to speak the language of the gospel to those who don't know Christ, we often spend too much energy trying to figure out what words to say. We need to focus on listening to the Spirit, the ultimate native speaker of the gospel, through a life of dependent prayer.

The early church was devoted to prayer. They knew that they couldn't do anything apart from the Spirit, so they waited in Jerusalem and prayed until the Spirit came on Pentecost. Then empowered to proclaim the gospel, they scattered all over the world.

Prayer wasn't just something that the early church did for the fifty days between the resurrection and the coming of the Spirit. Prayer was the beginning of *everything* they did. It was like breathing: they would inhale the Spirit through prayer and exhale the words of life through evangelism. As they prayed, they were given courage to speak even in the midst of life-threatening situations. They were ostracized, beaten, imprisoned, and even killed for proclaiming the gospel. Yet many were able to stare death in the face without flinching, not because they were naturally courageous people but because the Spirit gave them divine boldness and hope through prayer.

When we're afraid to tell people about Jesus, the answer isn't just to try harder but to draw near to God through prayer and to ask the Spirit to empower and embolden us. In 2 Timothy 1:7–8 Paul tells Timothy that the Spirit is the antidote to timidity. The Spirit is the source of power, love, and self-control who allows us to proclaim the gospel steadfastly, even in the midst of adversity. Rather than talking ourselves out of speaking or telling ourselves that everything is going to be OK, we need to listen to the Spirit call us to Christ, who is the source of our faith, the object of our hope, and the fountain of love that compels us to open our mouths.

The Spirit also directs our evangelistic efforts, giving us boldness and showing us when, where, and how to speak. In Acts 13 the church in Antioch was fasting and worshiping God when the Spirit spoke, directing them to send Barnabas and Paul to the gentiles. Later in his ministry, Paul wasn't sure where he should go next, but he knew that he needed to be led there by the Spirit. Luke describes the scene:

> Paul and his companions traveled throughout the region of Phrygia and Galatia, having been kept by the Holy Spirit from preaching the word in the province of Asia. When they came to the border of Mysia, they tried to enter Bithynia, but the Spirit of Jesus would not allow them to. So they passed by Mysia and went down to Troas. During the night Paul had a vision of a man of Macedonia

standing and begging him, "Come over to Macedonia and help us." After Paul had seen the vision, we got ready at once to leave for Macedonia, concluding that God had called us to preach the gospel to them. (Acts 16:6–10)

Notice that the Holy Spirit actually forbade them from proclaiming the gospel in certain regions because he was leading them to Macedonia. When thinking about evangelism, we often assume it's all about quantity. We're tempted to evaluate evangelism by how many conversations we are having with people, so we indiscriminately try to slip a gospel presentation into every conversation or to wallpaper the world with gospel tracts. (We don't want to be too critical of this approach; it's certainly better than never speaking of Jesus!) But perhaps a better way to engage in evangelism is to focus on listening to where the Spirit might be leading us, to what he wants us to say, and to whom he wants us to speak. Just like he called Paul to Macedonia to preach the gospel, the Spirit will lead us to where he's working *if we listen.* We need to stop thinking about evangelism as "bringing people to God" and realize that God is bringing *us* to people instead, already working in their lives and inviting us to harmonize with the Spirit.

For example, one day our friends Delano and Brian were having lunch at a restaurant and sensed that the Spirit wanted them to pay for another customer's lunch. They asked Jennifer, a server whom they knew because they were regulars at the restaurant, to bring them the customer's check and put it on Brian's debit card anonymously. Jennifer was surprised and delighted to participate in this act of kindness. However, about fifteen minutes later, she returned to Delano and Brian's table with tears in her eyes, visibly shaken.

She explained that the customer whose meal they paid for had just come from the doctor's office, where she had been told she had cancer. When the customer found out that the meal was paid for, she burst into tears and told the server that this was an affirmation that God loved her and was taking care of her. The customer told Jennifer (who wasn't a believer) about her faith in Jesus even in the face of death.

Jennifer asked Delano and Brian how they knew that the customer needed to be cheered up. They told her that they had never seen the woman before but that they had prayed at the beginning of their meal and sensed that God wanted them to pay for someone else's lunch. In that moment Jennifer saw the power of God and broke down in tears. She was so awestruck that she told many of her coworkers.

Over the next few weeks Jennifer and several other servers had questions about Jesus that they asked Delano whenever he came to the restaurant. Between bringing fish tacos to customers and mopping floors, they returned to Delano's table to discuss the biggest questions of life.

Delano sensed that the Spirit had given him a powerful gospel analogy by guiding him and Brian to pay for that customer's meal. He saw the situation as an analogy of God's grace and told Jennifer that, just as he and Brian had paid for another person's meal because of love, Jesus had died to bring us to a feast with God. His death was based on God's love rather than our merit. Jennifer was again deeply moved as she heard about the lavish grace of the God who had already paid for her sin and wanted to feast with her.

Shortly after this encounter Jennifer moved away, and Delano and Brian lost touch with her. They don't know if she ever came to believe in Jesus. However, they are confident that the Spirit was at work in her life and had showed them how to proclaim the gospel to her on that day. A moment that powerful couldn't have been orchestrated apart from the Spirit. When Delano and Brian stepped into the restaurant, they wanted to participate in the spoken word of God's mission. They could've tried to approach the situation in their own power and wisdom by handing out tracts to all the customers or trying to force a conversation. However, they chose the path of grace rather than grit, the power of the Spirit rather than human impotence.

If we want to participate in the verbal aspects of mission, we need to start by listening. There's a common saying that tells us we should listen twice as much as we speak, because God gave us two ears and one mouth. There's some wisdom to that statement. If we want to speak well, we need to listen well. We need to listen to the Spirit's work in the world and join him in what he's already doing. By relying on the guidance and power of the Spirit, we have the privilege of opening our mouths and singing the gospel to those who need to hear it.

7

LISTENING

Finding Your Place in God's Symphony

The Musical Instrument Museum (MIM) in Phoenix, Arizona, contains the largest and most varied collection of musical instruments in the world. It contains fifteen thousand different instruments from more than two hundred countries and territories—from a slender banjo-like instrument from China called a *sanxian* to its fatter cousin the *saraswati veena* from India. They have a Puerto Rican *guiro*, a *phet banam* from Nepal, a Turkish *ud*, and an ancient bone flute from Central Asia.

For most visitors these instruments are mysterious. Based on their shape and design, most people are able to tell that they are musical instruments of some kind. However, the particular sound they were intended to make and the technique that's required to make that sound are not easily discerned. If you were invited to learn how to play one of these mysterious instruments, how would you begin to figure out how?

You would probably start by observing how it had been made. You would pay attention to the materials and design and compare it to similar instruments you'd encountered. You would pick it up and experiment. Through trial and error you would see what kinds of sounds it makes. By attempting to play the instrument, you would experience some of its possibilities and limitations. You might try to find people who had played that instrument before and ask them to help you. But what if you could somehow get to know the *maker* of the instrument and understand their intention for it? With that information and enough time and attention, you could learn how to bring that instrument back to life, to make the beautiful music it was created for.

In the symphony of mission we are God's instruments. He's made each person and each community of believers to add a unique sound to the songs of stewardship, service, and spoken word. The process of discerning our role in God's symphonic mission isn't that different from figuring out how to play one of the instruments at the MIM.

First, we need to draw near to our maker and listen to his voice. Unlike the inanimate instruments at the MIM, we can intimately know our creator, his mission, and the purpose for which he created us. However, much like the curators of the MIM, God leaves a degree of mystery to our callings, not typically speaking to us through a voice from heaven but inviting us instead to experiment and explore, to seek counsel from others, and to observe the unique way that God has made us as we work out our part in his music.

The aim of this chapter is to help both individuals and communities discern their roles in the symphony of mission. We've been invited into God's grand symphony and called to play the songs of stewardship, service, and spoken word, but figuring out where God wants us to focus our time, talents, and treasures can be a challenge. Strings, woodwinds, brass, percussion? So many instruments—which do we choose? With so many problems in the world, which one should we engage first? We need to figure out what kind of instrument God has made us to be and the particular sounds he's called us to play.

This chapter gives a brief overview of the doctrine of vocation, a framework that helps readers discern the types of good works God created each of us to do by reflecting on where their gifts and passions can be used to address the pain of the world. It concludes by providing seven nuggets of wisdom for finding one's place in God's mission.

What Is a Calling?

The word *vocation* is derived from the Latin word *vocare*, which means "calling." It connotes being divinely ordained for a specific task. Though many of us may think of a calling as a personal quest for truly satisfying work, a biblical understanding of calling starts with God rather than with us. He calls us to join his good work. As Tim Keller says, "A job is a vocation only if someone else calls you to do it for them rather than for yourself. And so our work can be a calling only if it is reimagined as a mission of service to something beyond merely our own interests. . . . Thinking of work mainly as a means of self-fulfillment and self-realization slowly crushes a person."[1] Calling isn't primarily about serving ourselves but about glorifying God and loving our neighbors. It's not about "finding" ourselves but about losing ourselves in the worship of God and then finding the good works that we were created to do. In Scripture we see three dimensions of calling: the missional calling, the occupational calling, and the vocational calling. First, God calls a people to himself and to his mission. Second, he calls us to general good works and to faithfulness to the responsibilities he's placed before us. Third, he calls each of us to do the particular good works for which he's created us.

Missional calling: the identity we have been given. The most important aspect of calling is the call to be reconciled to God through the work of Christ (Rom. 1:6) and then to join his ministry of reconciliation (2 Cor. 5:17–21). It's to be adopted as a child of God by grace (Eph. 1:4–5) and then to join the family business of holistic mission (Eph. 1:10). To be a follower of Christ is to join his mission. To be chosen is to be sent. Throughout Scripture we see that the doctrine of *election* (another word for calling) is connected to the doctrine of mission. God chose the people of Israel so that they would be a light to the nations and a conduit of blessing. The same is true in the calling of his church. We are called and chosen to join the family business of mission.

Occupational calling: the work we must do. This is the broadest aspect of our calling. It's the general call to work and to be responsible for what God has set in front of us. Our "occupations" aren't unique to our personalities, gifts, and abilities but are the general things that we are called to do in God's world: pay bills, steward property, care for children, be generous to the poor, pursue justice, and obey all that God has commanded. This is the work that we *must* do because it's a part of our human responsibility. It's the general human calling to live a faithful, fruitful, and holy life by the power of the Spirit, but it isn't necessarily distinct to who we are.

Vocational calling: the work we were made to do. Despite the rhetoric many of us heard as children, we can't be anything we want to be when we grow up. God has made each of us to be a certain kind of person, uniquely equipped for particular good works. Before the creation of the world, God composed the symphony of mission and wrote a few particular parts for each of us to perform. Our vocation is the most specific aspect of calling; it is the call to engage in those particular good works for which God created us. Paul says, "For we are God's handiwork, created in Christ Jesus to do good works, which God prepared in advance for us to do" (Eph. 2:10). The rich wording

---

1. Timothy Keller, *Every Good Endeavor: Connecting Your Work to God's Work* (New York: Penguin Group, 2012), 2.

of this passage describes us as miniature masterpieces crafted by God for specific good works. The often-quoted verses that precede this passage (Eph. 2:8–9) answer the question of how we are saved: by God's grace not our good works. However, verse 10 tells us what we are saved *for*: the particular good works that God has planned for us. The word for *handiwork* in this passage is the Greek word *poiēma*, from which we get our English word *poetry*. Just as a poet deliberately labors over each word, God has deliberately shaped each aspect of our lives with intentionality and nuance. He has deliberately assembled the particular mix of experiences, personality traits, passions, and abilities that form our lives for the sake of his mission.

But how do we know which good works God created us for? How do we know what we were made to do? Where should we sit and what instruments should we play in God's symphony?

To understand the answers to these questions, we must listen to God, the great composer and conductor of the symphony. The first way to listen to the Spirit is through prayer and reading the Word in community. The Spirit gives us wisdom for how to live in light of the Word. Occasionally in Scripture and in the world today, we see God speaking in a clear, unmistakable way, giving people specific instructions for what he wants them to do in specific circumstances. I believe that still happens today, even though many of us haven't experienced it.

The typical experience of listening to God's call comes from listening to your life while living in community, paying attention to the unique way God has made you and the circumstances and opportunities he's placed in front of you. When we look at how something has been designed, we get a sense of the maker's intent. We know that shovels were intended for gardening rather than scooping food off our plates. The design of a pillow indicates that the maker wanted you to rest on it rather than use it as a wallet. The same is true for human beings. As we look at how God designed us and sovereignly orchestrated our circumstances, we see what kind of instruments he made us to be.

The rest of this chapter will focus on helping you reflect on your life. You can discern the good works you were created to do by paying attention to the way the great Composer has uniquely crafted your passions, gifts, burdens, opportunities, and circumstances.

Vocational Sweet Spot

The vocational sweet spot is a tool we've used to help people identify their callings. It helps people listen to their lives by identifying four categories that

Figure 7.1

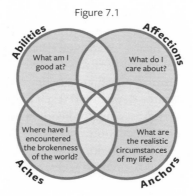

are typically good indicators of what God has created them for. There are many versions of this framework, but the one found in Amy Sherman's book *Kingdom Calling* is adapted here.[2]

The categories are:

Abilities: What are you good at?

Affections: What do you care about?

Aches: Where do you encounter the brokenness of the world?

Anchors: What are the realistic circumstances of your life?

Frederick Buechner writes, "The place that God calls you to is the place where your deep gladness and the world's deep hunger meet."[3] To identify the good works you were created for is to reflect on the things that give you great joy (affections) and see how they can be used to address some aspect of the world's brokenness (aches). For example, if someone finds great joy in teaching, they should look for ways to use that gift to push back against the effects of the fall. They may choose to teach social studies or civics to promote better political discourse. They may choose to display the sacrificial love of the cross by building a career in a struggling school. They might become a church planter and teach Scripture to a world that desperately needs to know God. All of these are ways for someone who is passionate about teaching to engage the world's problems.

Buechner's framework invites us to identify the overlap between our affections and the world's aches. Our framework includes two other categories:

2. Amy Sherman, *Kingdom Calling: Vocational Stewardship for the Common Good* (Downers Grove, IL: InterVarsity, 2011), 107–8.
3. Frederick Buechner, *Wishful Thinking: A Seeker's ABC* (San Francisco: HarperOne, 1993), 119.

abilities and anchors. Our abilities function as clues to our calling. By identifying the unique gifts that God has woven into our personalities and the skills we have acquired through experience, we are better able to discern the good works we were created to do. For example, if the hypothetical teachers mentioned above were more skilled in analyzing literature than explaining mathematics, this might be a good indicator they should teach English instead of algebra. God gave us particular strengths to use for his glory and the good of others.

Then there are anchors, the circumstances God has sovereignly brought into our lives that limit what we can do, including physical limitations, relational responsibilities, financial circumstances, educational credentials, and geographical realities.

This tool is not a mathematical equation that will automatically calculate your calling once you enter the data. Rather, each of these categories can function as a lens to help you see what God is doing and find clues about your calling. Or think of these categories as headphones to help you listen to your life. A degree of mystery will always remain when we ask questions of vocation, because God wants us to relate to him as children who draw near to our Father in dependence rather than as contractors carrying out a work order. Without a degree of mystery and uncertainty, there wouldn't be any faith. Think of these categories as ear-training exercises to help you hear the voice of the good Shepherd.

Abilities: What Am I Good At?

What are you good at? If you are able to answer this question honestly and humbly, you are well on your way to understanding the good works for which you were created. Reflecting about our vocation can create the perfect conditions for either dishonesty or pride, and this presents a challenge. We are often dishonest with ourselves when we try to identify our strengths. Rather than accurately assessing our lives, many of us have a subconscious bias toward the strengths that we perceive as the most important. If you are in a church that emphasizes preaching over other gifts, you may be tempted to see preaching as one of your strengths. If you live in the urban core of a large city, you may be tempted to esteem entrepreneurship over working as a craftsperson. This may seem a harmless bias, but it's not. It wastes time and withholds God-given gifts from the world. We need to assess our strengths honestly, without filtering them through the biases of our contexts.

Furthermore, when we spend time identifying our strengths, we're tempted to be prideful. Rather than being filled with gratitude, we're often filled with visions of grandeur. And pride can show itself in another more subtle way:

when we refuse to acknowledge our strengths, we implicitly show that we believe human strengths have a human origin. But if these gifts come from God, the giver of all talents, experiences, relationships, and faculties, it's not prideful to acknowledge them; it's just being honest. However, this whole process should be engaged in a posture of prayer. Confession and thanksgiving are vital practices that allow us to answer this question with honesty and humility.

How can you begin to reflect on this question? It can be as simple as sitting down and making a list of the abilities you have and how you have seen them displayed in your life. Ask questions like, Along with my natural gifts, what experiences and training have I received? God is the giver of both gifts and experience. He crafted the uniqueness of your personality, and he is the author of history. He uses many methods to equip us for his mission.

If you find this question challenging, here are a few exercises that might help:

1. Write a biography of fruitfulness. Spend some time reflecting on each stage of your life and identify the things you are best at. Ask yourself,
   What's my first memory of being good at something?
   What was I good at as a young child?
   In elementary school?
   As a teenager?
   In my 20s, 30s, 40s, and so on?
   After you've filled a few pages with examples of fruitfulness from different times of life, spend some time making observations. What are the common themes that show up over and over again? Since God has made you in a unique way for the sake of unique good works, you should be able to see expressions of that uniqueness in all the periods of your life.

2. Seek many counselors. Often those we are closest to know us better than we know ourselves and can function as a mirror to help us see how God has made us. "Plans fail for lack of counsel, but with many advisers they succeed" (Prov. 15:22). This isn't a promise that all failure will be averted if we have many counselors, but it does speak to the general pattern of God's creation: wisdom and discernment come through community.

   However, sometimes there's a downside to asking those who know us best. They often know us so well that they know what we want to hear and may not speak with the kind of candor we need. Furthermore, people tend to view us through the lens of who we were when we first got to know them. For example, there's a man on our team whom I met when he was a twenty-year-old intern. Recently I realized that I was still seeing him through that lens even though he's now a twenty-eight-year-old pastor with Christlike character and tremendous leadership ability. Any advice I gave over the past few years was probably skewed by my own false perspective.

It's often wise to seek counsel from someone you don't know too well, such as a pastor, spiritual director, or career coach, since they are typically less biased and not afraid to speak with candor.

3. Tests and assessments. There are also many tools and assessments that can help us reflect on our abilities. Some of these include Strengthsfinder, the Myers-Briggs Type Indicator, and the Disc Assessment. Along with other input, these tools can help us reflect on who God has made us to be and give us language to describe our strengths, gifts, and abilities. Of course, we should neither build our identities on the results of these assessments nor be afraid of them. They are simply tools to help us with self-reflection.

Affections: What Do I Care About?

Another important category to pay attention to is your emotions. What do you enjoy most? Our uniqueness is often displayed in our preferences. Some people love to work with their hands while others prefer to analyze with their minds. Some work best in teams while others prefer to work alone. Some can spend a whole afternoon reading books while others find their deepest joy in conversation. We might see these things as trivial preferences, but they can be strong indicators of how God made us. If God created us for particular good works, it makes sense that he would draw our attention to those works through a deep sense of delight.

Our negative emotions can also be strong indicators of calling. What makes you angry? What makes you sad? Some of us are inexplicably moved by some issues and not others. Why do you get so angry about systemic injustice but not about the struggle of single mothers? It might be because God has made you extra sensitive to one particular issue. Even our sinful or immature responses can be indicators of the unique perspective we have on life. For example, I know someone who hates disorganization and used to be quick to criticize churches, businesses, and homes that lacked order. When she was young, her critiques were harsh and personal; they lacked the fruit of the Spirit. As she grew in Christ and sought to put that sin to death, she found that she still sees disorganization with crystal clarity, but rather than giving harsh critiques and ascribing ill motives to others, she now sees those things as opportunities to serve in the unique way God has created her. With increased maturity and growth in Christlikeness, she has been used to display God's image and Christ's love through the order she brings to disorder.

How about you? If you had a free day, how would you spend it? What were your first memories of deeply enjoying something? What about the other seasons of your life? And what do your negative emotions tell you about the way God created you?

Aches: Where Do I Encounter the Brokenness of the World?

Most people are seeking work that satisfies them and allows them to use their strengths. There's nothing wrong with that; in fact, it's a good start. However, if we really want to participate in God's mission, the next step is to identify ways that we can use our gifts to engage some aspect of the world's brokenness, to pit our abilities and affections against the aches of the world.

We are surrounded by brokenness. In all likelihood there are people within a few square miles of where you are sitting right now who have cancer cells growing inside their bodies. Others are filing divorce papers. Others are lonely. Still others are typing racist comments on Facebook. Right now, as you read these words, struggling teachers are writing their resignation letters, and struggling high school students are resigning their dreams of college. Streams are being polluted, terrorists are plotting, false gospels are being advanced, children are being abducted, and parents are weeping.

How should we, as limited people, engage a world with seemingly limitless pain? Unspeakable brokenness has punctured the lungs of the world, and with every headline, we hear the world gasp for breath. The impact of the fall has caused injuries that affect every society, every home, and every individual. The world is hemorrhaging because of sin.

How should we respond to a world with so many wounds? Which injuries should we seek to mend with our limited strength and ability? We want to be good Samaritans who help the wounded strangers, but on this road it seems that *everyone* is wounded, including us! We are finite people who lack the time, talent, money, and influence to care for all of the world's wounds. We must make choices. To choose to be a nurse is to refrain from being a teacher. To give one hundred dollars to alleviate poverty is to refuse a one hundred dollar donation to end sex trafficking. We are surrounded by a world that desperately needs good news proclaimed and demonstrated through good works, but how do we decide what to focus on?

One of the great challenges of discerning our callings is finding the place where our skills and abilities intersect with the world's needs. Steven Garber, the author of *Visions of Vocation*, provides insight into how to narrow our focus, encouraging us to be attentive to the experiences of our lives. He says that one of the hardest and most important questions to ask is, "Knowing what you know, what are you going to do?"[4] In other words, you have become implicated by your experiences, especially your experiences with the brokenness of the world. We have all been through specific seasons of pain that have given us close encounters with specific effects of sin. Those encounters aren't necessarily random; they may be God's way of drawing attention to a specific place, people, or problem.

For example, I have a friend, Jessi, who is extremely intelligent, but as a child she struggled to read. It would take her hours to finish the same homework assignments that would take mere minutes for her classmates. Her struggles in school caused her to drop out at the age of sixteen and get her GED, because she realized that she had some learning disabilities that the school had never noticed or helped her with. But eventually she decided to go to college and study special education, and she completed her degree in just a few years, ahead of schedule. There's a beautiful irony in this, that the woman who struggled in school would choose, out of all available majors, to study education. But that's the mysteriously brilliant way God works through our pain. Jessi knows what it's like to struggle to learn, to have a mind that works differently, to be treated as "less than" by classmates and teachers. Knowing that pain and experiencing those struggles are what have equipped her to be a great teacher to children with special needs. Her struggle is what God used to draw her attention to their particular pain.

This is true for many people. Someone may become a nurse because he has sat next to the hospital beds of loved ones, or a manager because she has seen the damage of manipulative leadership, or a project manager because he has experienced a chaotic life. God is the one who "comforts us in all our troubles, so that we can comfort those in any trouble with the comfort we ourselves receive from God" (2 Cor. 1:4). The purposes behind our sufferings are too big and complex for us to understand fully, but we know that when God comforts us in our pain, he builds empathy and equips us to be his conduits of comfort to others. What aspects of the brokenness of the world have you encountered? These aspects might be clues to what you have been uniquely equipped to engage.

Generally speaking, we are most fruitful when we are actively engaging the problems that we've experienced for ourselves. Vocational faithfulness goes

---

4. Steven Garber, *Visions of Vocation: Common Grace for the Common Good* (Downers Grove, IL: InterVarsity, 2014), 162.

beyond just enjoying our work (although that is a good thing); it involves the intentional use of our skills and passions to push back against the thorns and thistles of sin, as a sign of what's to come when Jesus restores all things.

So, knowing what you've known, and having experienced what you've experienced, what are you going to do?

Anchors: What Are the Realistic Circumstances of My Life?

Many modern frameworks intended to help answer the question "What am I supposed to do with my life?" tend to be idealistic. They often say to "follow your dreams" without giving much attention to the responsibilities and realistic circumstances of one's life. They don't account for the limitations that come with chronic pain, the needs of young children, community, or level of education. Pursuing a sense of calling without giving thought to the real circumstances of life leads either to neglect (of family, health, friendships, etc.) or to disillusionment, when you conclude that these limiting circumstances are unfair obstacles that prevent you from doing what you were made to do.

These things are anchors. They are the real, often limiting circumstances that God sovereignly brings into your life. They could be physical, relational, financial, or any number of other limiting factors, such as chronic pain, a lack of academic credentials, the need to care for elderly parents or young children, or a lack of financial resources. These things might be trials that display God's power as he provides for you in unexpected and inexplicable ways. God could certainly heal chronic pain or provide an anonymous check. Sometimes he provides by taking away our limitations—but sometimes he provides by giving them.

Limitations, or anchors, may actually be indicators of the good works God has called us to. They bring focus to our lives by eliminating some of the potential options that our abilities, affections, and the world's aches open up to us. For example, a hypothetical teacher may be caring for elderly parents and young children. His highest level of education might be a bachelor's degree. These circumstances seem to take some options, such as teaching at a university in Dubai, off the table. Dubai's cost of living is too high for a large family, and the climate would be taxing on his elderly parents. His lack of a graduate degree would also probably prevent him from teaching at a university. Although God has the power to change the university standards and level of pay so that our hypothetical teacher could work in Dubai—and it takes faith to pray for God's provision in those situations—these limiting circumstances might just be God's provision, a way for our teacher to focus on the needs of the neighborhood where God has already embedded him. Circumstances often function as anchors to keep us from drifting in just any direction. They keep us rooted in particular places and focused on particular things.

We see this in the ministry of the apostle Paul. Though he wanted to take the gospel beyond Rome, there's no indication that he ever made it as far as Spain (which was his ultimate goal). God brought anchors into Paul's life, including arrest and imprisonment. This man, the ultimate missionary, could have taken the gospel to more unreached peoples, but he was stuck in jail. From a human perspective this seems like a waste. However, it was from that Roman prison cell that Paul wrote the letters to the Ephesians, Philippians, and Colossians, and to Philemon. As he was writing what he thought was merely personal correspondence, the Holy Spirit was guiding him into composing the very Scripture that's read each week by Christians all over the world, in places like Canada, Brazil, Nigeria, and China—places that Paul didn't even know existed. That's a *long* way beyond Rome!

God also brought the mysterious "thorn in the flesh" to Paul (2 Cor. 12:7–10). We don't know exactly what this thorn was—blindness, an aggressive adversary, chronic pain from former persecution—but we do know that it was a limiting circumstance that Paul wanted God to remove. Yet it turned out to be a gift that bound Paul to the freedom of depending on God's grace.

What are your anchors? What are the real circumstances of your life?

For whom are you responsible—children, spouse, older parents, employees, people in your community?

What are your financial circumstances (salary, debts, assets)?

What opportunities has God put in front of you?

What have you already committed to (contracts, church membership, a mortgage)?

What are your physical limitations? What are the physical limitations of your loved ones?

What kind of credentials do you have, and how do they limit you?

In what ways does your "place" (citizenship, language, etc.) impose limits?

It's important to acknowledge these things. God could eliminate them from your life, or he could call you to persevere through them. Either way, it's never wise to ignore them or shrug them off. You should count the cost and have a clear sense of calling as you move forward. However, these limiting factors might just be what God has brought into your life to focus your attention on something local and immediate in a particular neighborhood, industry, or issue.

Putting It Together

The vocational sweet spot isn't an infallible equation that will automatically result in clarity. Rather, it's a tool intended to help one think through some important aspects of life and how one might fit within the symphony of mission. No one can do everything; God has created each of us for particular good works, to be a particular kind of instrument that plays the music of the gospel for a listening world. By being attentive to your own real abilities, affections, and anchors and seeing how they overlap with the world's aches, you are being attentive to God's work in your life.

As you reflect on your vocational sweet spot, you may notice that it doesn't give you a specific career or cause. It's not rigid; a variety of good things could fit within it. The purpose of this reflection is to give you a broad understanding of the good works you were created to engage in. Set aside some time to work through these questions; perhaps take a half-day retreat or an hour each day for a week to prayerfully think through your vocational sweet spot. Do this in consultation with your community, especially those people who will be totally honest with you.

But once you have a broad sense of the good works you were created to do, how do you choose among them? Listen to God's Word and the Spirit through prayer. Move forward with your best sense of either God's specific guidance or the freedom he's given you to move forward in faith. Know that you are fallible and might just distort what you sense God is saying for selfish motives. Spend time seeking wisdom and counsel from those who know and love you.

Nuggets of Vocational Wisdom

In addition to listening to the counsel of others, it's important to seek out people in the body of Christ who have gained wisdom as they've pursued their own vocational faithfulness. Therefore, this chapter concludes with some nuggets of wisdom from others. These teachers range from thoughtful leaders to faithful servants in the marketplace to children. We hope these words of wisdom will provoke your thinking about your own place within the symphony.

Your Calling Is Not (Just) about You

Self-reflection is good. It's wise to spend time reflecting on your life and calling, identifying the unique ways God crafted your personality, experiences, gifts, and abilities. However, the potential danger is a drift toward self-absorption and selfishness. Self-reflection can be the seed of both fruitful work and narcissism. The latter happens when we think the ultimate purpose of our vocation is to find fulfilling and satisfying work. It's not.

Satisfaction can be a wonderful benefit of our calling and often serves to confirm that calling, but it isn't the main thing. The main thing is to love God by serving others. We're meant to wash our neighbor's feet, not to soak in a bubble bath of self-admiration.

The life of George Washington Carver is a great example of vocational faithfulness for the sake of others. He was a brilliant botanist and inventor who loved to learn, spend time outdoors, and make new things. These were his passions and gifts, and he saw them as things that should be not only enjoyed by him but also used for the sake of others. He deliberately chose to focus his research and innovation on developing agricultural technologies that could be used by former slaves and so empower them to thrive as farmers. Carver deeply enjoyed his work and often stopped to smell the flowers (literally). But he went on to study those flowers and found ways to draw out their potential. He cultivated plants that would be used for food, paper, soap, and paint and so contributed to the flourishing of the most vulnerable people in his world.

Don't Get Trampled by the Herd Mentality

Entrepreneurship. Community development. Urban ministry. AIDS in Africa. Refugees. Urban farming. Sex trafficking.

These are all examples of missional fads and focuses that have swept across the church over the past several years. Each new wave comes with a call to drop whatever you are doing and focus on the new issue of the day. You are presented with statistics, invited to conferences, and shown compelling videos with a deep-voiced narrator who tells you why this new cause is actually the most important issue in the world. Packaged inside this pitch is a not-so-subtle message: you will waste your life and contribute to the suffering of others if you don't join this particular cause right now.

Each time a new issue gains momentum, hordes of people drop whatever they were focused on to embrace the new cause. But this often results in decreased funding and a lack of personnel for the old cause unless the next tear-jerking video shifts the momentum back the other way. This herd mentality creates a lot of motion but very little movement.

Why do we bounce from cause to cause like a ping-pong ball? Sometimes it is because we have short attention spans and perseverance is not highly valued today. But much of the time it's because we are trying to find meaningful work in the world, whether through our employment or as volunteers. We think that our lives will be important if we are involved in one of the most important issues of the day. But this mentality is toxic. It elevates our status to that of quasi-saviors, while treating the issue like a product for our consumption, an elixir for significance.

What's wrong with working on the 149th most urgent issue in the world? What's wrong with living in the 83rd most influential city? God can raise up workers for all 148 other urgent issues just like he's raised you up for number 149. He has workers for Manhattan, just as he has workers for your hometown. We shouldn't ask what the most important issue is but should ask what God wants *us* to do in the place where he has placed us. How can we use our gifts and abilities to address the brokenness right in front of us? You cannot change the world, but you *can* choose to change tires and diapers. You don't have control over the impact your work will have, but you can make the decision to wake up each day as a servant who faithfully cultivates a little corner of God's garden to bless the people, places, and problems he's put in front of you. Your work may be forgotten in history, but it will never be forgotten by your Father.

A great example of this kind of faithfulness is seen in Andy, whom we mentioned in a previous chapter. He has been an insurance agent for thirty years. Although his job is more an occupation (work he must do) than a vocation (work he was made to do), he's remained faithful and intentional in it for three decades. He seeks to do his work with excellence, seeing it as extending God's protection for people when things go wrong. He writes good insurance policies that push back against the fall. His office is located in an economically distressed area, and he has intentionally rooted himself in that community.

Andy is faithful in his work as an insurance agent, but he's also a truly gifted evangelist and mentor. These seem to be the unique things God created him to do. Although he doesn't get paid to do these things, he's found ways to exercise his vocation (calling) outside of his employment. One of the main ways he does this is through a running club he started called the Bounding Moosen. Despite the silly name, there's some serious intentionality connected to this club. It pushes back against the fall by providing community amid the loneliness of the world and healthy exercise in a world of technological disembodiment. Furthermore, he's able to use his gifts of mentoring and evangelism during the club's weekly times together. Many people have come to see Andy as a father figure and through those interactions have come to know God as Father through the work of Christ.

Perhaps the most impressive trait that shines through Andy, both as an insurance agent and as a Bounding Moosen, is his faithfulness. He's heard dozens of pitches to get involved with other things, but he remains focused on the tasks God has put in front of him. While he cares about those other causes and supports them as he is able, he is undeterred from the specific good work God prepared in advance for him to do.

We do not *find* meaning in our work; instead, we *bring* meaning to our work. The lens of the gospel story allows us to see the significance of all of life because the whole world belongs to God. If you seek to display the glory of the Father through wise stewardship, the love of Christ through sacrificial service, and the power of the Spirit through the spoken word, then you have entered into the symphony of God's mission, which can be performed in any place and among all people. Your days are not wasted when they are spent cultivating the lives of a few children and serving a dozen neighbors on Loma Vista Drive. To work in middle management in middle America is a sacred task. It is not plain vanilla; it is a richly flavored life, soaked in the essence of gospel and filled with more meaning than you could ever imagine. Whether you're starting a business or starting a truck, living in Beijing, China, or Beeville, Texas, you have the opportunity to glorify God, love your neighbors, and care for the world. The only wasted life is the one spent chasing idols, even the idol of significance in the temple of service.

Articulate a Clear Vision for Your Life, but Write It in Pencil

In Matt Perman's book *What's Best Next?*, he encourages people to develop a clear "life goal," a vision statement that articulates their aim in life. He says, "You need to have an overarching, passionate, God-centered aim to your life—an overarching goal and message that flows from your mission and directs the priorities of your life."[5]

Essentially a life goal is a written statement that articulates your sense of calling. It provides focus in a world flooded with distraction. Whenever we are confronted with new opportunities or decisions in life—career changes, relocation, new volunteer opportunities—we can evaluate them by looking through the lens of our life goal or vision statement.

When we read Scripture, we certainly see a precedent for this kind of focus. Moses was dedicated to leading God's people. Esther was focused on protecting God's people. Solomon passionately pursued wisdom. Paul was committed to bringing the gospel to the gentiles. This clarity of calling guided their lives and shaped their decisions.

We also see this focus throughout history. Martin Luther King Jr. was one of the most gifted leaders in American history and could have engaged in any

5. Matt Perman, *What's Best Next? How the Gospel Transforms the Way Things Get Done* (Grand Rapids: Zondervan, 2014), 178.

number of issues, but he was implicated by his gifts and experience and so focused on civil rights. C. S. Lewis could have pursued any number of careers with his brilliant mind, but he focused on his gift of writing, even at the cost of more prestigious roles. Mother Teresa had the ears of the world's most influential people in the halls of power but chose to mend the wounds of the most vulnerable on the streets of Calcutta. As we follow in the footsteps of these people, we should consider imitating their clarity of vision and focus.

If you are unsure what your life goal should be, Perman encourages you to start with these two questions:

> What would I do if I had all the money I needed and could do whatever I wanted?
>
> What would I do if I could do only one thing for the next three years?

Once you have a sense of vision, try to articulate it in a succinct, memorable way. Write it down and look at it every day. Make it your screen saver. Incorporate it into a piece of art. Memorize it. Do whatever you can to keep it in front of you. Use it as a filter for the big decisions of life and the small decisions involved in planning your day.

This practice can be very helpful, but it does come with a few dangers. First, all good things (especially those we enjoy most) can move from being means of worship to objects of worship. John Calvin referred to the human heart as an "idol factory,"[6] and when not attended to, the heart can turn anything into the primary focus of our lives. Our life goal should be our secondary focus—only Jesus is primary. When these priorities are disordered, they result in the neglect of other important facets of life (family, neighbors, health, fellowship) and leave empty the parts of our souls that God alone can satisfy.

Second, you should (metaphorically speaking) write down your vision *in pencil*. The reality is that circumstances and assignments often change in the seasons of life. Furthermore, we tend to know God, ourselves, and the world better over time. A deeper sense of vocation often develops with deeper maturity. Your life goal should be evaluated and edited over time, not written in stone.

Third, don't be self-absorbed. In your attempt to find focus, don't turn your heart away from the rest of the world, treating other areas of life as less significant or unworthy of your time. Leave enough margin to support, encourage, and understand what else is going on in the world, especially

6. John Calvin, *Institutes of the Christian Religion*, trans. Ford Lewis Battles, ed. John T. McNeill (Philadelphia: Westminster, 1960), 108 (1.11.8).

among your family, friends, church, and community. Weep over Aleppo. Give some money to a friend's nonprofit. Understand what's on the ballot. Pray for a young church plant. Write an encouraging note to an excellent teacher. Create enough space within your own vocation to play at least a marginal role in the vocations of others. Give about 80 percent of your time, money, resources, and effort to your life goal; then leave about 20 percent available to support others. You need people, and they need you.

Employment That Fits Your Vocational Sweet Spot Is a Privilege Not a Promise

Imagine going to the grocery store to buy a loaf of bread. As you are checking out, you realize that the packaging is broken. You tell the cashier, and with warmth and joy she immediately finds you a new loaf. Having received the best customer service you have ever seen, you decide to ask her name and questions about her life. She says her name is Shirin and she's from Pakistan. Unsure of the region of Pakistan she's from, you ask what language she speaks. She replies that she speaks five languages, but Urdu is her native tongue. As you inquire further, she tells you she came to the United States because she had to flee persecution. When you ask what she did in Pakistan, she tells you that she was a doctor.

You ask why she doesn't practice medicine in the United States, and she simply states that her credentials don't transfer. She has to provide for her family and therefore can't afford to repeat medical school. She plans on becoming a registered nurse one day, but her current responsibilities don't allow her to seek the kind of employment that uses her skills and passions to meet the world's pain. However, with her medical background and the many languages she speaks, she's able to provide an important service to the world. She devotes her free time to volunteering for a local refugee resettlement agency, serving other refugees and helping them navigate the medical system in America.

It is a privilege to be employed in a job that enables our gifts to be a blessing to the world, but for many of us, the responsibilities and realities of life often prevent us from being paid to do the work that fits perfectly within our vocational sweet spot. Like Shirin, many of us will have to find ways to pursue our vocations outside of normal work hours. Artists may need to make financial statements on the weekdays and artistic statements on the weekends. Some might have to plan meetings during the day and plant gardens at night. This is the reality of life. It's not our birthright to have a job that makes perfect use of our gifts to make an impact on the world.

Should we try to pursue a job within our vocational sweet spot? Absolutely! We should work hard to find a way. However, this might be a slow process, and it might never happen at all. If there is some overlap between our official employment and our passions and abilities, we should rejoice, be grateful, and make the most of the opportunity. If that opportunity never comes, we should follow the example of Shirin. She found other ways to employ her gifts for the life of the world: as a volunteer and through informal relationships. While she did this, she treated her job at the grocery store as a sacred opportunity to serve God and her neighbors through excellent work.

There's No Back Door to Eden

Sin has brutalized the whole world. It is present in every country, city, neighborhood, industry, and human heart. No matter where we focus our missional efforts, we will encounter hardships and suffering. Everywhere we look, we find idols whose brutality would make Pharaoh blush, injustices that tangle and torment God's good world, and injuries untended and festering. All of life is filled with thorns and thistles. However, some people interpret the hardships of work and mission as indicators that they are engaged in the wrong kind of work. They say, "I'm just not passionate about it." Or, "If I were really called to this, it would come a lot easier." Or, "I'm just looking for work that I would truly enjoy." It's not wrong to look for work that's fruitful, meaningful, productive, enjoyable, and free of pain and complexity. The problem is that you will never find it—at least not completely—until Jesus returns and restores all things.

When people are looking for perfect and painless work, they are looking for Eden, the shalom we were meant to experience in God's good creation. Unfortunately, there's no back door to Eden. We will not find perfect shalom until Jesus makes all things new. The desire for such things is right and good, but it will not be satisfied in a new type of work, career, or calling. It can ultimately only be found in the coming reign of Christ.

The presence of pain and hardship is not necessarily an indicator that you should move on to greener pastures. Their presence might be the very reason God planted you in that field. Perhaps he put you there to trim some thorns and thistles as a harbinger of the future flourishing that he will bring to the whole earth.

Do Something

How much time have individuals spent pondering the question, What should I do with my life? How many thousands of hours have small groups spent devising plans to serve the city and debating the merits of various areas of missional focus? Beware of the paralysis of analysis! Months (sometimes years!) pass as churches hammer out the perfect strategic plan for missional engagement. Reflection is good, but it's important not to wait until you have everything figured out to start doing something.

And action itself often creates the best context for reflection. It keeps you oriented toward the Other rather than turning service into a self-centered activity. It provides hands-on experience that helps you understand God, yourself, and the complexities of the world. It reminds you that there's a world outside your head. Whether you are planning as an individual or as a member of a community, if you find yourself unsure of how God wants you specifically to participate in his mission, just start doing *something*—and keep listening.

Our friend Matteo didn't know what God wanted him to do with his life. He sensed that he might plant churches or do some sort of relief and development work in the future. In the meantime, he pursued a creative writing degree at ASU and wondered if he could use his creative gifts to serve the world. But he never imagined himself as a filmmaker.

In his twenties, Matteo asked big questions and prayed that God would give him wisdom to understand the trajectory of his life. He engaged in God's mission in a number of ways and stayed connected to community. This allowed him to better understand himself and gave him a greater sense of what his contribution to the world might be.

One day he decided to go hiking with some friends to Havasupai Falls in the Grand Canyon. He had just purchased a camera and was eager to learn a new craft. At the end of their day in the Grand Canyon, after they'd pitched their tents, it started to rain hard. As the river rose, so did the stress on the dam that was holding water back from the gorge. Eventually it burst and sent a flood rolling down through the canyon. Campers, in panic, scaled the canyon walls to get to higher ground. Matteo and his friends found refuge on a ledge about twenty feet higher than their original campground. As the water level continued to rise, they prayed, but Matteo also had the presence of mind to take pictures with his new camera of this beautiful, terrifying moment.

The group was eventually airlifted out of there by helicopter. As the rescue team moved them to safety, God was moving Matteo into a new place of mission. As he scrolled through the pictures in his camera, he realized he had been able to capture some amazing images. While most people would use photos like that to keep memories alive or to spark conversations, Matteo saw them as an opportunity to seek shalom. He organized an exhibition where people could come see his photos and other works from local artists. The money from the art sales went toward rebuilding the flood-damaged villages of the Havasupai tribes.

Matteo realized he had a knack for photography and even for cinematography, so he began to refine his craft. He took advantage of the new opportunities and connections that came from his divinely ordained encounter with a flash flood. He learned from other photographers, obtained new equipment, and started reflecting on ways that photography could be used for God's glory and the service of others.

Eventually Matteo founded an organization focused on visual peacemaking, which is the use of images to break down stereotypes people have of one another. He wanted to display the beauty of God's creation through images of God's beautiful world and to display the image of God in all people through humanizing photography. His images have been seen all over the world, both still photographs and full-length documentaries. He's now a filmmaker who injects each project with intentional stewardship, seeking to display the creativity and beauty of God. He finds ways to serve others sacrificially through his craft. He's even found rich redemptive analogies within the field of filmmaking that are springboards to conversations about the gospel. Matteo never planned on being a filmmaker, but he kept his eyes and ears open while engaging his hands in good work. We would do well to follow his example.

Conclusion

As we seek to participate in God's mission, it's wise to try to discern our particular callings, the types of good works that God created us to do. Just as a musician needs to identify early on what instrument to play, we need to identify what kind of instrument God has made us to be. In the process of discerning our callings, it can be helpful to reflect on our abilities, affections, aches, and anchors. However, as valuable as reflection is, we must resist the temptation to be paralyzed by overanalysis. In the next chapter, we will continue to reflect on how to find our places within God's mission. However, our focus will move from the big-picture questions of calling to the more narrow reimaginings of our personal lives in light of God's mission. These chapters are going to help you discern an area of missional focus for yourself and help you prayerfully dream up tangible ways to perform the songs of stewardship, service, and spoken word within that area.

8

PERFORMING

Participating in God's Symphony

Kim loves music. She's always humming or singing or using the closest piece of furniture for percussion. You know the type. A conversation with her is difficult because anything you say reminds her of a song. Her musical tastes are eclectic, to say the least, from Motown to Mozart. In a room full of instruments, she can pick up almost anything and fumble her way into a halfway decent sound. She goes just beyond "Chopsticks" on the piano, can play simple pop songs on the guitar, has a pretty good rhythm with the drums, and still remembers how to play a few songs on the clarinet from her days in the high school band. She can read music, articulate the finer points of music theory, and recommend an interesting album. However, Kim will never be able to make meaningful music unless she learns to focus on a single instrument and spends the thousands of hours necessary to master it.

When it comes to the symphony of mission, many of us are like Kim. We love God, understand his mission, and long to see him glorified among all people, in all places, and in all of life. We dabble in many aspects of mission—we sign up for the occasional volunteer opportunity, make year-end donations, and help neighbors when they have needs. However, like Kim, we lack the focus to engage a *specific* people, place, or problem with missional intentionality. This chapter will help you identify for yourself a specific area of missional focus and will discuss how to perform the songs of stewardship, service, and the spoken word in that particular context.

The Importance of Focus

Here's irony for you: right now, as I try to write this section about the importance of focus, I cannot seem to string together more than a few sentences
without shifting my attention somewhere else. I am a living example of the
problem as I sit at my computer paralyzed by distractions. My buzzing phone
is sending me countless invitations to inattention. I have dozens of unread
text messages with lunch confirmations, funny memes, and requests for information that could easily have been googled instead of sent to me. Instead of
writing, I'm tempted to scroll through Facebook to find out what hundreds of
friends are thinking at this moment. Is someone out there angry about political
events, eating a delicious sandwich, or sharing a profound quote? News alerts
call my attention to nuclear threats in North Korea, school shootings, celebrity
gossip, and speculation about the coming NFL season.

I want to focus on writing, but I need to work out where I will eat lunch
with my coworkers. I've already spent five minutes debating the merits of
the two hundred restaurants within ten minutes of my office. I'm trying to
choose which restaurant is the healthiest, but I'm confused about what kind
of diet is best. The voices of health gurus and their contradictions bounce
around my mind, turning a simple meal selection into a puzzle. Should I eat
meat? Avoid fat? Eliminate sugar? Where was the food sourced? There are
boatloads of podcasts, websites, and sample menus to choose from online, all
claiming to have the best protocol. And the volume of choices won't decrease
once I arrive at the restaurant. One page of the menu will offer more varieties
of food than most people in the 1700s would have seen in their entire lives.

Lunch is still a few hours away, so I have plenty of time to write. But as I
start typing, I become distracted by the conversations in the hallway, and I'm
tempted to join the debate about the best player in NBA history. Instead, I
will be disciplined and block them out by listening to music. But *what* music?
Latin, a playlist of my favorite songs, classical guitar, a famous symphony,
instrumental jazz, or Motown? As I scroll through Spotify, I'm paralyzed by
the abundance of choices. I have to choose just *one* song out of millions? The
simple act of trying to find music that will help me focus has left me utterly
distracted.

Each new day, we wake up and have to choose how we will spend the next
1,440 minutes. Our wealthy, Western world is filled with an overwhelming
number of options about how to spend our days. It's a buffet as long as an
airport runway, but each of us approaches it with a normal-size plate. We
spend a lot of time staring at the options, trying to pick what's best. Where
should I go on vacation? Which university should I attend? Where should I

live? Work? Worship? The abundance of options can be a gift, but it's often merely overwhelming. We can do so much, but we find ourselves doing very little or doing many things in a very distracted or mediocre way, like my friend Kim. This is the paralysis of analysis.

With distractions so common, we need to be more intentional than ever before, especially when it comes to choosing how to participate in God's mission. When we are overwhelmed by the sheer number of choices available to us, we often default to becoming one of four unhelpful types:

1. *The Menu Gazer.* Just like the person paralyzed by the abundance of choices at a restaurant, the menu gazer is always trying to find the perfect way to participate in God's mission and remains stuck in mere reflection and discussion. Sometimes individuals and communities will spend months or years trying to identify how they fit within God's mission. Overwhelmed by choices, they cannot move forward.

2. *The Ping-Pong Ball.* Some people or communities will be focused on one area of mission only to transition quickly to another, a choice typically based on the level of excitement associated with the cause. These people are "all in" at first but soon move on to the next thing, usually because their excitement has waned, the work is difficult, or they've heard a compelling pitch from an exciting new ministry or organization.

3. *The Sampler.* Costco is well known for its samples. There are folks who deliberately skip lunch to go and fill up on tiny cups of free food. Rather than having a full, nourishing meal, they settle for a dozen nibbles of pot stickers, tamales, and smoked sausage. Some people approach missional engagement in the same way. They are involved in dozens of opportunities to serve, but their service lacks intentionality and depth. They might volunteer at a homeless shelter once a year, throw a block party in their neighborhood every Christmas, try to bring up Jesus in the occasional work conversation, and give some money toward a church plant. They are right to assume that all of life is an opportunity for mission, but they lack a missional focus.

4. *The Cargo Net.* Some people have so many legitimate responsibilities that they feel like one of those cargo nets made of bungee cords, stretched in every direction at once. They don't have time or energy to add anything to their busy schedules and often feel overwhelmed by the many new opportunities to serve that the church and local nonprofits present to them. They don't have enough room in their lives to add one more thing, so they must focus on infusing what they're already doing

with missional intentionality. For example, a single mother who works multiple jobs and spends all of her other hours caring for her children probably can't be involved with high-commitment volunteer programs, but she could take the work she is already doing and find ways to fill it with stewardship, service, and spoken word.

Mission Focus: Engaging a People, Place, or Problem with Intentionality

Lesslie Newbigin makes a helpful distinction between missionary *dimension* and missionary *intention*. There is a missional *dimension* to our lives. Our friendships and families, our use of technology and money, our life in our neighborhoods and at work—all of these point to the new humanity renewed in Christ. However, a missional *intention* is also needed. We should embrace activities that have a deliberate focus on making the good news known. And Newbigin adds an important warning: "Because the Church *is* mission there is a missionary dimension of everything that the Church does. But not everything the Church does has a missionary intention. And unless there is in the life of the Church a point of concentration for the missionary intention, the mission-ary dimension which is proper to the whole life of the Church will be lost."[1]

What is true for the church is also true for each of us. Our whole lives wit-ness to the coming kingdom, and we will be either faithful or unfaithful in that witness. But if we are able to define a missional focus in our lives—a specific place, people, or problem that we are committed to engaging with missional intentionality—we will *truly* live out our missional vocation in all of life.

A mission focus differs from a vocation or calling in that it's not about the ideal work you were created to do; it's about the reality of your life right now. It's about identifying one area of your life here and now and intentionally seeking ways to bear witness through stewardship, service, and spoken word.

Place. One way to define your mission focus is by location. It could be a neighborhood, workplace, or coffee shop. One young stay-at-home mother spends a significant amount of time with her children at the park. By making that park her mission focus, she's been able to build relationships with other parents who go there regularly.

People. Another way to focus is to identify a particular group of people, such as coworkers, or people with shared interests, such as an artistic community, a group of Burmese refugees, or the other parents of your child's soccer team.

1. Lesslie Newbigin, *One Body, One Gospel, One World: The Christian Mission Today* (London: International Missionary Council, 1958), 43 (italics original).

Problem. Sin has affected every part of the world and has created an array of physical, social, and spiritual problems. You might define your role in God's mission by focusing on a specific problem, such as homelessness, lack of community, political tension, or autism.

Since all groups of people are connected to particular places and have specific problems, you won't find one of these three things without the other two. Therefore, some people might want to define all three *p*'s in their mission focus. For example, you might want to say that you are focusing on college students (people) in your dorm (place) who are plagued by consumerism and loneliness (problems). However, if it's simpler for you, define your mission focus by concentrating on just one category.

The purpose of a mission focus is to move you from the paralysis of perpetual reflection to active engagement. However, *some* reflection is important, and the following exercises are intended to help you narrow your options and choose that focus.

Three Helpful Exercises

Time Tracker. Look at what you spend your time doing. Most of us are already in many potential areas of mission, but we lack intentionality. So for this exercise, make a list of the activities that consume most of your time and where they happen. Brainstorm with other believers who could be potential partners in mission. Be as thorough as possible. You might even want to do this on a separate piece of paper so that you can add more activities.

Activity	Location	Hours per Week	Other Believers

You may have noticed that some areas of your life that might otherwise seem insignificant actually consume much of your time. Maybe you spend eight hours a week eating lunch or six hours at the gym. Your first impulse might be to cut those things out altogether. But pause before you do; those might be areas that just need to be infused with missional intentionality. Maybe you could join a soccer league with refugees instead of running on the treadmill for exercise or eat lunch with your coworkers each day rather than by yourself.

Mission Focus Brainstorm. Based on what you wrote on the Time Tracker, brainstorm potential areas of missional focus. Identify at least three people groups, places, and problems that could be your missional focus.

Places	People	Problems

Ice Cream Famine. For this next exercise, imagine that all the ice cream in the world will vanish forever unless you pick just *one* area of mission focus and then devote the next five years of your life to it. (Choose something that you could do right now, in this particular season of life.) For the sake of ice cream, what will you choose?

Now that you have defined your mission focus and saved the world from an ice cream famine, use that mission focus for the rest of the exercises. The questions that follow will help prepare you to perform the songs of stewardship, service, and spoken word in a particular area of focus. We encourage you to stick with whatever area you have identified until God makes it obvious that you should move on.

Performing the Song of Stewardship

As discussed in previous chapters, we participate in the stewardship movement when we seek to display the image of God through the work of our hands. Good work dramatizes the glory of God's character and the goodness of his creation, and it is a preview of his kingdom.

As people made in God's image, the way we work communicates something about God's character and kingdom. On the one hand, good work dramatizes his wisdom, creativity, provision, and other attributes. On the other hand, poor work distorts the picture of God that our lives are supposed to portray. Manipulative managers are a living heresy, portraying God as arbitrary and capricious. Distracted workers who do the bare minimum and spend a disproportionate amount of time surfing the web distort the image of God by portraying him as disengaged and not interested in his creation. Absent parents portray a distant God, selfish citizens smother the shalom of God's kingdom, and shoddy craftspeople depict an untrustworthy God.

A good practice is to reflect on what your work communicates about God. Take some time to write in your journal or discuss the following questions with your community:

What work must be done in your area of missional focus?

When that work is done well, what aspects of God's character will be displayed?

When that work is done well, how will it provide a preview of God's kingdom?

When that work is done poorly, what will it distort about God's character and kingdom?

What needs to be repented of? What needs to be built upon?

Along with reflecting on these questions, spend some time reflecting on the various aspects of God's character and kingdom. Then brainstorm ways to dramatize these in your particular area of focus. For example, if someone's missional focus is the barbershop where they work, they could reflect God's provision by providing free haircuts for unemployed people on their way to job interviews, by researching the best insurance plan for the barbershop employees, or by paying them generous wages. The same person might seek to display God's protection, creativity, and hospitality by arranging the furniture in a way that promotes community, conversation, and relationship. Perhaps they could remove the TV and replace it with a big chalkboard bearing a discussion question of the day. Those would be creative steps toward crafting a unique environment to display God's generosity, provision, and hospitality.

What does this look like in your area of missional focus? Use the table below or replicate it in your own journal.

God's Character	Creative Ways to Display God's Character through Your Work
Provision:	
Peace:	
Creativity:	
Hospitality:	
Protection:	
Restoration:	
Faithfulness:	
Knowledge:	
Communication:	
Mercy:	
Other:	

God's Kingdom	Creative Ways to Provide a Preview of God's Kingdom in Your Mission Focus
Reconciliation:	
Safety:	
Celebration:	
Healing:	
Gratitude:	
Joy:	
Love:	
Honoring the Most Vulnerable:	
Justice:	
Meaning:	
Other:	

Just as a gardener must engage in both the *proactive* work of planting and the *reactive* work of pulling weeds, we are called to magnify the brilliance of God's creation by developing its potential and providing reverent maintenance. Therefore, it's important to identify the aspects of God's creation that we're responsible for in our areas of focus. We need to identify what it looks like to (1) creatively cultivate and (2) faithfully maintain those things.

For example, if your mission focus is a local park, you might identify the need to cultivate the potential of the baseball diamond by organizing a family kickball league as a way to help neighbors get to know one another. What about faithful maintenance? Perhaps you will decide to take a walk through the park each day and pick up the trash on the ground or work with the city to paint over the graffiti.

Spend some time journaling or reflecting on the following questions:

Within my area of mission focus, what aspects of creation do I need to develop creatively?

Within my area of mission focus, what aspects of creation do I need to maintain faithfully?

What skills do I need to develop to be a better steward of God's world and showcase of his character?

Performing the Song of Service

In chapter 5 we reflected on how the love of Christ is displayed through lives of sacrificial service. All that we have is a gift from God, not just for our benefit and blessing but also for the flourishing of others. We need to reflect on ways we can use the everyday stuff of life for the flourishing of our neighbors, especially those in our areas of focus. We need to audit our lives, identify our resources, and then reimagine those resources as instruments of love for our neighbors.

The following two exercises will help you prayerfully and creatively dream up ways to love and serve your neighbor. The first exercise, Life Audit, helps you take a fresh look at your life and try to imagine ways to love and serve your neighbor every day. The second exercise, the Carrot Cake Game, builds on the Life Audit but adds a layer of creativity and out-of-the-box thinking.

Life Audit

When Jesus commands us to love our neighbors "as ourselves," he calls us to take stock of the ways in which we love ourselves and use those things as resources to bless our neighbors. Take thirty minutes to reflect on the following aspects of your life. Think of simple ways you could use these things to love the people in your area of mission focus. How could you use your life assets as instruments of love?

Life	Ideas for Intentional Love
Training/Education:	
Home:	
Mealtimes:	
Weekends:	
Mornings:	
Evenings:	
Vacation:	
Hobbies / Recreational Activities:	
Children's Activities:	
Physical Possessions:	
Connections/Relationships:	
Holidays/Celebrations:	
Technology:	
Money:	
Other:	

The Carrot Cake Game

Whether we realize it or not, each of us has many things at our disposal with which to bless and serve others. The Carrot Cake Game is an exercise in exploring what we have and connecting those things to the broken areas of our world. The name of the exercise comes from imagining what it was like the first time someone made carrot cake. (We have *no* idea how carrot cake was invented, but we're pretty sure it was not like it's imagined here.) Imagine a family invites their neighbors over for a meal, and one hour before the meal, they realize they don't have a dessert prepared. They search frantically through their cabinets and pantry to find ingredients and stumble across some flour, water, sugar, baking powder, and, well, carrots. They decide to combine these seemingly unrelated items together—and produce the world's first carrot cake.

Learning to love our neighbors creatively is a bit like inventing a new recipe. We look into the pantry of our lives, see what we have to work with, and imagine a new dessert that will show love to others. This doesn't take a stroke of genius or an eccentric personality. It just takes the ability to see three things:

1. the world's brokenness (problems),
2. your resources (gifts), and
3. some way to use your resources to address the brokenness (creative love).

If we just slowed down enough to reflect on the brokenness around us and the potential blessing embedded in something as simple as a bicycle, an iPhone, or a degree in accounting, our minds would be overwhelmed with the redemptive potential at our fingertips. There are more ideas out there than we could ever execute in our lifetime!

Here's how the game works:

Step 1: Make a list of the problems in your area of mission focus. Then create a stack of index cards with one problem written on each card (loneliness, racism, toxic political discourse, etc.). These are your brokenness cards.

Step 2: Take a second stack of cards and write down all the resources that God has blessed you with (bike, front yard, baking skills, etc.). This is similar to the resources you listed in the Life Audit exercise, but you should be even more specific here. Instead of writing "training/education," write something like "bachelor's degree in marketing." These are your resource cards.

Step 3: Shuffle both stacks of cards and then draw one resource card and one brokenness card.

Step 4: Spend time brainstorming ways to use that specific resource to address that specific aspect of the world's brokenness. Sometimes the combinations will be ridiculous—using a pancake recipe to help exhausted teachers isn't a very likely mission enterprise—but it is surprising how this exercise can stir the imagination by forcing you to see new relationships between your assets and your neighbors' needs.

Here are some examples of what this exercise might look like:

Example 1: Computer Repair for Refugees

Your Resource: The ability to repair computers

World's Brokenness: Refugees arriving with few possessions and struggling to navigate life in a new culture

Creative Love: Organize a group that collects and restores old computers for refugees and installs English language software and PowerPoint presentations with vital information about your city.

Example 2: Front Yard Gardens for Homelessness

Your Resource: A five-hundred-square-foot front yard

World's Brokenness: Lack of fresh vegetables for people experiencing homelessness

Creative Love: Grow a vegetable garden in your front yard and invite people experiencing homelessness to feast whenever they please.

Example 3: Playgroup for Lonely Young Mothers

Your Resource: Organizational/event-planning skills

World's Brokenness: Young mothers feeling isolated and alone

Creative Love: Create a playgroup that provides fun for kids and opportunities for mothers to build friendships.

Example 4: Mastering the Recipe for a Cold Workplace

Your Resource: Cooking ability and an oven

World's Brokenness: Unfriendly and cynical environment at work

Creative Love: Make each coworker's favorite dessert on his or her birthday and organize a time for everyone to enjoy the dessert and express appreciation for that coworker.

The point of this exercise isn't to come up with the "perfect" answer but to exercise the muscle of imaginative creativity. It's a chance to look at problems in an out-of-the-box way and cultivate the view that everything we have is a potential instrument of blessing. Now take some time to use the Carrot Cake Game to dream of ways to love your neighbor tangibly, sacrificially, and creatively.

Performing the Song of Spoken Word

In chapter 6 we discussed the importance of speaking the words of the gospel to those who don't know Christ. We reflected on the importance of avoiding formulaic, one-size-fits-all approaches to evangelism and embracing a kind of evangelism that's respectful, contextual, and led by the Spirit. As a matter of fact, you could think of evangelism as listening for what the Spirit is already doing in your particular context and then adding your voice to the song the Spirit is singing.

Identify the stories shaping the lives of people in your mission focus. These stories are probably influenced by a combination of ideologies, such as consumerism, individualism, and nationalism. For example, consumerism in the suburbs might be more materialistic—they may buy a boat they can't afford—while urban consumerism might emphasize experiences, like traveling the world. It's important to discern the story your mission focus people are living, so you can tell them a better story.

The Spirit has embedded clues to the gospel, echoes of the biblical story, even in the midst of idolatrous cultural stories. There are echoes of God's character everywhere, because all people are created in God's image and all creation bears witness to the creator. There are echoes of creation and the fall everywhere, because each person, every single day, experiences the overwhelming goodness of God's world and the devastating presence of sin and its effects. And in every cultural context there are people who provide an echo of God's restoration of creation. By serving, restoring, giving, and healing, these people point to the redeeming work of Christ.

To help identify the echoes of the biblical story embedded in your context, think about the following:

Echoes of God. Where are glimpses of God's character around you? Is there creativity in a coworker, hospitality in a neighbor, or wisdom in a local teacher? By identifying the ways in which the image of God is displayed through the image-bearers in your context, you will be able to engage in affirmational evangelism by honoring what you appreciate about them and showing them how they reflect God.

Echoes of Creation. What do people around you love about God's world? How are they experiencing the goodness of creation? For example, they may love gardening, woodworking, comic books, or new technologies. How can you affirm these good things and show how each is a gift from God?

Echoes of the Fall. What are the greatest struggles of the people in your social context? How are they experiencing the reality of a fallen world? Some people in physical pain need to hear about the risen Christ who entered into the human experience of pain on the cross and died to deliver us from death. Some people are angry about economic or ecological injustices and need to hear about the savior who endured injustice through his unjust arrest and execution and who will one day return to judge fairly and liberate all who are oppressed.

Echoes of Restoration. Where do you see examples of healing that might serve as an echo of the work of Christ? For example, you might know an employer who sacrifices some of her potential salary in order to provide benefits for her staff. Maybe you know of a family who has adopted a child and can tell them about how they reflect the God who adopts us into his family.

Once you have spent some time reflecting on the echoes of the gospel story in your cultural context, you can prayerfully reflect on ways to present the gospel. You can identify Jesus stories that will resonate with the questions being asked in your context. You can identify redemptive analogies and metaphors that illustrate the work of Christ. Furthermore, you can look for cultural stories embedded in your context that provide echoes of the gospel.

Saying Yes

Now that you have identified an area of mission focus and walked through some exercises to help you perform the songs of stewardship, service, and spoken word, the next step is to define how you will intentionally participate in God's mission each week. Dreaming up creative ideas to love your neighbors and communicate the gospel is worthless if those plans are never acted on. Take some time each week to prayerfully identify ways to bless your neighbors. As you do, you may find the following questions helpful.

Stewardship: How do I intend to display God's character through my work this week?

Service: How do I intend to serve sacrificially this week?

Spoken Word: How do I intend to speak of Jesus this week?

Alternatively, you could use the BLESS acronym each week. These questions originated with the Soma Communities in Washington but are used by many of the Surge Network churches in Phoenix.

B—Bless: Whom can I tangibly bless this week?

L—Listen: Whom should I intentionally listen to this week?

E—Eat: Whom should I eat with this week?

S—Speak: Whom should I intentionally share the good news with this week?

S—Sabbath/Celebrate: How should I rest this week? Whom can I invite to join me in that rest?

The questions you use to focus are not as important as regularly recommitting to intentional and active participation in God's mission. To keep from drifting into unintentional passivity, it's wise to define on a regular basis the ways you are saying yes to God's mission.

Saying No

Identifying an area of mission focus is good, but that goodness can be undermined if we don't take the time necessary to truly engage. Not only do we need to identify what we say yes to, but we need to decide what good things we will refrain from to make space in our lives for our focus area.

Make a list of things that you could remove from your life to free up more time, energy, and resources for intentionally engaging your mission focus. Are you coaching multiple sports teams, reading or watching the news more than once per week, eating at restaurants outside of your neighborhood, getting a bigger house, getting a master's degree, moving to another city, or teaching a class? All these things are good and hard to say no to. But by establishing your priorities ahead of time, you will be able to resist the opportunities that distract from your missional focus when they arise.

What Opportunities Will I Say No To?	Why Am I Saying No?
Example: Eating at restaurants outside my neighborhood.	Example: So that I can get to know the local restaurant's staff and frequent visitors.
Example: Getting a bigger house.	Example: So that I can live near the university.

While it's helpful to define specific things we intend to say yes and no to, we need to remember that we should not attempt to contain the Spirit with our plans. God may bring opportunities that we never expected, and we need to be ready to respond. It's wise to remain open to the Spirit's leading while preparing for mission.

Integration > Elimination

In the last exercise, you were encouraged to eliminate some things from your life. However, a more important practice than elimination is integration. Most aspects of our lives need to be infused with intentionality rather than eliminated altogether.

Each of us wears many hats—as friend, citizen, employee, church member, family member, neighbor, volunteer. Finding room for all these hats on *one* shelf can be difficult. We live in a society that fragments and separates our various roles. We have a specific time for work, which is often carried on away from our families. Many of us have sedentary jobs, so we have to go to the gym for exercise. Because we use automobiles and mobile technology so much, we can spend weeks without ever speaking to a neighbor. We should seek to simplify and reintegrate our lives, to create more space for authentic living and missional focus.

An audit of your fragmented life may reveal practical ways to create more overlap. Instead of eating at several different restaurants each month, consider focusing on one place and building friendships there. Perhaps you could integrate exercise and service; instead of working out in isolation, do some yard work for an elderly neighbor or work in the community garden. (And if you do this with your family or good friends, you've found another area of integration.)

You could try to live, work, and play in the same local neighborhood. This might mean living in a smaller or less polished house, but what if you chose your neighbors before you chose your neighborhood? What if fellowship, mission, and vocation were central factors in choosing where you lived? What if you traded in your Netflix binges for movie nights or book clubs? What if your social media was limited and integrated into your devotional life as your primary prayer list and as an instrument for writing encouraging notes to others?

My friend Max is a great example of someone with an integrated and intentional life. For several years he worked with international students at a major university and was known for excellent work. As he observed where God had placed him, he determined that international students would be his missional focus. So he looked at every facet of his life to find points of integration.

His exercise came from riding his bike to work, so he would ride through the international student-housing areas, taking time to pray over each apartment he passed. He lived, worked, and played in the same neighborhood. Most of his meals were strategically planned as opportunities to meet students, faculty, or other believers who had a similar mission focus. These meals happened either at his home (and included his whole family) or at one of the nearby restaurants that were owned by international people and frequented by international students.

Since he was working with international students, he tended to read books and watch movies about other cultures. He also focused his volunteer service on international outreach initiatives. He had other interests of course, but the majority of his time was spent in the same local area, with the same people, and focused on the same themes. Rather than choosing to eliminate important aspects of life, he chose to integrate them.

Reflect on the following areas of life and think of simple ways you can integrate your mission focus there.

Life	Ideas for Integration
Training/Education:	
Home:	
Mealtimes:	
Weekends:	
Mornings:	
Evenings:	
Vacation:	
Hobbies / Recreational Activities:	
Children's Activities:	
Physical Possessions:	
Connections/Relationships:	
Holidays/Celebrations:	
Technology:	
Money:	
Other:	

As we participate in God's symphony, we get the privilege of choosing to focus, of intentionally limiting ourselves so we can love our neighbors. A word of caution: we need such focus in our lives, but we also need room for Sabbath, for play and rest. A little variety in life is also good, so we can enjoy the diverse gifts of God's creation. Don't let the desire to be focused become an obsession or an idol. This will be discussed more in the next chapter.

9

SUSTAINING

Persevering in God's Symphony

Wherever you find a karaoke machine, you will probably also find someone singing a one-hit wonder like "Ice Ice Baby." In homes across North America, a person's genuine curiosity about who put the dogs in the backyard is typically met with a playful, amateur rendition of "Who Let the Dogs Out." At wedding receptions across the country, an awkward uncle inevitably rushes onto the dance floor and begins contorting himself to the song he's been waiting for all night: the "Macarena."

A one-hit wonder is catchy, makes a big splash, has a simplistic message, and is easy to sing. What it lacks in depth it makes up for in the breadth of its target audience. Too often our attempts to participate in God's mission resemble a one-hit wonder. Whether it's a short-term mission trip, a campaign with a catchy hashtag, a trendy evangelistic method, or a large rally for the cause of the day, many of us are susceptible to the type of missional engagement that's marked by short-lived enthusiasm.

But God's mission isn't short-term. It spans generations and has so many layers of depth that we cannot fully wrap our minds around it. It's complex and demands our full attention. It's like a symphony not made for the mere diversion of a moment but carefully crafted to endure for centuries. While it's easy to sing along with most one-hit wonders, it takes many hours of focused engagement (and sometimes painful endurance) to participate in a symphony. The same is true for the missional engagement that God calls us to. He doesn't call us to "make an impact," to "change the world," or even to "be radical."

He calls us to faithfully persevere through trials and not grow weary in doing good (James 1:12; Gal. 6:9). Sometimes God will make something big happen through our small acts of faithful obedience, but that's up to him not us.

In the last chapter, we discussed how important it is to discern an area of mission focus. Focus is hard, but faithfully maintaining that focus over a long period of time is even harder. Many Christians, especially in the West, bounce from one area of focus to another. It's hard to stay engaged when the enthusiasm and excitement of the new mission endeavor wear off and are replaced by the relative monotony of the long haul. Some bounce from one focus to another because they're bored; others wilt because they're worn out. Though we intend to make an impact, we can get discouraged when nothing seems to change despite all our sacrificial work.

How can we build up our endurance? How can we think about mission scripturally and long-term rather than chasing the short-term trends of the day? How can mission be sustained, engaged with intentionality and love for years, even decades, rather than mere days, weeks, or months? This chapter will focus on cultivating three practices to help you stay connected to Christ and engaged in his mission for the long run. These practices include subversive Sabbath, praying like a human, and the groan of lament.

Subversive Sabbath

A regular practice of Sabbath-taking is vital to sustaining missional engagement because it helps us refocus on God, recognize our creatureliness, and remember our neighbors. Sabbath is more than just taking a day off. It's the divinely ordained rhythm of the creation that includes six days of working and one day of resting. We set aside time to pray and play, to worship and be filled with wonder every one in seven days. It's hard to overstate the simplicity of this gift of rest: we just take one day a week to shift from worshiping God through our *work* to worshiping God through *rest*. It is not that one day is holy and the rest are not; rather, one day is holy so that all the rest can be as well.

We read about Sabbath first in Genesis 2:1–3. After six days of creating, God rested, not because he was exhausted but because he wanted to delight in the goodness of creation and to set the pattern of creation: a six and one rhythm of work and rest. The first command to honor the Sabbath comes in the Ten Commandments (Exod. 20:8–11; Deut. 5:12–15). Interestingly, this Sabbath commandment was so important for God's people that the law on Sabbath-breaking is listed among the prohibitions of things like murder and adultery. When Jesus came, the Sabbath changed for God's people. Jesus said that he was the source of rest, the Lord of the Sabbath, and that the Sabbath was made for humanity rather than humanity for the Sabbath (Mark 2:23–28). He offered abundant rest to all the weary, the deep rest that comes from union with Christ (Matt. 11:28). In Christ we have more freedom for how to practice the Sabbath than those who lived in the Old Testament, but the wisdom in following God's rhythm of creation remains. Christ uses the Sabbath as a channel of his grace to us.

Because of the breakdown of typical work hours and the workweek, we need to be more intentional than ever before in setting up rhythms of rest. Rather than having natural rhythms of night and day, work and rest, we now have our work (through mobile devices) always at our fingertips. It has never been so easy for work to seep into every crevice of life. Many of us no longer shape our rhythms of work and rest by the glow of the sun between sunrise and sunset but by the never-ending glow of our phones, the taskmasters in our pockets. It's not necessarily wrong to work at night or during the weekends. But since the cultural norms promoting Sabbath and rest have largely disappeared, paying attention to the need for rest in our lives and setting aside time for it are all the more important.

Eugene Peterson suggests that Sabbath should include at least two things: praying and playing.[1] First, we should take some time to reconnect with God through things like prayer, corporate worship, and feasting in his Word. Second, we should take some time to delight in the goodness of God's world by going on a hike, savoring a meal, playing a game, making music, or being silly with the kids. Sabbath is an opportunity for worship and wonder, for being in awe of God and of his creation. This is far more than taking a day off; it is an act of intentional worship that honors God and fuels our work for our neighbors. If we're serious about good work, we must be serious about good rest. If we are serious about participating in God's mission, we must also be serious about practicing Sabbath.

Refocusing on God

Those who don't practice Sabbath often think of the omission as a minor sin, or even as the innocent byproduct of their strong work ethic. However, the refusal to rest is treason within the kingdom of God. It's an attempt to colonize God's world, either by declaring one's self-sufficiency or by trusting in some other tyrant. Shunning God's gift of rest is planting the flag of idolatry in the soil of God's world.

1. Eugene Peterson, *Working the Angles: The Shape of Pastoral Integrity* (Grand Rapids: Eerdmans, 1987), 57.

The ugly irony of self-sufficient missional activity is that it undermines the very purpose of mission, which is the worship of God. Yet somehow we often forget mission's purpose even as we engage in its activities. The purpose of stewardship is to display the glory of God, not our own glory. The purpose of service is to display the love of Christ, not to be seen as a hero for our loving actions. The purpose of the spoken word is to announce the good news of Jesus, not to celebrate our own eloquence or influence. When our missional engagement is done in our own strength, we begin to cut corners and refuse to rest. When we attempt to be self-reliant rather than dependent on the Spirit, rest is typically the first thing to go. Simultaneously, we overestimate our strength—acting as if we don't really need rest—and underestimate God's strength—acting as if God could not accomplish his mission without us. But because we aren't God, we cannot do what only God can do—*we cannot save the world*.

Sometimes our refusal to rest comes not from our sense of self-sufficiency but from our enslavement to an idol. Some of us feed the hungry in an attempt to satisfy our own cravings for significance. Others use the noble work of overseas missions as an excuse to feed the idol of experience and to fill their Instagram feed with images of exotic places. Some people start a company to seek the economic flourishing of their city but then slowly drift into building an altar to the god of consumerism. The currents of life can slowly pull us toward idolatry, but God has thrown us a rope: the practice of Sabbath.

This practice subverts the potential idols of our lives and provides unhindered space for praying, reading the Word, giving thanks, and gathering with others to celebrate God's abundance. It provides the slowness that we need to examine our hearts and reorient all of life toward God. Sabbath is the gift of a whole day to step out of our work and delight in God's work. It's a time literally to stop and smell the roses, savor a meal, take a nap without an alarm, make art, and play whimsical games. It's a day to remind all our senses of God's goodness.

The Sabbath is also a time of deliberate inefficiency that reminds us how much we need God. If you cease from work for one full day each week, you will "lose" 2,600 days of work over fifty years. What could you accomplish in that amount of time? How much more productive could you be? You could get a master's degree, volunteer at a community center, or earn tens of thousands of dollars to put to good use. But the inefficiency is deliberate; in it God reminds us that the mission is dependent on *God's* strength, not ours. With less time to work, we find ourselves more dependent on our Lord, the one who knows how to take our bread and fish and feed the masses. The Sabbath chips away at the illusion that if we just work hard enough or put in enough hours, we can accomplish the mission. But while we take our Sabbath rest, God continues to work, reminding us that the mission belongs to him.

Recognizing Our Creatureliness

It's not enough just to recognize that we are not God; we need to go further and identify what we really are—humans. We are not machines to be optimized for ultimate efficiency. While we can grow in productivity, we cannot hack ourselves out of our humanity.

To recognize that we are human is to accept that we are limited. Unlike robots, we need things like food, sleep, beauty, community, safety, and variety. We are not being honest with ourselves, nor honoring our creator, when we fail to attend to these truly human needs. There are times when the call to discipleship requires us to suffer deprivation for the glory of God and the good of our neighbor, but we shouldn't be deceived into equating sleeplessness with sanctification or stoic workaholism with discipleship. In *The Liturgy of the Ordinary*, Tish Warren Harrison says, "In our workaholic, image-barraged, over-caffeinated, entertainment-addicted, and supercharged culture, submission to our creatureliness is a necessary and often overlooked part of discipleship."[2] We often imagine discipleship as a call to trust Jesus enough to lay down our lives for the sake of the gospel, but sometimes it's a call to trust Jesus enough to lay down our heads on our pillows because we *believe* the gospel. We spend a third of our lives sleeping. Our need for that sleep proves we are not God—and it displays his trustworthiness.

Our bodies fall apart each day, and we need God to restore us through the daily rhythm of eating, drinking, and sleeping. The same is true with our souls. Each week they are ripped by the idolatry, pain, brokenness, and injustice of a fallen world, and the Sabbath is the weekly rhythm through which God stitches us back together through corporate worship, community, feasting, and delighting in the goodness of God's creation. Sabbath restores us, slows us down, and reminds us that we are not God. We submit to God by submitting to our limitations and taking time to receive the gifts that restore and invigorate us.

However, we're often tempted to neglect God's gift of rest, choosing to work every day of the week and to endure sleepless nights in pursuit of our goals. We're tempted to replace good food with prepackaged super supplements, messy community with polished social media, and slow wonder with efficient entertainment. Often, even as we seek to engage in God's mission, we cut corners by cutting out the creational rhythms of rest in the quest for efficiency and success.

2. Tish Warren Harrison, *The Liturgy of the Ordinary: Sacred Practices in Everyday Life* (Downers Grove, IL: InterVarsity, 2016), 152.

Ironically, deep rest is necessary for fruitful work. A day away from our checklists often results in fresh ideas and new perspectives. Nothing provides a better motivation for good work than a heart filled with awe, wonder, and gratitude toward God, and the Sabbath creates the space for cultivating that heart.

Remembering Our Neighbors

We also practice Sabbath for the sake of witness and justice. At first glance the command to stop working once a week might seem out of place next to the commands to not murder, steal, lie, or commit adultery. It may seem like the Sabbath is insignificant compared to the others. However, we must remember that these commands were given just after God's people were delivered from the economic oppression of Pharaoh, who had refused to give the people rest and continually increased their quotas of work. By giving his people the Sabbath, God created an embodied practice that reminded people each week that the oppressive reign of Pharaoh, marked by scarcity, anxiety, and endless toil, was finished. The tyranny of Pharaoh was replaced by the grace of God, and so by abundance, worship, fellowship, and feasting.

We might not live in Egypt under the tyranny of Pharaoh, but the modern world has its own tyrants. Our constantly buzzing phones, twenty-four-hour news cycles, and endless opportunities for consumption are the hallmarks of false gods who, like Pharaoh, steadily increase our quotas and demand more of us. This dehumanizing system of "more" is life draining to everyone but is especially costly to the most vulnerable of people. Our demand for the cheapest products robs the poor of their wages; the waste from our consumption robs the world of clean water; our hurried schedules rob children of human interaction when we make the iPad the third parent. We live in a frenetic world of speed, productivity, and consumption, which leaves us exhausted and disoriented.

The Sabbath creates an alternate rhythm of life that bears witness to the flourishing we will experience when Jesus returns. To enjoy the Sabbath is an act of resistance to the tyrants of our times and an invitation to others to join us in a different way of life. Walter Brueggemann writes, "Sabbath is the cornerstone of faithful freedom. Such faithful practice of work stoppage is an act of resistance. It declares in bodily ways that we will not participate in the anxiety system that pervades our social environment. We will not be defined by busyness and acquisitiveness and by the pursuit of more, in either our economics or our personal relations or anywhere in our lives."[3] Perhaps one of the most subversive ways we can bear witness to the world is by

3. Walter Brueggemann, *Sabbath as Resistance: Saying No to the Culture of Now* (Louisville: Westminister, 2014), 32.

engaging in Sabbath one day each week. By turning off the phone and turning toward people, taking a long nap instead of taking yet another meeting, and giving thanks with friends instead of debating politics on social media, we give people a picture of the peace of Christ and the coming Sabbath rest that will define his new creation.

This is not something just for us to do in our hidden corner of the world; it's something we are to invite others into. Just as the Israelites were called to extend the blessings of Sabbath to the gentiles in their land and just as Jesus feasted with tax collectors and prostitutes, we have the opportunity to extend the blessings of Sabbath to others, especially to the most vulnerable and oppressed people we know.

Can you imagine what that would be like? Can you imagine a community that answers no to our culture's loud demands for more, instead setting aside a day of playing games, singing to God, making art, getting lost on walks, and having long, lingering conversations over a good meal? Can you imagine if, in this weekly rhythm of feasting, we deliberately included those who were homeless, children with special needs, newborn infants, and elderly people in their last days? Can you imagine multiple languages raised together in prayer? Can you imagine a community of people who spend more time looking into the faces of their fellow image-bearers than looking at images on a screen? What could be a more countercultural witness than being well rested, unhurried, unworried people who choose to trust in God rather than in their own sufficiency?

A commitment to Sabbath is a way to renew our commitment to working in God's ways of justice, mercy, wisdom, and creative stewardship. As Eugene Peterson says,

> Lest any of us [oppress] our neighbor or husband or wife or child or employee, we are commanded to keep a Sabbath. The moment we begin to see others in terms of what they can *do* rather than who they *are*, we mutilate humanity and violate community. There is no use claiming "I don't need to rest this week and therefore will not keep a Sabbath": our lives are so interconnected that we inevitably involve others in our work. Sabbath-keeping is elemental kindness. Sabbath-keeping is commanded to preserve the image of God in our neighbors so that we see them as they are, not as we need them or want them.[4]

By keeping the Sabbath, we are remembering that we are human—and that our neighbors are too.

4. Peterson, *Working the Angles*, 71.

Praying Like a Human

One of the most important practices of Sabbath is prayer, though it shouldn't be reserved for just one day—it should permeate our whole lives. Our engagement in God's mission is sustained by the power of God through prayer. When we don't have regular rhythms of prayer where we seek God's strength, we can be tempted to find other sources of "power," like time management, trendy methodologies, pandering to the wealthy, or working unreasonable hours.

Prayer focuses the work of mission and gives us access to the power we need to carry it out. It shapes our character and strengthens our resolve. It's the means by which God molds and guides us. Few would disagree about the importance of prayer. But few of us feel that we, personally, have a strong prayer life. We struggle to be attentive in prayer, probably not because we think it's unimportant but because we really don't know *how* to pray. We must learn to pray like a human, not like a computer.

A computer is an inanimate object that transfers information back and forth with some distant server. It lacks emotion, relationship, imagination, and attentiveness to place. Most of all it lacks the five human senses (or fifteen, depending on whom you ask).

Many of us imagine prayer as something to do hunched over, alone in a room, with eyes closed and hands folded. Where did we get this idea? Not from the Bible! At best, this formula might keep us from being distracted, but at worst, this is the posture for praying like a computer. It will tend to make our prayers dull, focused merely on transferring information to God as if he were a dusty server in a distant land. To pray like this is to disconnect ourselves from our senses, ignore our environment, and disengage ourselves from the beauty and brokenness of God's world. This isn't how we were meant to pray.

Praying with all senses. God has given you sight, smell, hearing, taste, and touch. From Israel's feasts to the taste of communion bread to the waters of baptism, we see hundreds of biblical examples of worship that engage all of our senses. Our prayer lives will be more truly human if we pay attention to our senses. Confess your sin while you stand beside a dumpster. Climb a mountain overlooking your city to pray for the communities in it.

Praying in all places. How about seeking out the places linked to the content of your prayers? Perhaps you could craft a daily prayer walk, where different landmarks remind you to pray for specific things. A playground might remind you to pray for your children. A bakery might remind you to pray for your daily bread. A memorial, a statue, or a museum might remind you of some historical tragedy or injustice and so help shape your prayers of lament for the world's brokenness and your pleas for God to restore his wounded creation.

Praying in all of life. Too often we restrict our prayers to the so-called sacred parts of life, saving them to be performed in church buildings and at set devotional times. But we live our whole lives before God's face, including the humdrum stuff like driving to the office and weeding the garden. Why not pray about these things? How about turning your Facebook feed and news headlines into your prayer list? How could your prayers acknowledge God as the source of all the goodness, joy, truth, and beauty you encounter in your conversations with neighbors, when a project at work unexpectedly goes well, or when you finish reading a really good book?

Praying with all emotions. God knows when we are afraid, angry, confused, ashamed, or sad. Since our hearts are not hidden from God, we should follow the example of the Psalms and bring these deep emotions to the Lord. When you are angry about ridiculous public discourse on the internet, bring that anger to God. When you are struggling with doubt, know that God isn't afraid of your questions. When you look at your bank account and feel fear, use that fear as an occasion to cling to God.

The Bible invites us to worship God in the fullness of our lives. We are free to pray like real humans, with human senses and feelings. We should meet with God in meaningful places. Prayer should engage the full scope of our lives, from filet mignon to foreign policy. *Boring* should not be a word to describe our conversations with the God who gave us the Grand Canyon, March Madness, honey badgers, and the color turquoise. The problem isn't our weak intentions; it's our flabby imaginations. If the gospel is about the redemption of all creation, and if God's mission engages all of life, then shouldn't our prayers touch all of our activities and all of our days?

The Hopeful Groan of Lament

As this book draws to a close, we wish we could promise you that if you'll just engage in God's mission with intentionality and prayerfulness, you will always have a huge impact. We wish we could say that faithfulness always leads to fruitfulness and that if you engage in the stewardship, service, and spoken word movements, you will inevitably become an instrument for changing the world. But the truth is that all across the world, Christians are faithfully participating in God's mission and yet falling well short of changing the world.

Despite the best efforts of my friend Jean, who works in drug rehabilitation, there's still one little girl whose last glance of her mother was of needle-scarred arms hanging limp as she overdosed on heroin. Despite the best efforts of A Rocha and other Christian environmental agencies, there are lobbyists defending a known carcinogen that will harm a child in the womb. Somewhere right now a marriage is ending with signatures scribbled on divorce documents, despite the fact that the couple had a small group who walked closely and prayed fervently with them.

Even when we have a strong sense of vocation and deliberately give our lives to focused mission, we usually still fall short of changing the world. Even the best teachers don't reach every student, the best policies have unforeseen negative effects, and the best doctors lose patients. How do we keep going when we've tasted the hard realities of life and mission in a fallen world?

Learning to Live Proximately

Here Steven Garber is helpful. He talks about our need to make peace with the "proximate," the here-and-now realities of our lives. Garber urges Christians to work toward *some* change, *some* justice, *some* restoration, even though we can't make everything right, right here and now. Christians are called to be signs of a *coming* kingdom.

Jesus can, and will, wipe away every tear from our eyes and restore all that's broken when he returns. We can't bring ultimate healing or change to our world—only Jesus can do that. We must learn to trust in his future restoration rather than in our present abilities.

In the meantime, we are called to put our hands to the plow, to work hard for justice and the common good, not as ultimate solutions but as witnesses to the One who will renew all things: "Whatever our vocation, it always means making peace with the proximate, with something rather than nothing—in marriage and in family, at work and at worship, at home and in the public square, in our cities and around the world. That is not a cold-hearted calculus; rather it is a choice to live by hope, even when hope is hard."[5] All of our missional activity is an enacted prayer for the coming kingdom.

The world is filled with underfunded teachers, confused policy makers, and struggling entrepreneurs who sought to change the world but came to realize that the world is brutal and not so easily changed. Most of us eventually have to come to terms with the reality that we are not heroes, but like Garber often says, we're mere hints of hope. Like Jesus, we offer signs of and windows toward the kingdom. He healed only some of the blind and lame. He raised some of the dead—but they died again. His works pointed to a kingdom that had begun to come and yet was still coming.

5. Steven Garber, *Visions of Vocation: Common Grace for the Common Good* (Downers Grove, IL: InterVarsity, 2014), 203.

Once people come to the realization that the best we can hope for is proximate justice—some good, some justice, some reconciliation, signs and windows—they tend to respond with several different postures toward the world. Some of these postures are beautiful, showing that they have taken on the yoke of Christ. Other postures are deformed because they are not braced by the gospel. Let us look at some of these.

The folded arms of cynicism. Cynical Christians accurately see the brokenness of the world and know that utopian visions are for fools. Their mantra is, "The reason this will never work is . . ." They are usually intelligent, articulate, and masters of deconstruction, often somewhat disappointed by their own failures and extremely disappointed in the failures of others. These people are not people of action, and they rarely engage the brokenness of the world beyond their words and thoughts. They have strength enough for demolition but not for building. They like to think of themselves as realists, but they functionally deny the *real* resurrection of Christ and his *real* power to affect the world.

The shrug of apathy. Other Christians respond to the brokenness of the world with a shrug. Their mantra is, "Oh well. You can't do everything." These people can watch the world news with popcorn in their hands; they're interested in issues but not deeply concerned with people. They understand their inability to get involved with every cause and have made peace with their finitude. But the shrug of apathy is dehumanizing in two ways. First, in order to cultivate apathy one must stop seeing people as people and instead see them as issues. People without food become the issue of hunger; people with disease become the issue of health care. But God's image-bearers are more than mere topics of interest! Second, to be apathetic toward suffering is to dehumanize oneself, stifling what the brokenness of the world *should* make one feel. To numb one's heart from feeling the world's pain is to become less human. An apathetic shrug dishonors the God who created humanity in his own image.

The turn of the simplistic. Some respond to the wounds of the world by simply turning away from pain or by convincing themselves that things aren't that bad. They close their eyes, plug their ears, and simply avoid the evidence of brokenness. Sometimes they distract themselves with busy schedules or entertainment, making the world noisy to drown out the groans of creation. They sometimes engage important issues but always from a safe distance, shielding themselves with simplistic ideologies and media that confirm their own biases. They are unwilling to mourn, wrestle deeply, and hold things in tension. The motto of the simplistic is, "If they would just . . ." Whether it's the free market, evangelism, government regulation, education, systemic injustice, or personal responsibility, the simplistic avoid the complexity of the world by identifying *one thing* (whatever it is) as the answer to everything.

The busy hands of activism. These people must be commended for actually doing something, even if their confident visions of changing the world are somewhat naive and overstated. They believe innovation, hashtags, campaigns, funding, policies, strategies, techniques, and awareness will, when arranged in the most creative and inspiring way, make everything better. They engage themselves in good work but do so shallowly. They evaluate the merit of their work by the level of their own passion and the volume of their activity rather than by how their work actually helps others. They have not learned to slow down, weep, lament, understand complexity, or even confess how they've contributed to the world's pain. Their pursuit of justice and the common good might be somewhat helpful, but they often rush to action without sufficient reflection and relationship. Their work is often perceived as condescending, especially among the most vulnerable, because their naive optimism makes light of the tragic presence of sin and suffering in the world.

The Hopeful Groan of Lament

But there *is* a legitimate response to the world's suffering. It is shaped by the gospel, takes into consideration both the brokenness and beauty of the world, and balances our finitude against the limitless power of Christ. This is the hopeful groan of lament, the ability to groan with creation about the deep pain of the hurting world while also responding faithfully to God's call to pursue shalom in his world now and to look forward to the return of Christ. Romans 8:18–30 paints such a picture, of creation and humanity groaning together and waiting for a future day of glory when the bound world will be set free.

In the biblical practice of lament, prayer acknowledges and mourns the reality of a sin-ravaged world, expressing grief, frustration, and anger over things such as sin, death, tragedy, personal trouble, and national disaster. It uses powerful and emotive imagery to describe the nature of brokenness and cries out for God to intervene. Lament ends by refocusing on God's character.

We see prayers of lament throughout Scripture, including in the life of Jesus, but they are primarily found in the Psalms and Prophets. Over a third of the Psalms are laments, teaching God's people to assess the idolatry, injustice, and pain in the world honestly. They also teach us that we can bring our deepest and rawest emotions to God without pretense. God already knows our hearts, so we can bring the darkest parts to him, weeping—and even yelling—in his presence. We don't come to God flippantly or with a lack of reverence, nor do we come without hope. All but one psalm of lament (Ps. 88) expresses some hope or trust in God, but this is not a naive hope that covers hardship and pain with platitudes.

In order to be genuinely hopeful and to trust in God's future restoration, we first need to have an honest and prayerful encounter with the brutalities of the world. Lament is about having our eyes wide open, seeing clearly both the effects of sin in the world and also God's future restoration. These who see the world clearly and honestly are able to cry out to God about the death of a dear friend, the moral failings of a coworker, or the thousands of hours of work that seem to have barely moved the needle. If we are going to persevere in this harsh world and stay engaged in God's mission, then we need to have some way of dealing with the pain, failure, and tragedy that often accompany our best attempts at participating in God's mission. Those who don't come to God honestly about the horrors of this world will be tempted to apathy, naivety, frenetic busyness, or simplistic solutions. However, if we can come to God with soaked cheeks, cracked voices, and honest cries, we may just be able to lean into God's mission with perseverance and sober hope.

People who exercise the hopeful groan of lament pursue proximate justice in just a few areas. Though they care deeply about brokenness wherever they find it, they realize they can't engage in everything. Their concerns don't merely turn into worry or anxiety but to prayer. They weep and lament when they watch the news or hear of another cancer diagnosis or read about systemic injustice. They give their hearts to others in empathy and to God in prayer, even if that's all they have to give. Knowing they cannot change *everything*, they still seek to do *something*. They work now while they wait with longing for the one who will make all things new.

Steven Garber writes, "We know in our deepest places how hard it is to keep our eyes open to the complexity of the broken world around us, to keep feeling the pains of a world that is not the way it is supposed to be and, knowing the difficulty, choosing to engage it rather than being numbed by it."[6] As we are confronted by the cold reality of a broken world, let's pay attention to our posture and let that posture be shaped by both the cross and the resurrection. Let us heed the words of Paul, who admonished the church in Corinth as they tried to figure out how to live between the resurrection of Christ and the renewal of all things: "Be steadfast, immovable, always abounding in the work of the Lord, knowing that in the Lord your labor is not in vain" (1 Cor. 15:58 ESV).

6. Garber, *Visions of Vocation*, 222.

Conclusion: Symphony in the Subway

On a gray Friday morning in January 2007, more than a thousand people attended a concert to hear Joshua Bell, the Grammy-winning concert violinist, perform six pieces of classical music. *But most of them didn't know about the concert until it was over.* They walked right past the musical genius in the subway station without really seeing or hearing him, distracted by the text messages on their phones or by their own urgent search for a bagel.

Gene Weingarten describes in the *Washington Post* a social experiment to have Joshua Bell spend forty-three minutes playing classical masterpieces in L'Enfant Plaza just outside the subway station in Washington, DC.[7] One of the world's finest musicians was incognito, dressed in "jeans, a long-sleeved T-shirt and a Washington Nationals baseball cap." Some of the most beautiful music in the world was being given for free, but very few people recognized what was being offered or gave it any attention. Most ignored the music entirely or just shrugged and walked away. Only *seven* of the 1,097 passersby stopped to listen!

This is often our own experience as we perform in the symphony of mission. As we engage in stewardship, service, and spoken words, the world often shrugs and walks by. Rather than beholding the glory of God through the song of stewardship, they pass by, their attention fixed on something—anything—else. Rather than pausing to behold the love of Christ through the song of service, they scurry away and attend to their usual tasks. Rather than listening to the proclamation of the gospel through the song of the spoken word, they see us as a nuisance, a panhandler with selfish motives. Sometimes it's easy to get discouraged by the lack of impact our efforts make.

But we don't participate in God's mission because of the size of the crowd we attract. Whether seven or seven thousand people respond to the music of mission, we know that there's One who is always present: Jesus, our rescuer and our King. He has promised that he will always be present with the church as it makes disciples of all nations (Matt. 28:18–20). We participate in God's mission out of an overflow of our love for the One who is our primary audience and out of the overflow of *his* love for our neighbors. In the long journey of mission, in the challenges of performing his music before an often ambivalent and occasionally hostile world, we need the endurance that can be sustained only by constant fellowship with God, the composer and conductor of the symphony of mission.

7. Gene Weingarten, "Pearls before Breakfast: Can One of the Nation's Great Musicians Cut through the Fog of a D.C. Rush Hour? Let's Find Out," *Washington Post*, April 8, 2007, https://www.washingtonpost.com/lifestyle/magazine/pearls-before-breakfast-can-one-of-the-nations-great-musicians-cut-through-the-fog-of-a-dc-rush-hour-lets-find-out/2014/09/23/8a6d46da-4331-11e4-b47c-f5889e061e5f_story.html?utm_term=.b66a8377708d/.

RECOMMENDED
RESOURCES

Arias, Mortimer. *Announcing the Reign of God: Evangelization and the Subversive Memory of Jesus*. Philadelphia: Fortress, 1984.

Barrs, Jerram. *The Heart of Evangelism*. Wheaton: Crossway, 2005.

Bartholomew, Craig G., and Michael W. Goheen. *The Drama of Scripture: Finding Our Place in the Biblical Story*. 2nd ed. Grand Rapids: Baker Academic, 2011.

Bauckham, Richard. *The Bible and Mission: Christian Witness in a Postmodern World*. Grand Rapids: Baker, 2003.

Berry, Wendell. *Our Only World*. Berkley: Counterpoint, 2015.

Borthwick, Paul. *Great Commission, Great Compassion: Following Jesus and Loving the World*. Downers Grove, IL: InterVarsity, 2015.

Bosch, David J. *Transforming Mission: Paradigm Shifts in Theology of Mission*. Maryknoll, NY: Orbis, 2006.

Brueggemann, Walter. *Sabbath as Resistance: Saying No to the Culture of Now*. Louisville: Westminster, 2014.

Card, Michael. *A Sacred Sorrow: Reaching Out to God in the Lost Language of Lament*. Colorado Springs: NavPress, 2005.

Conn, Harvie. *Evangelism: Doing Justice and Preaching Grace*. Philipsburg, NJ: P&R, 1992.

Crouch, Andy. *Culture Making: Recovering Our Creative Calling*. Downers Grove, IL: InterVarsity, 2013.

Dawn, Marva J. *Keeping the Sabbath Wholly: Ceasing, Resting, Embracing, Feasting*. Grand Rapids: Eerdmans, 1999.

Dickson, John. *The Best Kept Secret of Christian Mission: Promoting the Gospel with More Than Our Lips*. Grand Rapids: Zondervan, 2010.

Escobar, Samuel. *The New Global Mission: The Gospel from Everywhere to Everyone*. Downers Grove, IL: InterVarsity, 2003.

Flemming, Dean E. *Contextualization in the New Testament: Patterns for Theology and Mission*. Downers Grove, IL: InterVarsity, 2005.

———. *Recovering the Full Mission of God: A Biblical Perspective on Being, Doing, and Telling*. Downers Grove, IL: InterVarsity, 2013.

Foster, Richard. *The Celebration of Discipline: The Path to Spiritual Growth*. San Francisco: HarperOne, 2018.

Garber, Steven. *Visions of Vocation: Common Grace for the Common Good*. Downers Grove, IL: InterVarsity, 2014.

Gelinas, Robert. *Living Sacrifice: The Cross as a Way of Life*. Denver: Wolgemuth & Associates, 2015.

Goheen, Michael W. *The Church and Its Vocation: Lesslie Newbigin's Missionary Ecclesiology*. Grand Rapids: Baker Academic, 2018.

———. *Introducing Christian Mission Today: Scripture, History, and Issues*. Downers Grove, IL: InterVarsity, 2014.

———. *A Light to the Nations: The Missional Church and the Biblical Story*. Grand Rapids: Baker Academic, 2011.

———. "The Missional Calling of Believers in the World: The Contribution of Lesslie Newbigin." In *A Scandalous Prophet: The Way of Mission after Newbigin*, edited by Thomas F. Foust, George R. Hunsberger, J. Andrew Kirk, and Werner Ustorf, 37–54. Grand Rapids: Eerdmans, 2001.

Harrison, Tish Warren. *The Liturgy of the Ordinary: Sacred Practices in Everyday Life*. Downers Grove, IL: InterVarsity, 2016.

Keller, Timothy. *Every Good Endeavor: Connecting Your Work to God's Work*. New York: Penguin Group, 2012.

King, Martin Luther, and Coretta Scott King. *Strength to Love*. Minneapolis: Fortress, 2010.

Love, Rick. *Glocal: Following Jesus in the 21st Century*. Eugene, OR: Cascade, 2017.

Miller, C. John. *Outgrowing the Ingrown Church*. Grand Rapids: Zondervan, 1986.

Nelson, Tom. *Work Matters: Connecting Sunday Worship with Monday Work*. Wheaton: Crossway, 2011.

Newbigin, Lesslie. *Foolishness to the Greeks: The Gospel and Western Culture*. Grand Rapids: Eerdmans, 1986.

———. *The Gospel in a Pluralist Society*. Grand Rapids: Eerdmans, 1989.

Padilla, C. Rene. *Mission between the Times: Essays on the Kingdom*. 2nd rev. ed. Carlisle, UK: Langham, 2010.

Perman, Matt. *What's Best Next? How the Gospel Transforms the Way Things Get Done*. Grand Rapids: Zondervan, 2014.

Peterson, Eugene. *Working the Angles: The Shape of Pastoral Integrity*. Grand Rapids: Eerdmans, 1987.

Plantinga, Cornelius, Jr. *Not the Way It's Supposed to Be: A Breviary on Sin*. Grand Rapids: Eerdmans, 1995.

Rah, Soong-Chan. *Many Colors: Cultural Intelligence for a Changing Church*. Chicago: Moody, 2010.

———. *Prophetic Lament: A Call for Justice in Troubled Times*. Downers Grove, IL: InterVarsity, 2015.

Reformed Ecumenical Synod. *The Church and Its Social Calling*. Grand Rapids: Reformed Ecumenical Synod, 1980.

Roberts, Bob. *Glocalization: How Followers of Jesus Engage the New Flat World*. Grand Rapids: Zondervan, 2009.

Sherman, Amy. *Kingdom Calling: Vocational Stewardship for the Common Good*. Downers Grove, IL: InterVarsity, 2011.

Sicks, Chris. *Tangible: Making God Known through Deeds of Mercy and Words of Truth*. Colorado Springs: NavPress, 2013.

Smith, James K. A. *Letters to a Young Calvinist*. Grand Rapids: Brazos, 2010.

Srygley, David. *From Cloisters to Cubicles: Spiritual Disciplines for the Not-So-Monastic Life*. Bloomington, IN: WestBow, 2015.

Stevens, R. Paul. *The Other Six Days: Vocation, Work, and Ministry in Biblical Perspective*. Grand Rapids: Eerdmans, 1999.

Stone, Bryan. *Evangelism after Christendom: The Theology and Practice of Christian Witness*. Grand Rapids: Brazos, 2007.

Stott, John R. W., and Christopher J. H. Wright. *Christian Mission in the Modern World*. Downers Grove, IL: InterVarsity, 2016.

Swoboda, A. J. *Subversive Sabbath: The Surprising Power of Rest in a Non-Stop World*. Grand Rapids: Brazos, 2018.

Webber, Robert E. *Ancient-Future Evangelism: Making Your Church a Faith-Forming Community*. Grand Rapids: Baker, 2003.

Willard, Dallas. *Spirit of the Disciplines: Understanding How God Changes Lives*. New York: HarperCollins, 1999.

Wolters, Albert M. *Creation Regained: Biblical Basics for a Reformational Worldview*. 2nd ed. Grand Rapids: Eerdmans, 2005.

Wright, Christopher J. H. *Mission of God's People: A Biblical Theology*. Grand Rapids: Zondervan, 2010.

Wright, Tom. *Bringing the Church to the World: Renewing the Church to Confront the Paganism Entrenched in Western Culture*. Minneapolis: Bethany, 1993.